CBT FOR PSYCHOSIS

Cognitive Behaviour Therapy (CBT) for psychosis is constantly changing and evolving. Recently, in what is sometimes called the 'third wave', therapy has become more concerned with the individual's relationship to their experience, rather than with the content of it. This more process–orientated approach appears to tap into universal psychological processes. The aim is to reduce distress by changing the function of the experience, rather than necessarily the experience itself. Written by some of the leading figures from around the world, *CBT for Psychosis: Process-Orientated Therapies and the Third Wave* brings the reader the latest developments in the field.

Presented in three parts, *CBT for Psychosis* first explores theoretical perspectives on recent developments in cognitive behavioural therapies. Part two examines specific therapeutic approaches, including metacognitive training, mindfulness, acceptance and commitment therapy, compassion focused therapy and the method of levels. Finally, part three presents two critical perspectives: the first offering a reflection on the experience of receiving CBT, and the second looking ahead to possible future developments.

Offering a cutting-edge collection of theoretical, therapeutic and critical perspectives, *CBT for Psychosis: Process-Orientated Therapies and the Third Wave* will be of great interest to clinical and counselling psychologists, both practising and in training, as well as psychiatrists, nurse therapists, occupational therapists and other healthcare professionals working with people experiencing psychosis.

Caroline Cupitt is Head of Psychology for the Psychosis Clinical Academic Group at South London and Maudsley NHS Foundation Trust, UK. She has worked as a clinical psychologist in services for people experiencing psychosis for more than twenty years. She is also editor of *Reaching Out: The Psychology of Assertive Outreach* (Routledge).

THE INTERNATIONAL SOCIETY FOR PSYCHOLOGICAL AND SOCIAL APPROACHES TO PSYCHOSIS BOOK SERIES

Series editors: Alison Summers and Anna Lavis
Series advisor for the monograph strand: Andrew Moskowitz

ISPS (The International Society for Psychological and Social Approaches to Psychosis) has a history stretching back more than five decades, during which it has witnessed the relentless pursuit of biological explanations for psychosis. This tide has been turning in recent years and there is growing international interest in a range of psychological, social and cultural factors that have considerable explanatory traction and distinct therapeutic possibilities. Governments, professional groups, people with personal experience of psychosis and family members are increasingly exploring interventions that involve more talking and listening. Many now regard practitioners skilled in psychological therapies as an essential component of the care of people with psychosis.

A global society active in at least twenty countries, ISPS is composed of a diverse range of individuals, networks and institutional members. Key to its ethos is that individuals with personal experience of psychosis, and their families and friends, are fully involved alongside practitioners and researchers, and that all benefit from this collaboration.

ISPS's core aim is to promote psychological and social approaches to understanding and treating psychosis. Recognising the humanitarian and therapeutic potential of these perspectives, ISPS embraces a wide spectrum of therapeutic approaches from psychodynamic, systemic, cognitive, and arts therapies, to need-adapted and dialogical approaches, family and group therapies and residential therapeutic communities. A further ambition is to draw together diverse viewpoints on psychosis and to foster discussion and debate across the biomedical and social sciences, including establishing meaningful dialogue with practitioners and researchers who are more familiar with biological-based approaches. Such discussion is now increasingly supported by empirical evidence of the interaction of genes and biology with the emotional and social environment especially in the fields of trauma, attachment, social relationships and therapy.

Ways in which ISPS pursues its aims include international and national conferences, real and virtual networks, and publication of the journal *Psychosis*. The book series is intended to complement these activities by providing a resource for those wanting to consider aspects of psychosis in detail. It now also includes a monograph strand primarily targeted at academics. Central to both strands is the combination of rigorous, in-depth intellectual content and accessibility to a wide range of readers. We aim for the series to be a resource for mental health professionals of all disciplines, for those developing and implementing policy, for academics in the social and clinical sciences, and for people whose interest in psychosis stems from personal or family experience. We hope that the book series will help challenge excessively biological ways of conceptualising and treating psychosis through the dissemination of existing knowledge and ideas and by fostering new interdisciplinary dialogues and perspectives.

For more information about ISPS, email isps@isps.org or visit our website, www.isps.org.

For more information about the journal *Psychosis* visit www.isps.org/index.php/publications/journal

MODELS OF MADNESS
Psychological, social and biological approaches to schizophrenia 1st edition
Edited by John Read, Loren R. Mosher & Richard P. Bentall

PSYCHOSES
An integrative perspective
Edited by Johan Cullberg

EVOLVING PSYCHOSIS
Different stages, different treatments
Edited by Jan Olav Johanessen, Brian V. Martindale & Johan Cullberg

FAMILY AND MULTI-FAMILY WORK WITH PSYCHOSIS
Gerd-Ragna Block Thorsen, Trond Gronnestad & Anne Lise Oxenvad

EXPERIENCES OF MENTAL HEALTH IN-PATIENT CARE
Narratives from service users, carers and professionals
Edited by Mark Hardcastle, David Kennard, Sheila Grandison & Leonard Fagin

PSYCHOTHERAPIES FOR THE PSYCHOSES
Theoretical, cultural, and clinical integration
Edited by John Gleeson, Eión Killackey & Helen Krstev

THERAPEUTIC COMMUNITIES FOR PSYCHOSIS
Philosophy, history and clinical practice
Edited by John Gale, Alba Realpe & Enrico Pedriali

MAKING SENSE OF MADNESS
Contesting the meaning of schizophrenia
Jim Geekie and John Read

PSYCHOTHERAPEUTIC APPROACHES TO SCHIZOPHRENIA PSYCHOSIS
Edited by Yrjö O. Alanen, Manuel González de Chávez, Ann-Louise S. Silver &
Brian Martindale

BEYOND MEDICATION
Therapeutic engagement and the recovery from psychosis
Edited by David Garfield and Daniel Mackler

CBT FOR PSYCHOSIS
A symptom-based approach
Edited by Roger Hagen, Douglas Turkington, Torkil Berge and Rolf W. Gråwe

EXPERIENCING PSYCHOSIS
Personal and professional perspectives
Edited by Jim Geekie, Patte Randal, Debra Lampshire and John Read

PSYCHOSIS AS A PERSONAL CRISIS
An experience-based approach
Edited by Marius Romme and Sandra Escher

MODELS OF MADNESS
Psychological, social and biological approaches to psychosis 2nd edition
Edited by John Read and Jacqui Dillon

SURVIVING, EXISTING, OR LIVING
Phase-specific therapy for severe psychosis
Pamela Fuller

PSYCHOSIS AND EMOTION
The role of emotions in understanding psychosis, therapy and recovery
Edited by Andrew Gumley, Alf Gillham, Kathy Taylor and Matthias Schwannauer

INSANITY AND DIVINITY
Studies in psychosis and spirituality
Edited by John Gale, Michael Robson and Georgia Rapsomatioti

PSYCHOTHERAPY FOR PEOPLE DIAGNOSED WITH SCHIZOPHRENIA
Specific techniques
Andrew Lotterman

CREATIVITY AND PSYCHOTIC STATES IN EXCEPTIONAL PEOPLE
The work of murray jackson
Murray Jackson and Jeanne Magagna

ART THERAPY FOR PSYCHOSIS
Theory and practice
Katherine Killick

CBT FOR PSYCHOSIS
Process-orientated therapies and the third wave
Caroline Cupitt

MONOGRAPHS:

PSYCHOSIS, PSYCHOANALYSIS AND PSYCHIATRY IN POSTWAR USA
On the borderland of madness
Orna Ophir

MEANING, MADNESS AND POLITICAL SUBJECTIVITY
A study of schizophrenia and culture in turkey
Sadeq Rahimi

CBT FOR PSYCHOSIS

Process-Orientated Therapies
and the Third Wave

Edited by Caroline Cupitt

Routledge
Taylor & Francis Group

LONDON AND NEW YORK

First published 2019
by Routledge
2 Park Square, Milton Park, Abingdon, Oxon OX14 4RN

and by Routledge
711 Third Avenue, New York, NY 10017

Routledge is an imprint of the Taylor & Francis Group, an informa business

British Library Cataloguing in Publication Data
A catalogue record for this book is available from the British Library

Library of Congress Cataloging in Publication Data
Names: Cupitt, Caroline, 1966- author.
Title: CBT for psychosis : process-orientated therapies and
the third wave / Caroline Cupitt.
Description: Milton Park, Abingdon, Oxon ; New York,
NY : Routledge, 2018. | Includes bibliographical references and index.
Identifiers: LCCN 2018004294 (print) | LCCN 2018005315 (ebook) |
ISBN 9781315294858 (Master e-book) | ISBN 9781138239869 (hbk : alk.
paper) | ISBN 9781138239876 (pbk : alk. paper) | ISBN 9781315294858 (ebk)
Subjects: LCSH: Psychoses—Treatment. | Cognitive therapy.
Classification: LCC RC512 (ebook) | LCC RC512 .C86 2018 (print) |
DDC 616.89/1425—dc23
LC record available at https://lccn.loc.gov/2018004294

ISBN: 978-1-138-23986-9 (hbk)
ISBN: 978-1-138-23987-6 (pbk)
ISBN: 978-1-315-29485-8 (ebk)

Typeset in Times
by Keystroke, Neville Lodge, Tettenhall, Wolverhampton

Front cover photo: Brendan Wilson

CONTENTS

List of illustrations   ix
Notes on contributors   xi
Acknowledgements   xv

Introduction   1
CAROLINE CUPITT

PART 1
Theoretical perspectives   7

**1 Metacognition in psychosis: Implications for developing
    recovery oriented psychotherapies**   9
PAUL H. LYSAKER AND ILANIT HASSON-OHAYON

**2 Emerging perspectives on the role of attachment and
    dissociation in psychosis**   25
KATHERINE BERRY, SANDRA BUCCI AND FILIPPO VARESE

PART 2
Specific therapeutic approaches   45

3 Metacognitive training: Targeting cognitive biases   47
RYAN P. BALZAN, STEFFEN MORITZ AND BROOKE C. SCHNEIDER

4 Mindfulness in CBT for psychosis   64
KATHERINE NEWMAN-TAYLOR AND NICOLA ABBA

CONTENTS

5   **Acceptance and Commitment Therapy**   79
    ERIC M. J. MORRIS

6   **Compassion-Focused Therapy for relating to voices**   98
    CHARLES HERIOT-MAITLAND AND GERRARD RUSSELL

7   **A principles-based approach using the Method of Levels**   115
    SARA J. TAI

PART 3
Critical perspectives   133

8   **A step in the right direction or a missed opportunity?**   135
    RACHEL WADDINGHAM

9   **Where next for CBT and psychosis?**   150
    CAROLINE CUPITT AND ANNE COOKE

    Index   168

ILLUSTRATIONS

Figures

3.1 'Girl' stimuli set for 'fragmentation exercise' in the JTC module 51
3.2 Example of a 'BADE exercise' (picture order is 3, 2, 1) 52
3.3 'Pool scene' from the memory/overconfidence module; people often falsely recall items (e.g., towels; sunhat) with high confidence despite them not being depicted in the picture 53
4.1 Mindful and unmindful relationship to psychosis 67
4.2 Formulation-based rationale for mindfulness (details have been changed to preserve anonymity) 69
6.1 Sessional measures: (a) social safeness and (b) dissociation 111
6.2 Emotional outcome measures: depression, anxiety and stress 112

Table

1.1 MERIT elements 18

NOTES ON CONTRIBUTORS

Nicola Abba is a Consultant Clinical Psychologist working in acute care in the NHS, and lectures at the University of Southampton, UK. She is an accredited CBT therapist and incorporates mindfulness into her clinical practice with people with distressing psychosis.

Ryan Balzan is a Clinical Psychologist and Postdoctoral Research Fellow at Flinders University in Adelaide, Australia. He is interested in improving our understanding of the underlying psychology of psychosis (particularly on the formation of beliefs), and investigates the efficacy of psychological treatments for psychosis including metacognitive training, cognitive behaviour therapy and cognitive remediation.

Katherine Berry is a Senior Lecturer at the University of Manchester, UK, Clinical Psychologist and co-Director of the Complex Trauma and Resilience Research Unit (C-TRU) within Greater Manchester Mental Health NHS Foundation Trust, UK. Her main area of expertise is attachment theory and therapeutic relationships in people with a diagnosis of psychosis. She currently works on the Manchester clinical psychology training programme and as a clinical psychologist in mental health rehabilitation.

Sandra Bucci is a Senior Lecturer at the University of Manchester, UK, an Honorary Consultant Clinical Psychologist with Greater Manchester Mental Health NHS Foundation Trust and co-Director of the Complex Trauma and Resilience Research Unit (C-TRU) within Greater Manchester Mental Health NHS Foundation Trust, UK. Her main research interests are understanding the mechanisms involved in voice-hearing, and developing innovative ways of extending the reach of healthcare interventions for people with psychosis, primarily through harnessing technology.

Anne Cooke is a Consultant Clinical Psychologist and a Director of the Doctoral Programme in Clinical Psychology at Canterbury Christ Church University, UK. She was the editor of the British Psychological Society report, *Understanding Psychosis and Schizophrenia*. She is interested in the power of ideas, particularly the idea of mental illness.

Caroline Cupitt is Head of Psychology for the Psychosis Clinical Academic Group at South London and Maudsley NHS Foundation Trust, UK. She has been working as a clinical psychologist in services for people experiencing psychosis for more than twenty years. She was editor of a previous book, *Reaching Out: The Psychology of Assertive Outreach.*

Ilanit Hasson-Ohayon is a Rehabilitation Psychologist, Associate Professor and co-director of the community clinic at the Department of Psychology at Bar-Ilan University in Israel. She is author of over 80 peer reviewed articles in the field of mental health, mainly concerned with how people cope with serious mental health problems. She both practices and supervises psychotherapy.

Charles Heriot-Maitland is a Clinical Psychologist, researcher and trainer. He holds an MRC Research Fellowship at the University of Glasgow, where he is currently researching the application of Compassion-Focused Therapy for people experiencing distress in relation to psychosis. He is also a Director of Balanced Minds, a UK organisation providing compassion-focused therapy, supervision, consultation and training.

Paul H. Lysaker is a Clinical Psychologist with over 30 years of experience providing psychotherapy to adults diagnosed with psychosis. He is also an active researcher and an author of more than 400 peer reviewed articles related to the psychological processes involved in the experience of psychosis.

Steffen Moritz is a Psychologist and heads the Neuropsychology Unit at the Department of Psychiatry and Psychotherapy of the University Medical Center, Hamburg, Germany. His main interests are group and online intervention programmes for people diagnosed with schizophrenia, depression and obsessive-compulsive disorder.

Eric M. J. Morris is Director of the Psychology Clinic, La Trobe University, Melbourne, Australia. Eric's research focuses on Acceptance and Commitment Therapy for people recovering from psychosis, carers, and as a workplace intervention for mental health workers. He is a co-editor of *ACT and Mindfulness for Psychosis*, and co-author of *ACT for Psychosis Recovery*.

Katherine Newman-Taylor is a Consultant Clinical Psychologist with Southern Health NHS Trust and Associate Professor at the University of Southampton, where she is course director for the advanced CBT programmes. Her clinical work and research focuses on CBT for psychosis, including mindfulness and attachment-based imagery.

Gerrard Russell has worked in a variety of industries and roles, from lead musician in a rock band, through engineer, to fashion designer. At the age of 40 he had an intense spiritual ('kundalini') experience, and at the age of 50 started hearing distressing hostile voices. His contributions to this book are grounded in the wisdom of personal lived experience.

Brooke C. Schneider is a Research Psychologist in the Neuropsychology Unit at the Department of Psychiatry and Psychotherapy of the University Medical Center, Hamburg, Germany, and a psychotherapist in private practice. Her main research interests are the development of interventions for depression and psychosis, as well as cognitive changes due to ageing.

Sara J. Tai is Senior Lecturer at the University of Manchester and a practicing Consultant Clinical Psychologist. She has extensive clinical and research experience of working internationally in multi-cultural inner-city areas and in training clinicians in psychological interventions. Her research focuses on the science and practice of psychological treatments using both clinical trials and qualitative research methodologies.

Filippo Varese is a Lecturer at the University of Manchester, UK, Clinical Psychologist and Director of the Complex Trauma and Resilience Research Unit (C-TRU) within Greater Manchester Mental Health NHS Foundation Trust, UK. His research interests focus on the relationship between life adversity and severe mental health difficulties, the psychological mechanisms responsible for this association and the evaluation of psychological therapies for trauma-related difficulties in those with psychosis.

Rachel (Rai) Waddingham hears voices, sees visions and was once disregarded as 'mad'. Informed by the principles of the Hearing Voices Movement, she has developed innovative projects in the youth, community and prison sectors. An Open Dialogue practitioner, Chair of Intervoice and Vice Chair of ISPS UK; Rai is a trainer, consultant and practitioner who is committed to societal change.

ACKNOWLEDGEMENTS

I would like to thank Alison Summers, Nigel Bunker, Tony Morrison and Paul Wilson for their help in developing the original proposal for this book. Thanks also to Alison Summers, Anna Lavis and Sunil Nandha who gave very helpful comments on earlier drafts, and to Brendan Wilson for the cover photo.

Most of all, thanks are due to David Hutchens for his help and support throughout the project.

INTRODUCTION

Caroline Cupitt

Cognitive Behaviour Therapy (CBT) for psychosis is said to have started in 1952 with a single case study by Aaron T. Beck (Beck, 1952). It was not until the late 1980s however, once CBT for other conditions was firmly established, that attention turned more firmly to the experience of psychosis. The pioneers took as their starting point what were known as the two hallmark symptoms: hallucinations and delusions. What followed were a number of treatment manuals which outlined the approach (including Kingdon & Turkington, 1994; Fowler et al., 1995; Chadwick et al., 1996). If Behaviour Therapy is thought of as the first wave of CBT, this can be thought of as part of the second wave, in which a symptom-based approach to CBT for psychosis emerged as a significant force (Hagen et al., 2011). Proponents argued against the idea of a syndrome of psychosis, suggesting that CBT should be targeting specific individual symptoms.

During the 1990s, researchers worked hard to establish the efficacy of CBT for psychosis through a series of randomised controlled trials, many of which were conducted in the UK. These generally showed modest effect sizes, although the positive effects often outlived the therapy itself (Wykes et al., 2008). However, there was a debate about the measures used to evaluate CBT in these trials. As with research on the effectiveness of medications, the most commonly used outcome measure was the Positive and Negative Syndrome Scale (PANSS), which assesses a wide range of psychotic experiences – many of which are not the focus of CBT. What is more, the published manuals describing CBT for psychosis explicitly state that the therapy aims to reduce distress rather than symptoms. Arguably CBT was being evaluated as if it was a neuroleptic medication, rather than on its own terms (Birchwood & Trower, 2006). Nevertheless, this early work clearly established that CBT can be an effective method for working with psychotic experience.

As the results flowed through into guidance in the UK (NICE, 2002), the US (APA, 2004), Canada (CPA, 2005), Australia and New Zealand (RANZCP, 2005), Spain (Working Group, 2009) and elsewhere, there was hope that people within the mental health system experiencing psychosis could finally begin to expect a psychological approach to their distress. Unfortunately, despite CBT becoming widely recommended, access to the therapy has remained limited. There are many reasons for this, not least the limited numbers of suitably trained therapists available in many healthcare systems – but continued controversy about its effectiveness has also played a part, with some having argued that its effectiveness has been seriously overstated (Lynch et al., 2010). There are others who point out that in CBT generally, content-orientated cognitive change has not been shown to add very much to the effectiveness of previously established behavioural approaches (Longmore & Worrell, 2007).

Given this context, it is therefore of no surprise that CBT-trained clinicians and researchers have sought to extend and improve the approach. This work has been informed by an increasing volume of studies demonstrating that voice hearing and unusual beliefs are common in the general population (Romme & Escher, 1989). Once the experiences themselves are not viewed as inherently distressing, there is the exciting possibility that they may not be *symptoms* at all, but rather aspects of human experience that only sometimes become problematic. The traditional focus on a person's appraisal of their unusual experiences now does not seem to go far enough: the underlying processes by which we all relate to difficult experiences are brought now into question.

The beginning of this change appears with an increased understanding of the role of metacognition. Morrison & Wells (2000) investigated the strategies people use to suppress unwanted intrusive thoughts, known as thought control. They found that people experiencing psychosis used more worry and self-punishment to control thoughts than the general population. It follows that understanding more about thinking, and specifically the uncontrollable nature of many mental events, offers the possibility of freeing people from the distress they may experience on hearing an unwanted voice. Metacognitive Training (Chapter 3) applies this understanding in a very accessible and normalising way. It is distinctive in taking an educational approach and regards change in metacognition to be central to relieving psychosis-related distress.

At a similar time, mindfulness techniques were being established for the treatment of depression. Chadwick (2006) saw these as offering another route to changing someone's relationship to psychotic experience, in this case using experiential exercises. Although at first these two developments appear very different, they share an emphasis on adopting a new stance in relation to experience. Someone in the midst of a distressing psychotic experience is being asked to observe the process without seeking to suppress or change the experience. Developing this kind of 'decentering' capacity is of course a part of traditional CBT (Hofmann et al., 2010), but previously it was typically spoken of in terms of rationalising thoughts. The introduction of mindfulness techniques provided a means to enable people to develop greater metacognitive awareness without simultaneously requiring them to change the content of thoughts or voices.

The more effectively someone is able to develop and utilise skills to unhook from a distressing experience, the less likely they are to rely on habits of experiential avoidance, which in turn creates the possibility of accepting – rather than battling against – the elements of experience that a person cannot change. Here we more firmly enter what is commonly considered the 'third wave' of CBT. Acceptance is not based on passivity or resignation, but instead on an understanding of the mind and its uncontrollable nature. CBT would previously have focused on reducing voice power and control by seeking to change someone's appraisal of the voice hearing experience. Now the horizon has expanded and a more relational approach is taken, in which the *process* of engagement with the experience is targeted, rather than a person's appraisal of that experience. In Acceptance and Commitment Therapy (ACT) this is spoken about as attention to context in order to change the function of psychological events (Hayes et al., 2006). It is an approach that values acceptance over change, albeit recognising that acceptance then brings with it change.

A difficulty with the concept of acceptance is that it can make it all sound too easy. Research tells us that the quality of someone's relationship with an unwanted voice is very similar to their other relationships (Hayward, 2003). Many people have suffered severe trauma and their voice content often reflects this. If trauma occurred early in life it may have affected someone's ability to conceptualise their own and others' mental states. It may also have made it difficult to relate to others with trust and confidence, be they embodied or just a voice (Chapter 2). In these circumstances, asking someone to accept the nature of their experience without also wishing to change it will not be straightforward. It requires people to considerably expand their repertoire of coping, in the context of a safe and secure relationship. One way of describing that change is in the development of more compassionate responses for the self and other (Chapter 6).

Collectively all these developments have at times been referred to as 'third wave CBT for psychosis'. However, they do not all identify as CBT or as third wave approaches (Chapter 9). For example, Compassion Focused Therapy, whilst described as arising from within the cognitive behavioural tradition, is now an approach in its own right (Gilbert, 2010). In other reviews of third wave CBT, different therapies may be included, and others left out. For example, in his review Kahl (2012) includes Behavioural Activation as a third wave approach. Although at first this might seem odd, there are striking connections between some third wave approaches and traditional Behaviour Therapy. For some, the third wave is part of a return to and reinvigoration of what would otherwise have been known as Radical Behaviourism (Chapter 5).

Difficulties defining third wave CBT have led some to argue that the concept should be abandoned. Hofmann et al. (2010) argue that these developments are simply an extension of what has always been 'a family of CBT approaches', which have in common the idea that cognition exerts a causal effect on behavior and emotion. Whilst there certainly is a debate to be had, there nevertheless does appear to have been an evolution in CBT over the last ten years which merits attention. It has excited clinicians, many of whom have adopted these new approaches in advance of their being subject to robust evaluation.

This book takes a pragmatic view, including the cognitive behavioural approaches that a practising clinician or client is most likely to encounter. It understands the third wave as having a focus on process rather than content, and being more concerned with someone's relationship to experience than the content of experience itself. Since this is a change of emphasis in CBT, rather than an entirely new idea, metacognition is included for this is where it all appears to start. Metacognition is important because thinking about thinking is the start of moving away from a focus on the content of thoughts. It has led to a form of therapy called Metacognitive Training (Chapter 3), in which people are explicitly taught about thinking. What is more, the principles learnt apply to all thinking and do not single out psychosis as a special case. As such, the approach steps firmly away from a symptom-focused perspective. However, this may only be the first step in understanding the role of metacognition in psychosis, which has the potential to take us into wider questions about the nature of the self (Chapter 1).

The Method of Levels (Chapter 7) is included in this book, although it is only part of the family of cognitive behavioural approaches in its broadest sense. It is a metacognitive form of therapy, which seeks to change someone's relationship to experience. It therefore seems to make the same kind of departure from traditional cognitive behavioural therapies that we see in the other, more obviously third wave approaches. It is also trans-diagnostic in approach, again moving us away from a focus on symptoms.

Mindfulness-based approaches (Chapter 4) and Acceptance and Commitment Therapy (Chapter 5) are centre-stage, widely regarded as third wave approaches. We begin with mindfulness because it forms part of the other, and yet is often also practised as an adjunct to traditional CBT. ACT is rapidly becoming the first order third wave approach, in part due to its originators' enthusiasm for the term (Hayes, 2004).

Compassion Focused Therapy (Chapter 6) also critiques the emphasis previously given to cognition within CBT, but is different in that it takes an evolutionary perspective. It explicitly seeks to work with the older affiliative motives and emotions, albeit using recognisably CBT techniques (Gilbert, 2014). Again it offers a trans-diagnostic approach and also the beginnings of a more social view of mental distress.

A book on process-orientated therapy and the third wave of CBT would not be complete without some critical reflection on these diverse developments. This comes firstly from someone who has experienced CBT (Chapter 8) and in the final chapter (Chapter 9) we ask the question of where next for both CBT and psychosis?

References

American Psychiatric Association (2004). *Practice guideline for the treatment of patients with schizophrenia*. Washington DC: APA.

Beck, A. T. (1952). Successful outpatient psychotherapy of a chronic schizophrenic with a delusion based on borrowed guilt. *Psychiatry, 15,* 305–312.

Birchwood, M. & Trower, P. (2006). The future of cognitive-behavioural therapy for psychosis: Not a quasi-neuroleptic. *British Journal of Psychiatry, 188,* 107–108.

Canadian Psychiatric Association (2005). Clinical practice guidelines: Treatment of schizophrenia. *The Canadian Journal of Psychiatry, 50*(13) Suppl. 1.

Chadwick, P. (2006). *Person-based cognitive therapy for distressing psychosis*. Chichester: Wiley

Chadwick, P., Birchwood, M, & Trower, P. (1996). *Cognitive therapy for delusions, voices and paranoia*. Chichester: Wiley.

Fowler, D., Garety, P. A., & Kuipers, L. (1995). *Cognitive behaviour therapy for psychosis: Theory and practice*. Chichester: Wiley.

Gilbert, P. (2010). Compassion focused therapy: The CBT distinctive features series. London: Routledge.

Gilbert, P. (2014). The origins and nature of compassion focused therapy. *British Journal of Clinical Psychology, 53*(1), 6–41.

Hagen, R., Turkington, D., Berge, T. & Gråwe, R.W. (2011). *CBT for psychosis: A symptom-based approach*. Hove: Routledge.

Hayes, S. C. (2004). Acceptance and Commitment Therapy, Relational Frame Theory, and the third wave of behavioral and cognitive therapies. *Behavior Therapy, 35*, 639–665.

Hayes, S. C., Luoma J. B., Bond F. W., et al. (2006). Acceptance and commitment therapy: Model, processes, and outcomes. *Behaviour Research Therapy, 44*, 1–26.

Hayward, M. (2003). Interpersonal relating and voice hearing: To what extent does relating to the voice reflect social relating? *Psychology and Psychotherapy: Theory, Research and Practice, 76*, 369–383.

Hofmann, S. G., Sawyer A. T. & Fang, A. (2010). The empirical status of the 'new wave' of cognitive behavioral therapy. *Psychiatric Clinics of North America, 33*,701–710.

Kahl, K. G., Winter, L. & Schweiger, U. (2012). The third wave of cognitive behavioural therapies: What is new and what is effective? *Current Opinion in Psychiatry, 25*, 522–528.

Kingdon, D. & Turkington, D. (1994). *Cognitive behavioral therapy of schizophrenia*. Hove: Lawrence Erlbaum Associates.

Lynch, D., Laws, K. R. & McKenna, P. J. (2010). Cognitive Behavioural Therapy for major psychiatric disorder: Does it really work? A meta-analytical review of well-controlled studies. *Psychological Medicine, 40*, 9–24.

Longmore, R. J. & Worrell M. (2007). Do we need to challenge thoughts in cognitive behavior therapy? *Clinical Psychology Review, 27*, 173–187.

Morrison, A. P. & Wells, A. (2000). Thought control strategies in schizophrenia: A comparison with non-patients. *Behaviour Research and Therapy, 38*(12), 1205–1209.

National Institute for Clinical Excellence (2002). *Schizophrenia: Core interventions in the treatment and management of schizophrenia in primary and secondary care*. London: NICE.

Romme, M. & Escher, S. (1989). Hearing voices. *Schizophrenia Bulletin, 15*(2), 209–16.

Royal Australian and New Zealand College of Psychiatrists Clinical Practice Guidelines Team for the Treatment of Schizophrenia and Related Disorders (2005). Royal Australian and New Zealand College of Psychiatrists clinical practice guidelines for the treatment of schizophrenia and related disorders. *Australian and New Zealand Journal of Psychiatry, 39*, 1–30.

Working Group of the Clinical Practice Guideline for Schizophrenia and Incipient Psychotic Disorder. Mental Health Forum, coordination (2009). *Clinical Practice Guideline for Schizophrenia and Incipient Psychotic Disorder*. Madrid: Quality Plan for the National Health System of the Ministry of Health and Consumer Affairs. Agency for Health Technology Assessment and Research. Clinical Practice Guideline: CAHTA. Number 2006/05–2.

Wykes, T., Steel, C., Everitt, B. & Tarrier, N. (2008). Cognitive behaviour therapy for schizophrenia: Effect sizes, clinical models and methodological rigor. *Schizophrenia Bulletin, 34*(3), 523–537.

Part 1

THEORETICAL PERSPECTIVES

1

METACOGNITION IN PSYCHOSIS

Implications for developing recovery oriented psychotherapies

Paul H. Lysaker and Ilanit Hasson-Ohayon

Psychosis in its many different forms leads to myriad psychological and social challenges that affect not only the lives of persons diagnosed with these conditions, but also the lives of their friends, families, and others in their communities. Our scientific understanding of the course of psychosis, however, has taken an optimistic turn in the last several decades. While it was once firmly asserted that people with psychosis could only hope to have a life in which, at best, they were 'stable' and free from acute disturbances in emotion, cognition, and behaviors, careful field research found that many recover (Leonhardt et al., 2017; Silverstein & Bellack, 2008).

In exploring how to characterize recovery, disparate groups have agreed on at least two things. First, recovery can mean different things to different people. Recovery can involve objective phenomena such as symptom remission or the attainment of psychosocial milestones, and subjective experiences including self-appraisals of an acceptable quality of life and the recapturing of a coherent sense of oneself as a valuable person in the world. Second, regardless of what kind of achievements constitute recovery, the person diagnosed with psychosis must feel a sense of ownership of their recovery. This is to say that the person diagnosed with mental illness must be 'in charge' of their own recovery. Recovery is thus a matter for the whole person. It is more than a person 'fixing' or finding solutions for one or more dilemmas: it requires persons to make their own sense of what they are experiencing in the moment and decide what they want to do about it. Recovery requires that the person be an active agent in that process.

The recognition that recovery is possible and should be the goal of treatment has spurred on efforts to understand the barriers to recovery. After all, if services are to promote recovery, a clear idea of what stands in the way would seem necessary. To date, some of the most widely identified obstacles to recovery from psychosis include anomalous experience such as experiences of permeable boundaries around the self, neurocognitive impairments, isolation, and poverty, as well

9

as trauma history and stigma or stereotyped ideas. In this chapter, we will go beyond this work and look at another set of barriers to recovery and their implications for developing treatments. We are referring here to reduced metacognitive capacities or difficulties forming a sufficiently complex sense of self and others, needed to decide how to respond to the challenges of psychosis and – more broadly – life itself. We will focus on these reduced capacities as they are intimately tied with the potential of persons to be active agents in their recovery. Indeed, helping to restore metacognitive function could help many not only decide what recovery means to them but also to take charge of that process.

To explore the implications of studies on reduced metacognitive capacities for developing psychotherapy, we will first offer a definition and then detail literature supporting the role of metacognition in psychosis. We will explore the implications of this for developing cognitively oriented psychotherapy for psychosis, both in theoretical and technical terms. We will lastly describe recent efforts to operationalize a recovery oriented metacognitive approach to psychotherapy, offering thoughts on how the metacognitive approach can be distinguished from others on the basis of its focus on meaning-making and a person's sense of self in the human community.

Metacognition

The construct

In this chapter, we use the term 'metacognition' to conceptualize and operationalize the processes involved when persons notice and integrate information about themselves and others. However, the term is complex and requires some consideration of its use in different disciplines. By the strictest definition, a metacognition is a cognition about other cognitions. It was first used in education research, to look at learners' awareness of their own learning (Flavell, 1979). The use of the term metacognition has since been expanded, for example, to deal with self-regulation (Dinsmore et al., 2008), attentional biases (Wells, 2000), and the ability to monitor and correct behavior and one's own reasoning (Moritz et al., 2007). Taking all of these activities into account, a broader understanding of metacognition has emerged as a larger process in which information is integrated into complex representations of the self and others (Lysaker & Dimaggio, 2014). Here metacognition is seen as a spectrum of activities which, at one end, involves awareness of discrete mental experiences such as specific thoughts, feelings or wishes, and at the other end the integration of those discrete experiences into a larger complex sense of oneself and others. These different ends of the spectrum are also not conceptualized as completely independent activities. The larger senses we form of ourselves are based on awareness of discrete elements of experience, just as we assign meanings to our discrete experience on the basis of our larger sense of ourselves.

This view stresses the representational nature of reflection, emphasizing that the metacognitive process allows us to form a sense of ourselves and others by bringing together an ocean of pieces of information across unique settings over time, rather than being a mirror of reality. It also emphasizes that metacognition is a crucial and not a causal activity. It is intimately tied to meaning-making, which is essential to survival. Metacognition is not an academic activity but is the basis for how one decides what to pursue, with whom, where, and when. Metacognition occurs and evolves intersubjectively. Metacognition requires that selected states and experiences are given meaning and expressed in ways that can be shared and acknowledged between people, in real or imagined interactions (Tomasello et al., 2005; Cortina & Liotti, 2010). Finally, metacognition describes the processes which make available a sense of self and others from moment to moment depending on slightly or grossly changing circumstances.

Different terms in the broad field of psychology have been used to refer to similar phenomena. These terms, which include mentalizing, theory of mind, and social cognition, all share similarities with metacognition. However, the concept of metacognition differs from those terms in several conceptual ways. First, while theory of mind and social cognition are expressly concerned with the correct detection of a thought or feeling, metacognition concerns the integration of those details into a whole; one whose coherence, rather than pure accuracy, is at issue. In contrast to mentalizing, metacognition explicitly distinguishes from one another the formation of integrated ideas of the self, the formation of an integrated sense of other people, and the use of that knowledge. Metacognition also differs from mentalizing in that it understands reduced metacognitive capacities can result from multiple factors, including decrements in neurocognition, social isolation, and stigma. It does not share the view that decrements in reflectivity occur almost exclusively in the context of disturbed attachment and emotion dysregulation (Fonagy et al., 2004). From this view, metacognition may have a bidirectional relationship with both attachment security and emotional regulation.

Operationalization and research in psychosis

One of the first efforts to operationalize the construct of metacognition was offered by Semerari et al. (2003). Influenced by work in attachment (Main, 1991), this group created the Metacognition Assessment Scale (MAS). The MAS offered several advances in the study of metacognition. First, it made the leap of using the term metacognition to describe the processes that go beyond momentary self-awareness and allow emergence of a broader sense of self. Second, it differentiated different forms of metacognition on the basis of their foci: the self (Self-reflectivity); other people (Awareness of the mind of the other); and the use of metacognitive knowledge to respond to emergent psychological and social challenges (Mastery). It also offered an additional subscale concerned with awareness of other, namely Decentration, which concerns the awareness that events can be understood validly from multiple perspectives. This brought to light that our sense of ourselves and others requires the ability to shift back and forth from one's own perspective to the valid and differing perspectives of others. As originally

11

applied, the MAS was used as a tool to detect the frequency of successful meta-cognitive acts during psychotherapy.

Applying this conceptualization and operationalization of metacognition to the field of psychosis, Lysaker et al., (2005) created the Metacognition Assessment Scale-Abbreviated (MAS-A). The MAS-A is an adaptation of the MAS and retained the general four-scale structure, though Decentration was designated as an independent scale because of its centrality as an outcome. The MAS-A contains four scales: Self-reflectivity (S), Understanding other's minds (O), Decentration (D), and Mastery (M). There were major changes from the MAS to the MAS-A. The most substantial change was that MAS-A revised the original MAS items so that each scale was transformed into an ordinal scale. Each item of the S, O, and D scales of the MAS-A represents a mental act which involves a higher level of integration than the item below it. In other words, each ascending item requires a new element to be integrated into one's self of self, others, and the larger community respectively. For example, the fourth item of the S scale (a sense of self as having distinct cognitive operations and nuanced affective states) produces a more integrated sense of self than the third item level (self as composed only of cognitive operations), but which is less integrated than the fifth item (a sense of self experiencing affective states as changing and thought processes as subjective). For the M scale, each item now represents a response to distress which requires a higher level of metacognitive activity than the one below it. This allowed the MAS-A to assess a person's maximal capacity and assign a single value separately to the S, O, D, and M scales of the MAS-A.

Research using the Metacognition Assessment Scale-Abbreviated

Research using the MAS-A has suggested it has adequate psychometric properties (Lysaker & Dimaggio, 2014), and that it reflects mental processes which are distinct from social cognition (Lysaker et al., 2013; Hasson-Ohayon et al., 2015). The use of this scale has enabled studies to examine the prevalence and effects of reduced metacognitive capacities in psychosis. This work has found that MAS-A scores of persons given a diagnosis of first episode or prolonged psychosis have more significant reductions in metacognitive capacities than persons with prolonged non-psychiatric medical conditions or substance abuse disorders (Lysaker, Leonhardt et al., 2014; Lysaker, Vohs et al., 2014), minor anxiety and affective disorders (WeiMing et al., 2015), and community members without mental health conditions (Hasson-Ohayon et al., 2015; Popolo et al., 2017). Reductions in metacognitive capacities have also been noted in other mental health conditions, including depression (Ladegaard, et al., 2014), post-traumatic stress disorder (Lysaker, Dimaggio et al., 2015), borderline personality disorder (Lysaker et al., in press), and bipolar disorder (Popolo et al., 2017). Metacognition as a process of integration has been found to be more closely related to function than specific dysfunctional metacognitive beliefs (Popolo et al., 2017).

Research has reported that reductions in metacognitive capacities negatively affect functional competence (Lysaker, McCormick et al., 2011), subjective recovery (Kukla et al., 2013), therapeutic alliance (Davis et al., 2011), stigma (Nabors et al., 2014), physical activity levels (Snethen et al., 2014), reasoning bias (Buck et al., 2012), hedonic response to life (Buck et al., 2014), clinical insight (Lysaker et al., 2005) and intrinsic motivation (Luther et al., 2016a) in psychosis, regardless of levels of symptom severity. Reductions in metacognitive capacities have also been found to predict future levels of vocational function (Lysaker, Dimaggio et al., 2010), negative symptoms (Hamm et al., 2012; Lysaker et al., 2015; McLeod et al., 2014) and intrinsic motivation (Luther et al., 2016b), regardless of baseline functioning. A recent meta-analysis (Arnon-Ribenfeld et al., in press) affirmed the existence of associations between reductions in metacognitive capacities with symptomatic and psychosocial functioning in persons diagnosed with schizophrenia.

Of note, in a broader historical framework, it has been suggested that these findings linking disruptions in function with disturbances in metacognition bear a striking similarity to some of the original conceptualization of the concept of schizophrenia. In particular, parallels have been drawn between this metacognitive model and Bleuler's (1950) contention that the disruption in goal directed behavior in what he termed schizophrenia, was largely the result of disturbances in associative process or the ability to link ideas together via associative threads (Lysaker & Klion, 2017). Thus, the self as an agent is related to the ability to reflect upon oneself and others and use these reflections in order to facilitate recovery.

Four implications for developing forms of psychotherapy for psychosis

The treatment target is a capacity which can improve over time

Given that reductions in metacognitive capacities represent an immediate barrier to recovery, psychotherapies that successfully enhance metacognition and opportunities for healthier function and recovery are needed. The metacognitive research paradigm, noted above, offers important directions for how to conceptualize the interventions, processes, and outcome of any developing psychotherapy. To begin, it tells us that metacognition is a continuous, not a categorical variable; metacognition is a capacity which can wax and wane. As such, this offers what we think is the first major implication for treatment: namely treatment should not approach metacognition as something someone has or does not have. Instead treatment should approach metacognition as something a person possesses to a varying degree and something they can acquire more of over time. In addition, metacognition is perceived as a multi-dimensional phenomenon that includes the four related dimensions presented above. As such, one can have high self-reflection abilities but low ability to understand others' minds, or vice versa.

Importantly, since metacognition here is understood as an ability, rather than a knowledge set, to enhance metacognition treatment would need to offer persons opportunities to think about themselves, others, and about the use of that knowledge. By having opportunities which are repeated over a period of time, persons might become more able to think about themselves and others and use that knowledge in more complex and flexible ways. Using the metaphor of physical therapy, psychotherapy may most effectively impact metacognition when it offers patients the opportunity to practice acts that are difficult for them, with the result that incrementally they become more able to perform those acts in the flow of life.

Because it is a matter of personal sense making, and not the grasping of facts, treatment cannot be conceptualized as primarily following a curriculum. Treatment cannot mainly seek to 'teach' patients to perform these acts, nor direct them to think certain things. Moreover, treatment would not treat metacognition as something to educate patients about. Rather, therapy should provide the patient with a therapeutic space to *experience* and perform metacognitive acts. A related point is that since metacognition is conceptualized as a capacity for integration, treatment would also necessarily need to focus on the quality of individuals' thinking as information is being synthesized rather than based on concrete thoughts in isolation. Since there are naturally many different ways of thinking about oneself and others, and because there is never an ultimately true single unchanging way of seeing oneself, metacognitively oriented therapies need to be sensitive to the processes of subjective meaning-making. Treatment should seek to help persons become better able to assemble information in an integrative holistic manner, rather than direct them to a specific conclusion. Ultimately this therapy would likely have to be concerned with how meaning is being made – that is, the extent to which that meaning is complex and integrated. It also calls for the understanding that meaning is generally expressed in personal narratives. Further, those personal narratives are themselves not a matter of correctly relaying historical events or affirming elements of the dominant social discourse, but are a way of personally understanding life events in a holistic and flexible way (Hasson-Ohayon et al., 2017). This is consistent with James et al. (2016), who found reductions in metacognitive capacities and dysfunctional thoughts separately affect psychosocial function.

Interventions should match a patient's metacognitive capacity

If metacognition is a capacity which varies between people, a second set of implications is that metacognitively oriented psychotherapies must offer interventions that match patients' capacities for different types of metacognition. This would require the assessment of metacognition and responsiveness to changes within and between sessions; the metacognitive research paradigm, noted above, offers a methodology for doing this. Specifically, the MAS-A used to study metacognition in psychosis, as described above, offers two more separate advances for metacognitively oriented therapies trying to deal with this issue. First, it offers a way to think about differing capacities for metacognition, separating out patients' capacities to think about themselves from their abilities to think about others, then separating out both of those from the capacity to use that knowledge to respond to psychological and social challenges (mastery). Thus, using this scale, metacognitive therapies can respond to metacognition as more than a monolithic phenomenon. It allows for responding differently to someone with reductions in specific metacognitive capacities; for example in Mastery as opposed to someone who struggles with both Self-reflectivity and Mastery.

Beyond this the MAS-A also offers a framework for intervention. As noted above, the Self-reflectivity (S), Understanding others' minds (O) and Mastery (M) scales offer clearly delineated levels of metacognitive capacity, which would allow a therapist to determine at what point reflections might exceed the patient's capacity for that metacognitive domain. To illustrate, we will discuss the S scale. As noted above, each level of the S scale involves a somewhat more complex and integrated reflection upon self-experience. Specifically, the first and second levels (S1 and S2) differ in that the second level involves the understanding that a set of experiences exists within the boundary of the mind, whereas at the first level there is no solid sense of how experiences may be internal or external. At the third level (S3), the mental experiences boundaried by the mind at the second level are now perceived as different from one another. Whereas at the second level we only have particles of mental activities, now there are discrete small groupings of those particles. For example, a person at this level is able to tell the difference between a memory and a wish. At the fourth level (S4), these different mental operations are further distinguished and larger affects can be perceived and differentiated from one another. Thus, metaphorically, at the fourth level we have moved from discrete atoms of experience to larger molecules of experience. At the fifth level (S5), persons can see their mental experiences, including larger affects, changing over time and can tell that their thought processes are subjective and changeable. At the sixth level (S6), these changing mental states are understood in the context of a reality which can contradict or accommodate changing mental states. At the seventh level (S7), all of those activities are understood as interacting in a specific way in a narrative episode. Then, at the eighth level (S8), persons are able to compare and see similarities between the ways mental activities within the context of reality interact with each other in similar ways across different narrative episodes. In other words, there is the detection of nuanced patterns. Finally, at the ninth level (S9), persons are able to see different clusters of related and unrelated narrative episodes spread out across the lifespan. Taken as a whole, the MAS-A thus allows us to see that metacognition is not about getting one's story 'right.' The MAS-A, in particular, outlines a series of increasingly complex mental acts which allow persons to access self-experience within the flow of life; the very process necessary to effectively manage one's own recovery from psychosis.

Turning to the issue of intervention, this framework thus allows for therapists to concretely share thoughts which do not overtax patients' abilities to integrate and think about themselves and others, and to use that knowledge when facing challenges. For example, for a patient unable to see changing mental states and how their thoughts and feelings are changeable and subjective (S5), it would potentially be folly to ask them to doubt their thoughts. Similarly, for the patient unable to integrate experience and see within their own mind larger nuanced affects, asking them to describe their feelings would also be useless. Instead, for the patient functioning at a level in which they have the ability to see different mental operations but not larger affects, therapists might limit their reflections to these discrete mental operations until the ability to name affects might emerge. At higher levels, the therapist can disclose his or her own thoughts and feelings, acting from an intersubjective framework, allowing for both increasing self-reflection and understanding of others.

Goals and outcome will fluidly emerge with time

If metacognitive capacity emerges over time, the next major implication for developing treatments is that patients' goals, in and out of therapy, are likely to be fluid and may change dramatically. Patients with more impoverished metacognition are likely to have goals which are general and difficult to connect with actions they may take as an agent. It is likely, in particular, that at lower levels of meta-cognitive mastery, by definition, patients may have very limited ways to under-stand psychological challenges or at best struggle to use unique knowledge of themselves and others to think about what directions make the most sense for them in their recovery. Thus, therapy can begin with patients unaware of psychiatric needs or with patients holding what seem like unrealistic goals. It also places an onus on the therapist not to insert their own goals into the work, which could unintentionally impede the emergence or sustenance of agency. Thus, a major aspect of therapy is for the therapist to accept the patient's story and facilitate a joint meaning-making process. This requires that the therapist be willing to change his or her own story of the patient so a new one will develop (Hasson-Ohayon et al., 2017).

Therapy focusing on metacognitive processes, therefore, needs to be attentive to emerging wishes and desires which may be contradictory, complimentary, or unrelated and what patients want to do about them. Similarly, what patients expect of therapists is likely to be fluid and changing. Further, the actions which meet these goals may be completely outside of therapy, as with enhanced metacognition, patients simply decide they need to do certain things and do them independently without consulting therapists – something that would fully align with what it means to direct one's own recovery.

Explicit attention is needed to promote reflection about intersubjective processes

Finally, the kinds of metacognitive activities measured in the research described above (e.g., deciding what one feels, wants, or how that fits into actual life events) are fundamentally intersubjective acts and always carried out in conjunction with other people, either with others directly or with others in mind. Generally, the ideas we form about ourselves and others are constructed in order to be shared with, or to respond to, the ideas of other people (Cortina & Liotti, 2010). More often than not, we explicitly or implicitly anticipate the responses of others to what we think about ourselves and other people. These other people could include immediate loved ones or rivals, others who are distant, or memories of persons who have died.

A final implication we will draw from the work on metacognition in psychosis is that psychotherapies which target metacognition need to consider that the ideas of self and others being formed in those therapies are taking place within the therapeutic intersubjective space, between the therapist and patient (Buck et al., 2015; Hasson-Ohayon et al., 2017). This would require continuous attention to the therapeutic relationship and the process of shared meaning development. In other words, such therapies require joint consideration of the relationship within which ideas about the patient are being formed. This is to say there has to be reflection about the changing ideas of the patient, but also on the environment in which those ideas are forming. This would seem again to require a framework in which the therapist is not 'teaching' the patient how to think, or even worse, what to think. There is a unique joint interaction and the product of that interaction will have to be in part unique to the characteristics of both parties in the dyad. The therapists' reflection on their own subjectivity and the willingness to self-disclose relevant feelings and thoughts can enhance the process of facilitating metacognition (Hasson-Ohayon, 2012; Hasson-Ohayon et al., 2017).

Metacognitive Reflection and Insight Therapy (MERIT): An illustration of an emerging form of therapy that targets metacognition in psychosis

MERIT: Structure and principles

One therapy which explicitly seeks to promote recovery from psychosis by enhancing metacognition is Metacognitive Reflection and Insight Therapy (MERIT) (Lysaker & Klion, 2017). MERIT assumes that recovery from psychosis is to be expected, regardless of how ill, demoralized, or disorganized patients may seem at the start of treatment. It also assumes patients are active agents in their own recovery during all phases of illness and that the therapist's role is one of an equal participant or consultant. It is thus a therapy for any consenting patient with psychosis and not only for patients who meet certain preconditions. MERIT is defined by eight elements, each of which is assumed to uniquely assist adults with psychosis to recapture atrophied, damaged, or perhaps previously not attained metacognitive abilities. As described elsewhere (Lysaker & Klion, 2017), the elements were developed through international dialogue among experts on performing and supervising psychotherapy across many different settings, including the authors of this chapter.

Table 1.1 MERIT elements

Designation	Element Name	Element Type
E1	Patient's Agenda	Content
E2	Therapist's Mind	Content
E3	Narrative Episode	Content
E4	Psychological Problem	Content
E5	Interpersonal Relationship	Process
E6	Progress	Process
E7	Stimulation of self-reflectivity and awareness of others	Superordinate
E8	Stimulation of Mastery	Superordinate

Taken as a whole, MERIT is an integrative framework that assists practitioners, from a range of perspectives, to tailor their practice in order to enhance meta-cognition. Each of the eight elements describes a measurable activity that should occur organically within every given session. Each reflects a process that can occur regardless of the unique dilemma a patient is experiencing. Thus, MERIT does not offer prescribed activities to be performed in a certain order. It is not a step-by-step guide, nor does it offer a specific curriculum. While the elements are synergistically related to each other, each is to be considered on its own and therapists are expected to be able to keep all elements in mind as the session progresses. These elements of MERIT are summarized in Table 1.1.

Research evidence

Although MERIT is still an emerging therapy, several studies have presented evidence that this therapy can be delivered under routine conditions and accepted by patients with psychosis (de Jong et al., 2016; de Jong et al., in press; Vohs et al., in press). One qualitative study has also revealed high levels of patient satisfaction along with improvements in sense of agency and the ability to manage and respond to emotional distress (Lysaker, Kukla et al., 2015). de Jong et al. (2016, in press) and detailed case studies have reported that participation in MERIT was associated with improved metacognitive capacity in patients with prolonged and early phases of psychosis (Arnon-Ribenfeld et al., in press; Hamm & Firmin, 2016; Hasson-Ohayon et al., in press; Hillis et al., 2015; James et al., in press; Leonhardt et al., 2016; Leonhardt et al., in press; van Donkersgoed et al., 2016). Bargenquast and Schweitzer (2014) also reported on the success of delivering a metacognitively oriented psychotherapy inspired by MERIT to adults with prolonged psychosis, with a therapy course ranging in length from 11 to 26 months. Finally, in a small Randomised Controlled Trial (RCT) Vohs et al. (in press) reported that participants with first episode psychosis with poor clinical insight who received six months of MERIT had a treatment completion rate of 80%. There were clinically and statistically significant improvements in objective measures of clinical insight without any concurrent increases in depression or demoralization.

Convergence and divergence with CBT

As an integrative framework, MERIT is intended to be applicable and usable by practitioners of a variety of therapies, including Cognitive Behavioral Therapy (CBT). Considered in that light, MERIT shares with the practices of mindfulness and Acceptance and Commitment Therapy (ACT), a focus on persons' relationship to their experience. MERIT and these therapies, sometimes called third wave CBT, are concerned with matters that go beyond individual thoughts and call for curiosity about mental experience with the expectations that persons' responses to life challenges will be unique. MERIT, however, is overtly focused on joint reflection about self-experience in the moment, as it occurs in the relationship with the therapist and across patients' personal narratives. It offers the context needed for events in the here and now to have personal meaning. Unlike ACT, MERIT de-emphasizes abstractions and looks to the larger complex web of mean-ings which span a unique life. Like mindfulness, MERIT is interested in patients' experiences as they occur in the mind in the moment, in response to the therapist's mind, etc. Unlike mindfulness, MERIT goes further and asks what those mental experiences mean in relation to one another, again in the context of the unique life of the patient. This is to say that MERIT is interested in how patients synthe-size or do not synthesize those experiences into a larger, flexible, and evolving sense of self and others in the world. An interesting point here is that MERIT may also regard self-knowledge differently than other second and third wave CBT. The self-knowledge that emerges from MERIT is not a knowledge of a true, as opposed to a false, sense of self but more of a complex sense of self, one that is diverse and potentially contradictory, and so is better able to respond to what develops in life.

Finally, in contrast to both second and third waves of CBT, MERIT stresses a somewhat different form of psychotherapeutic relationship. MERIT proposes unambiguously a non-hierarchical relationship in which meaning is made inter-subjectively. This is to say that advances happen when matters are reflected upon in a metaphorical space between people. Deepening self-experience in MERIT does not occur when an idea is first formed in the mind of the therapist and then shared with the patient. It is understanding which emerges from and within the encounter of two unique beings. Therapy thus has to begin with reflection about patients' experiences, especially their basic wishes and desires. This may be dif-ficult and time-consuming for patients who are out of touch with those wishes and desires, and in MERIT there is no shortcut for understanding what patients seek. For example, a MERIT therapist might ask a patient, 'What do you want me to understand?' before asking 'What do you want me to do?' These interpersonal and intersubjective elements of MERIT may often leave therapists with a period of confusion as they seek to understand the fragmented and anguished experience of another with no clear curriculum to follow to tell them what is best for the patient. Thus, MERIT may diverge from CBT in that it has additional emotional requirements which involve acceptance of fundamental vulnerability on the part of therapists.

Discussion and future directions

In this chapter, we have reviewed research on metacognition in psychosis and presented a theoretical and empirical basis for the connection between the forming of integrative senses of self and others and concurrent and prospective levels of function. We also interpreted this work as suggesting that therapies need to be adapted to enhance metacognition. We further argued that this work suggests that such therapies need to consider metacognition as a capacity that therapists must assess and focus on, according to patients' unique experiences. We have also suggested that metacognitive research tells us that such therapies should be responsive to fluid and evolving goals while also explicitly reflecting upon the interpersonal processes which enable metacognition to emerge. As an illustration, we presented one emerging therapy explicitly concerned with metacognition in psychosis.

Taken as whole, we suggest that emerging therapies focused on metacognition may also diverge from existing forms of CBT in several important ways. First, it seems unlikely that there will be a single recommended period for these kinds of therapies. Given patients' unique histories of cognitive compromise, stigma, trauma, demoralization, etc., it seems certain different amounts of exposure to therapy will be needed. These therapies are also likely to be at odds with skills-based approaches which primarily seek to 'get' people to think and do certain things. For many patients, deciding what 'things' they need to do or think may only reinforce their lack of agency and position as stigmatized and marginalized adults. Patients may seek to learn certain things or acquire certain kinds of knowledge and certainly therapists could assist accordingly. The key point would be that in a truly metacognitively focused therapy those requests would emerge organically and not be a function of the agenda of the therapist or curriculum of the therapy. Rather the plan is to explore the patient's agenda and meaning as a means to pursue and maintain personal defined goals.

Finally, since metacognition is about meaning creation which is beyond any specific approach to therapy, and since different people make meaning in different ways, metacognitively oriented therapies necessarily would have to be integrative, allowing therapists to flexibly respond to what is happening in the moment. This may be threatening and overwhelming to some therapists, requiring them to be able to think in the moment and manage their own confusion and sense of personal vulnerability. It may also unlock therapist creativity and allow therapists to be able to know the whole person with psychosis, ultimately leading to a more fulfilling professional life.

References

Arnon-Ribenfeld, N., Hasson-Ohayon, I., Lavidor, M., Atzil-Slonim, D., & Lysaker, P.H. (2017). The association between metacognitive abilities and outcome measures among people with schizophrenia: A meta-analysis. *European Psychiatry, 46*, 33–41.

Arnon-Ribenfeld, N., Bloom, R., Atzil-Sloman, D., Peri, T., de Jong, S., & Hasson-Ohayon, I. (2017). Metacognitive Reflection and Insight Therapy (MERIT) among people with schizophrenia: Lessons from two case studies. *American Journal of Psychotherapy*.

Bargenquast, R. & Schweitzer, R. (2014). Enhancing sense of recovery and self-reflectivity in people with schizophrenia: A pilot study of Metacognitive Narrative Psychotherapy. *Psychology and Psychotherapy: Theory, Research and Practice, 87*(3): 338–356.

Bleuler, E. (1950). *Dementia praecox or the group of schizophrenias*. New York: International Universities Press.

Buck, K.D., Buck, B.E., Hamm, J.A. & Lysaker, P.H. (2015). Martin Buber and evidence-based practice: Can the lion really lie down with the lamb? *Psychosis 8*(2), 156–165.

Buck, K.D., McLeod, H.J., Gumley, A., Dimaggio, G., Buck, B.E., Minor K., James, A.V. & Lysaker, P.H. (2014). Anhedonia in prolonged schizophrenia spectrum patients with relatively lower vs. higher levels of depression disorders: Associations with deficits in social cognition and metacognition. *Consciousness and Cognition, 10*(29c), 68–75.

Buck, K.D., Warman, D.M., Huddy, V. & Lysaker, P.H. (2012). The relationship of meta-cognition with jumping to conclusions among persons with schizophrenia spectrum disorders. *Psychopathology 45*(5), 271–275.

Cortina, M., & Liotti, G. (2010). The intersubjective and cooperative origins of consciousness: An evolutionary-developmental approach. *J Am Acad Psychoanal Dyn Psychiatry, 38*(2), 291–314.

Davis, L.W., Eicher, A.C., & Lysaker, P.H. (2011). Metacognition as a predictor of therapeutic alliance over 26 weeks of psychotherapy in schizophrenia. *Schizophrenia Research, 129*(1), 85–90.

Dinsmore, D.L., Alexander, P.A., & Louglin, S.M. (2008). Focusing the conceptual lens on metacognition, self-regulation, and self-regulated learning. *Educational Psychology Review. 20*, 391–409.

Flavell, J.H. (1979). Metacognition and cognitive monitoring: A new area of cognitive-developmental inquiry. *American Psychologist, 34*, 906–911.

Fonagy, P., Gergely, G., & Jurist, E.L. (2004). *Affect regulation, mentalization and the development of the self*. London: Karnac Books.

Hamm, J.A., Renard, S.B., Fogley, R.L., Leonhardt, B.L., Dimaggio, G., Buck, K.D. & Lysaker, P.H. (2012). Metacognition and social cognition in schizophrenia: Stability and relationship to concurrent and prospective symptom assessments. *Journal of Clinical Psychology, 68*(12), 1302–1312.

Hamm, J.A. & Firmin, R.L. (2016). Disorganization and individual psychotherapy for schizophrenia: A case report of Metacognitive Reflection and Insight Therapy. *Journal of Contemporary Psychotherapy, 46*(4), 227–234.

Hasson-Ohayon, I. (2012). Integrating cognitive behavioral-based therapy with an intersubjective approach: Addressing metacognitive deficits among people with schizophrenia. *Journal of Psychotherapy Integration, 22*(4), 356.

Hasson-Ohayon, I., Avidan, M., Mashiach–Eizenberg, M., Kravetz, S., Rozencwaig, S., Shalev, H. & Lysaker, P.H. (2015). Metacognitive and social cognition approaches to understanding the impact of schizophrenia on social quality of life. *Schizophrenia Research, 161*(2–3): 386–391.

Hasson-Ohayon, I., Kravetz, S., & Lysaker, P.H. (2017). The special challenges of psychotherapy with persons with psychosis: Intersubjective metacognitive model of agreement and shared meaning. *Clinical Psychology and Psychotherapy, 24*(2), 428–440.

Hasson-Ohayon, I., Arnon-Ribenfeld, N., Hamm, J.A. & Lysaker, P.H. (2017). Agency before action: The application of behavioral activation in psychotherapy with persons with psychosis. *Psychotherapy, 54*(3), 245.

Hillis, J.D., Leonhardt, B.L., Vohs, J.L., Buck, K.D., Salvatore, G., Popolo, R., Dimaggio, G. & Lysaker, P.H. (2015). Metacognitive Reflective and Insight Therapy for people in early phase of a schizophrenia spectrum disorder. *Journal of Clinical Psychology, 71*(2), 125–135.

James, A., Leonhardt, B., & Buck, K.D. (in press). Metacognitive Reflection and Insight Therapy for schizophrenia: A case study of an individual with a co-occurring substance use disorder. *American Journal of Psychotherapy.*

James, A.V., Hasson-Ohayon, I., Vohs, J., Minor, K.S., Leonhardt, B.L., Buck, K.D., George, S. & Lysaker, P.H. (2016). Metacognition moderates the relationship between self-appraisal and social functioning in prolonged schizophrenia independent of general psychopathology. *Comprehensive Psychiatry, 69*, 62–70.

de Jong, S., van Donkersgoed, R., Pijnenborg, G.H.M. & Lysaker, P.H. (2016). Metacognitive Reflection and Insight Therapy (MERIT) with a patient with severe symptoms of disorganization. *Journal of Clinical Psychology, 72*(2), 164–174.

de Jong, S., van Donkersgoedd, R.J.M., Timmerman, M.E., aan het Rot, M., Wunderinke, L., Arendsa, J., van der Gaag M., Aleman., A, Lysaker, P.H., & Pijnenborg, G.H.M. (in press). Metacognitive reflection and insight therapy (MERIT) for patients with schizophrenia. *Psychological Medicine.*

Kukla, M., Lysaker, P.H. & Salyers, M. (2013). Do persons with schizophrenia who have better metacognitive capacity also have a stronger subjective experience of recovery? *Psychiatry Research, 209*(3), 381–385.

Ladegaard, N., Lysaker, P.H., Larsen, E. & Videbech, P. (2014). A comparison of capacities for social cognition and metacognition in first episode and prolonged depression. *Psychiatry Research, 220*(3), 883–889.

Leonhardt, B.L., Benson, K., George, S., Buck, K.D., Shaieb, R., & Vohs, J.L. (2016). Targeting insight in first episode psychosis: A case study of Metacognitive Reflection Insight Therapy (MERIT). *Journal of Contemporary Psychotherapy, 46*(4), 207–216.

Leonhardt, B.L., Huling, K., Hamm, J.A., Roe, D., Hasson-Ohayon, I., McLeod, H., & Lysaker, P.H. (2017). Recovery and serious mental illness: A review of current clinical and research paradigms and future directions. *Expert Review of Neurotherapeutics, November, 17*(11): 1117–1130.

Leonhardt, B.L., Ratliff, K., & Buck, K.D. (in press). Recovery in first episode psychosis: A case study of metacognitive reflection and insight therapy (MERIT). *American Journal of Psychotherapy.*

Luther, L., Firmin, R.L., Vohs, J.L., Buck, K.D., Rand, K.L & Lysaker, P.H. (2016a). Intrinsic motivation as mediator between metacognitive deficits and impaired functioning in schizophrenia. *British Journal of Clinical Psychology, 55*(3), 332–347.

Luther, L., Firmin, R.L., Minor, K.S., Vohs, J.L., Buck, B., Buck, K.D. & Lysaker, P.H. (2016b). Metacognition deficits as a risk factor for prospective motivation deficits in schizophrenia. *Psychiatry Research, 245*, 172–178.

Lysaker, P.H., Carcione, A., Dimaggio, G., Johannesen, J.K., Nicolò, G., Procacci, M., & Semerari, A. (2005). Metacognition amidst narratives of self and illness in schizophrenia:

Associations with insight, neurocognition, symptom and function. *Acta Psychiatrica Scandinavica, 112,* 64–71.

Lysaker, P.H. & Dimaggio, G. (2014). Metacognitive capacities for reflection in schizophrenia: Implications for developing treatments. *Schizophrenia Bulletin. 40*(3), 487–491.

Lysaker, P.H., Dimaggio, G., Carcione, A., Procacci, M., Buck, K.D., Davis, LW. & Nicolò, G. (2010). Metacognition and schizophrenia: The capacity for self-reflectivity as a predictor for prospective assessments of work performance over six months. *Schizophrenia Research, 122*(1–3), 124–130.

Lysaker, P.H., Dimaggio, G., Wicket-Curtis, A., Kukla, M., Luedtke, B.L., Vohs, J., Leonhardt, B.L., James, A.V & Davis, L.W. (2015). Deficits in metacognitive capacity are related to subjective distress and heightened levels of hyperarousal symptoms in adults with Posttraumatic Stress Disorder. *Journal of Trauma and Dissociation, 26,* 1–15.

Lysaker, P.H., George, S., Chadoin-Patzel, K.A., Pec, O., Bob, P., Leonhardt, B.L., Vohs, J., James, A., Wickett-Curtis, A., Buck, K.D. & Dimaggio, G. (2017). Contrasting metacognitive, social cognitive and alexithymia profiles in adults with borderline personality disorder, schizophrenia and substance use disorder. *Psychiatry Research, 257:* 393–399.

Lysaker, P.H., Gumley, A., Luedtke, B., Buck, K.D., Ringer, J.M., Olesek, K. & Dimaggio, G. (2013). Social cognition and metacognition in schizophrenia: Evidence of their independence and linkage with outcomes. *Acta Psychiatrica Scandinavica, 127*(3), 239–247.

Lysaker, P.H., Kukla, M., Belanger, E., White, D.A., Buck, K.D., Luther, L., Firmin, R.L. & Leonhardt, B. (2015). Individual psychotherapy and changes in self-experience in schizophrenia: A qualitative comparison of patients in metacognitively focused and supportive psychotherapy. *Psychiatry, 78*(4), 305–316.

Lysaker, P.H., Kukla, M., Dubreucq, J., Gumley, A., McLeod, H., Buck, K.D., Minor, K.S., Luther, L., Leonhardt, B.L., Belanger, E.A., Popolo, R. & Dimaggio, G. (2015). Metacognitive deficits predict future levels of negative symptoms in schizophrenia controlling for neurocognition, affect recognition, and self-expectation of goal attainment. *Schizophrenia Research, 168*(1–2), 267–272.

Lysaker, P.H. & Klion, R. (2017). *Recovery, meaning-making, and severe mental illness: A comprehensive guide to Metacognitive Reflection and Insight Therapy.* New York: Routledge.

Lysaker, P.H., Leonhardt, B.L., Brüne, M., Buck, K.D., James, A., Vohs, J., Francis, M., Hamm, J.A., Salvatore, G., Ringer, J.M. & Dimaggio, G. (2014). Capacities for theory of mind, metacognition, and neurocognitive function as independently related to emotional recognition in schizophrenia. *Psychiatry Research, 30; 219*(1), 79–85.

Lysaker, P.H., McCormick, B.P., Snethen, G., Buck, K.D., Hamm, J.A., Grant M.L.A., Nicolo, G. & Dimaggio G. (2011). Metacognition and social function in schizophrenia: Associations of mastery with functional skills competence. *Schizophrenia Research, 131*(1–3), 214–218.

Lysaker, P.H., Vohs, J., Hamm, J.A., Kukla, M., Minor, K.S., de Jong, S. & Dimaggio, G. (2014). Deficits in metacognitive capacity distinguish patients with schizophrenia from those with prolonged medical adversity. *Journal of Psychiatric Research, 55,* 126–132.

Main, M. (1991). Metacognitive knowledge, metacognitive monitoring, and singular (coherent) vs. multiple (incoherent) models of attachment: findings and directions for future research. In: P. Harris, J. Stevenson- Hinde, C. Parkes (Eds.), *Attachment across the life cycle.* New York: Routledge. pp. 127–159.

McLeod, H.J., Gumley, A.I., MacBeth, A., Schwannauer, M. & Lysaker, P.H. (2014). Metacognitive functioning predicts positive and negative symptoms over 12 months in first episode psychosis. *Journal of Psychiatric Research*, 54, 109–115.

Moritz, S., Woodward, T.S., Burlon, M., Braus, D. & Andresen, B. (2007). Attributional style in schizophrenia: Evidence for a decreased sense of self-causation in currently paranoid patients. *Cognitive Therapy and Research, 31*, 371–383.

Nabors, L.M., Yanos, P.T., Roe D., Hasson-Ohayon, I., Leonhardt, B.L., Buck, K.D. & Lysaker, P.H. (2014). Stereotype endorsement, metacognitive capacity, and self-esteem as predictors of stigma resistance in persons with schizophrenia. *Comprehensive Psychiatry, 55*(4), 792–798.

Popolo, R., Smith, E., Lysaker, P.H., Lestingi, K., Cavallo, F., Melchiorre, L., Santone, C. & Dimaggio, G. (2017). Metacognitive profiles in schizophrenia and bipolar disorder: Comparisons with healthy controls and correlations with negative symptoms. *Psychiatry Research*, 257, 45–50.

Semerari, A., Carcione, A., Dimaggio, G., Falcon, M., Nicolo, G., Procacci, M. & Alleva, G. (2003). How to evaluate metacognitive function in psychotherapy? The metacognition assessment scale and its applications. *Clinical Psychology and Psychotherapy, 10*, 238–261.

Snethen, G., McCormick, B.P. & Lysaker, P.H. (2014). Physical activity and psychiatric symptoms in adults with schizophrenia spectrum disorders. *Journal of Nervous and Mental Disease, 202*(12), 845–852.

Silverstein, S.M. & Bellack, A.S. (2008). Scientific agenda for the concept of recovery as it applies to schizophrenia. *Clinical Psychology Review, 28*(7), 1108–1124.

Tomasello, M., Carpenter, M., Call, J., Behne, T. & Moll, H. (2005). Understanding and sharing intentions: The origin of cultural cognition. *The Behavioral and Brain Sciences, 28*, 691–735.

van Donkersgoed, R.J., de Jong, S. & Pijnenborg, G.H.M. (2016). Metacognitive Reflection and Insight Therapy (MERIT) with a patient with persistent negative symptoms. *Journal of Contemporary Psychotherapy, 46*(4), 245–254.

Vohs, J.L., Lysaker, P.H., Francis, M., Hamm, J., Buck, K.D., Olesek, K., Outcalt, J., Dimaggio, G., Leonhardt, B., Liffick, E., Mehdiyoun, N. & Breier, A. (2014). Metacognition, social cognition, and symptoms in patients with first episode and prolonged psychosis. *Schizophrenia Research, 153*, 54–59.

Vohs, J.L., Leonhardt, B.L., James, A.V., Francis, M.M., Breier, A, Mehdiyoun, N., Visco, A.C. & Lysaker P.H. (in press). Metacognitive Reflection and Insight Therapy for early psychosis: A preliminary study of a novel integrative psychotherapy. *Schizophrenia Research.*

WeiMing, W., Yi, D., Lysaker, P.H. & Kai, W. (2015). The relationship among the metacognitive ability, empathy and psychotic symptoms in schizophrenic patients in a post-acute phase of illness. *Chinese Journal of Behavioral Medicine and Brain Science 24*(2), 128–131.

Wells, A. (2000). *Emotional disorders and metacognition: Innovative cognitive therapy.* New York: John Wiley and Sons.

2

EMERGING PERSPECTIVES ON THE ROLE OF ATTACHMENT AND DISSOCIATION IN PSYCHOSIS

Katherine Berry, Sandra Bucci and Filippo Varese

Vulnerability to developing distressing psychotic experiences has been linked to a range of adverse socio-environmental circumstances, including poverty, social deprivation, urbanisation, discrimination or minority status, victimisation, substance misuse, unemployment and exposure to war conflicts (e.g., Read et al., 2008; van Os et al., 2010). Although adverse experiences occurring at any point over an individual's lifespan can influence the emergence of psychotic experiences, researchers have paid particular attention to the impact of experiences occurring in childhood and adolescence. This preferential focus on early adversities is motivated by two factors. First, the exposure to these adversities precedes the peak risk period for the emergence of full-blown distressing psychosis, which occurs most often in early adulthood (Baldwin et al., 2005). This minimises (but does not completely exclude) the possibility that exposure to life adversity could simply represent an indirect consequence of psychosis, rather than be a contributor to the development of psychotic experiences (for a commentary of the criteria used to determine causality in this research area, see Bentall & Varese, 2012). Second, given the importance of childhood and adolescence in shaping individuals' trajectories towards psychological and emotional adjustment and resilience in later life, the investigation of early contextual risk factors for psychosis has the appeal of providing the basic building blocks for a much needed developmental perspective of psychosis liability that does not only account for biological factors, but also social and environmental contributors as well as mediating psychological mechanisms.

In recent decades, growing interest has been shown in the potential impact of interpersonal adversities in childhood, such as abuse, neglect, peer victimisation and early separation from, or loss of, primary caregivers. Several meta-analytic studies suggest that these potentially traumatic experiences can dramatically increase the risk of developing psychosis (e.g., Varese et al., 2012b). Whilst early evidence for this relationship has largely relied on cross-sectional data and relatively small participant samples, a growing number of investigations have replicated these findings in both longitudinal cohort studies (e.g., Cutajar et al., 2010) as well as large-scale epidemiological studies demonstrating clear dose-response relationships (i.e., the more traumas experienced in childhood, the stronger the risk of developing psychosis later in life; e.g., Shevlin et al., 2007). To paraphrase psychologist John Read, one of the researchers that most contributed to this research area, the notion that childhood trauma might represent a robust risk factor for psychosis is not a fringe hypothesis, but an undeniable certainty supported by empirical evidence (Read, 2013).

The notion that childhood adversities and other traumatic experiences can influence the development, course and severity of psychosis has increasingly informed recommendations for clinical practice calling for the routine assessment of trauma and trauma-related difficulties in this clinical population, and the delivery of appropriate trauma-focused therapies to ameliorate trauma-related distress in people with psychosis (e.g., NICE, 2014). Psychological interventions such as Eye Movement Desensitization and Reprocessing (EMDR) therapy, prolonged exposure and Trauma-Focused Cognitive Behaviour Therapy (TF-CBT) are increasingly being evaluated for their safety and efficacy in terms of improving post-traumatic symptoms in people with psychosis (e.g., van den Berg et al., 2015; Sin et al., 2017). Furthermore, preliminary evidence indicates that the severity of psychotic symptoms can also decrease with the provision of these trauma-focused interventions, suggesting that the amelioration of trauma-related symptoms and processes may have a knock-on effect on the severity of characteristic symptoms of psychosis, such as paranoia (e.g., de Bont et al., 2016). These findings are corroborated by a series of cross-sectional studies of people with clinical psychosis and non-clinical samples, indicating that the relationship between trauma exposure and the presence or severity of psychotic experiences is mediated by post-traumatic stress symptoms (e.g., Hardy et al., 2016). However, the expanding literature on the psychological mediators of the relationship between trauma and psychosis has also highlighted that other psychological sequelae of childhood adversity could play an influential role in the pathways leading to the development of hearing voices and other distressing psychotic symptoms. In turn, psychological therapies considering these additional processes may represent fruitful treatment options for people with distressing psychosis. We will elaborate on these clinical implications towards the end of the chapter but feel that it is first important to provide the theoretical context and empirical evidence behind our thinking.

Dissociation and insecure attachment are amongst the most widely investigated mediators of the trauma-psychosis relationship (Williams, Varese, Berry & Bucci, under review). Within the body of empirical studies in this area, attachment and dissociation have often been conceptualised as relatively independent processes, possibly implicated in the etiology of different psychotic experiences (e.g., Bentall et al., 2014). However, in this chapter we set out alternative proposals suggesting that disorganised attachment specifically, and the predisposition to dissociate, are closely and meaningfully related phenomena (Liotti, 2004), and that

26

their combined action can, in some individuals, lead to heightened vulnerability to developing psychosis. Here, we will first provide an overview of empirical studies of the relationship between dissociation and symptoms of psychosis, focusing in particular on voice hearing, as this phenomenon has been most frequently linked to heightened dissociation. We will then describe how the development of dissociation is in turn influenced by specific attachment representations that are commonly observed in individuals with complex trauma histories, and how attachment theory (Bowlby, 1969) and dissociation could provide a meaningful framework for understanding possible pathways leading to distressing voices and other psychotic symptoms. After highlighting priorities for future research to test the most pressing hypotheses proposed, importantly we summarise how cognitive behavioural interventions for psychosis can be adapted to incorporate work with dissociation and attachment in people with a history of reported early adversity. Whilst many of the ideas we present in terms of clinical implications will resonate with other chapters in this book, here we focus on the science behind the recommendations for practice.

Dissociation

There is considerable variation in the way in which dissociation is conceptualised in the literature. In general, dissociation is used as a catch-all term to describe a range of psychological phenomena characterised by a 'lack of normal integration of thoughts, feelings and experiences into the stream of consciousness and memory' (Bernstein & Putnam, 1986, p. 727). These experiences are found in non-clinical as well as help-seeking individuals, and are not necessarily indicative of a need for care. Despite this, dissociative experiences can be distressing and problematic, and within current diagnostic classification systems, they represent a core component of several psychiatric disorders (e.g., dissociative disorders such as Dissociative Identity Disorder and Depersonalisation or Derealisation Disorder, but also specific trauma and stress-related presentations such as the Post-Traumatic Stress Disorder (PTSD) dissociative subtype introduced in the latest revision of the Diagnostic and Statistical Manual (APA, 2013). There has been considerable debate as to whether dissociation is best represented as a single continuum of severity or as several aetiologically and phenomenologically distinct 'subtypes', typically referred to as 'compartmentalisation' and 'detachment' (Holmes et al., 2005; Brown, 2006). The former implies that mild or fleeting dissociative experiences common in non-clinical individuals, for example absorption, represent the 'lower boundary' of more pervasive and potentially disabling dissociative experiences, such as identity alteration and extreme depersonalised states. There is also considerable variation in the extent to which different authors and empirical studies regard dissociation as, for example, a general trait-like disposition, a potentially functional 'mechanism' in response to threat, or as the endpoint of some pathogenic process or psychological dysfunction that requires care. Mindful of these debates, we accept that the description of dissociation we

27

will provide here may not always be compatible with other perspectives represented in the extensive literature on dissociative phenomena. In the context of the current chapter, we use the term 'dissociation' broadly and descriptively to indicate states of consciousness characterised by a sense of separation within certain elements of one's current experience and mental functioning captured by multifactorial measures that are used widely in both research and clinical settings (e.g., the Dissociative Experiences Scale). We align ourselves with theoretical and clinical perspectives that regard dissociation as a potentially adaptive response to unbearable or inescapable life adversities, but that can become a source of concern and distress when such a method for coping with adversities becomes chronic, uncontrollable and/or interferes with the person's functioning, values and life goals.

Dissociation and trauma

Many authors and empirical studies have sought the origin of dissociation in the traumatic histories that are often described by individuals reporting pervasive dissociative experiences. Dissociation is in fact frequently observed both during and in the immediate aftermath of traumatic events (i.e., peri-traumatic dissociation), and survivors can experience a heightened predisposition to dissociate long after the original trauma (e.g., Dalenberg et al., 2012). The link between trauma and dissociation has been the subject of extensive theoretical debate and empirical scrutiny, with some regarding this association as spurious (explainable, for example, in terms of confounding factors such as fantasy proneness (Merckelbach & Muris, 2001), and others as consistent with the alleged action of an in-built 'defence mechanism' that allows people to reduce the overwhelming emotional and cognitive consequences of traumatic experiences (for a critical appraisal of these theoretical debates and associated empirical research, see Dalenberg et al., 2012).

There is considerable evidence suggesting that the link between early adversities and dissociation might not be an artefactual one (Dalenberg et al., 2012). For example, the findings of cross-sectional studies suggesting a robust association between histories of childhood abuse and adult dissociation (e.g., van IJzendoorn & Schuengel, 1996) have been corroborated by a growing number of longitudinal investigations and studies that sought objective confirmation of self-reported trauma histories (Dalenberg et al., 2012). Heightened dissociation has been linked to a wide range of traumatic life experiences. Although trauma may not always be necessary for dissociation to occur, empirical studies indicate that the risk of experiencing pervasive dissociative phenomena is particularly elevated in individuals exposed to severe interpersonal adversities, such as acts of abuse, maltreatment or victimisation perpetrated by close family members or significant others. For example, Betrayal Trauma Theory argues that traumas are particularly toxic if they involve a breach of trust from a significant other. Findings of studies on betrayal trauma suggest that the association between interpersonal traumatic experiences characterised by high interpersonal closeness and dissociative phenomena is particularly robust relative to those between dissociation and other types of traumas studied (e.g., Hulette et al., 2011; Gómez et al., 2014). Betrayal trauma is important here as it is a theoretical model that views dissociation as an adaptive response that minimises the distress and conflict faced when perpetrators are also the very same persons or institutions on which the victim depends for their survival or well-being (Freyd, 2008). In the light of the evidence from these empirical studies, traumatic events that occur in the context of salient relationships at critical stages of development (e.g., within child-caregiver relationships in childhood, but also within valued peer and romantic relationships in adolescence and early adulthood) can be regarded as particularly influential to the development of dissociation and related-phenomena.

Dissociation, hearing voices and other psychotic experiences

Given the growing interest in the role played by early interpersonal adversities in psychosis, it is not surprising that dissociation has come under increasing empirical scrutiny within the psychosis literature (for a detailed analysis of the varied perspectives on the interplay between trauma, dissociation and psychosis, see Moskowitz et al., 2009). Meta-analytic findings indicate that dissociative experiences are commonly elevated in people experiencing psychosis (O'Driscoll et al., 2014), with several studies suggesting that these heightened levels of dissociation are unlikely to simply be caused by the presence of psychotic symptoms as they are often predicted by trauma exposure (e.g., Schäfer et al., 2006; Varese et al., 2012a).

In addition to the above findings, numerous investigations have attempted to examine whether dissociation may be associated with increased proneness to experience specific psychotic symptoms, most notably hallucinations (and voice-hearing, more specifically). For example, cross-sectional studies have indicated that dissociative experiences are particularly prevalent amongst voice-hearers relative to service users with psychosis who do not currently experience voices or who have never heard voices (e.g., Goff et al., 1991; Perona-Garcelán et al., 2012a; Perona-Garcelán et al., 2014; Varese et al., 2012a). Studies which examined the predictors of hallucinatory experiences over the course of daily life in people with psychosis have similarly observed increased levels of dissociation during hallucinatory episodes (Varese et al., 2011). In our recent systematic review and meta-analysis of all cross-sectional studies, we found evidence of a robust association between dissociation and voice-hearing not only in individuals with psychosis, but also in studies with non-clinical samples and those who received other psychiatric diagnoses (Pilton et al., 2015). It has been argued that dissociation could represent a candidate process to explain the association between trauma and hearing voices (e.g., Moskowitz & Corstens, 2008; Altman et al., 1997; Anketell et al., 2010). This has been supported by the findings of recent cross-sectional studies suggesting that dissociation mediates the relationship between childhood adversity and the proneness to hearing voices in both clinical (Perona-Garcelán et al., 2012a; Varese et al., 2012a) and non-clinical samples (e.g., Perona-Garcelan et al., 2012b; Cole et al., 2016). Longitudinal evidence to further support this indirect 'dissociative pathway' linking childhood adversity to voices is currently lacking. However, in a recent prospective study, Geddes, Ehlers and Freeman (2016) found that peri-traumatic dissociation (in conjunction with other variables) predicted the onset of hallucinatory experiences in adult survivors of adult interpersonal assaults.

Despite these encouraging findings, it has been highlighted that the exact processes through which dissociation leads to the formation of voices remain unspecified in both theoretical models and the empirical literature (Steel, 2017). Studies have often cited generic mechanistic explanations such as that provided by Allen et al. (1997), who proposed that the experience of trauma-induced dissociation could increase an individual's vulnerability to developing psychotic symptoms by depriving them of 'internal and external anchors'. This would increase the individual's sense of feeling disconnected from their world, interpersonal relationships and intrapersonal self, leading to impaired reality-testing and states of confusion, disorganisation, and disorientation which appear to mirror, or increase proneness to, psychotic experiences.

More recently, there has been speculation that the cognitive underpinnings of dissociation could interact or overlap with those that promote hallucinatory experiences (e.g., Bentall & Varese, 2013; Varese et al., 2012a), but studies specifically examining this proposal are extremely sparse. In a rare study of this kind, Varese, Barkus & Bentall (2012a) tested service-users with psychosis on self-report measures of dissociation and experimental measures of 'reality discrimination', or source monitoring. This refers to the ability to accurately discriminate between internally and externally generated mental events, which has often been found to be anomalous in clinical and non-clinical hallucination-prone individuals (Bentall, 1990; Brookwell et al., 2013). This study found tentative evidence suggesting that dissociation and reality discrimination difficulties independently contribute to hallucination-proneness, but further research is required to replicate these findings and explore the overlap between dissociation and the numerous cognitive anomalies that have been linked to hallucinatory experiences in previous experimental studies. (For a review, see Waters et al., 2012.)

To summarise, considerable evidence supports the existence of a robust association between dissociative phenomena and hearing voices. However, it should be noted that although considerable research has focused on potential links with voices, this does not preclude the possibility that dissociation could also be implicated in the formation and maintenance of other psychotic experiences. For example, in a recent study by Longden and colleagues (2016), dissociation and childhood trauma histories were found to be linked not only to voice-hearing, but also to hallucinatory experiences in other sensory modalities. Furthermore, mediation studies with clinical and non-clinical participants have indicated that dissociation and related phenomena mediate the relationship between early adversity and psychotic experiences more generally (e.g., Evans et al., 2015; Berenbaum et al., 2008). In a recent study by our research group (Pearce et al., 2017), we found that dissociation was a robust mediator of the impact of childhood interpersonal trauma on paranoia, even when controlling for the co-variation between voices and paranoia. This suggests that additional research is required to further explore the role of dissociation in increasing vulnerability for other potentially distressing psychotic experiences, and that therapeutic interventions that consider dissociation may not only be beneficial in people with psychosis struggling with distressing voices, but also those with other clinical presentations.

Attachment theory

The potential influence of relationships and early relational trauma on the experi- ence of psychosis has led a growing number of researchers to apply Bowlby's (1969) attachment theory to the understanding of voices (Berry et al., 2007; Berry & Bucci, 2016; Longden et al., 2012; Read & Gumley, 2008). According to attach- ment theory, early experiences of caregiving influence later methods of regulating distress and interpersonal functioning in adulthood via the development of internal working models, which are essentially cognitive and emotional representations of the self in relation to others, such as 'I am worthy of love and attention' and 'other people can be trusted'. Suboptimal caregiving, including both subtle but frequent disruptions in caregiving and more extreme experiences of neglect and abuse, have all been identified as aetiological precursors of more negative representations of the self and others and associated difficulties in relating to others and regulating negative affect (Bifulco et al., 2002; Whiffen et al., 1999). Conversely, responsive and sensitive enough caregiving results in a secure attachment style, which is associated with a positive self-image, capacity to manage negative affect and appropriate levels of comfort or autonomy in interpersonal relationships (Hazan & Shaver, 1987). Clearly both of these possibilities have important implications for someone's future relationship to caregivers, including mental health services.

Different types or dimensions of so-called insecure attachment have been identified in both the child and adult psychology literatures. Most commonly, adult insecure-attachment has been conceptualised in terms of two dimensions: insecure-anxious and insecure-avoidant attachment. Anxious attachment is associ- ated with a negative image of the self, an overly dependent interpersonal style, fear of rejection and a tendency to become overwhelmed by negative affect. High levels of anxious attachment are hypothesised to develop in response to caregivers who are inconsistently available or relate over-intrusively towards the infant. Avoidant attachment is associated with a negative image of others, interpersonal hostility, social withdrawal and minimisation of affect. High levels of avoidant attachment are hypothesised to develop in response to caregivers who are consist- ently emotionally unavailable, critical and rejecting towards the infant (Granqvist et al., 2010). In addition to the so-called organised attachment patterns of secure, anxious and avoidant styles, researchers have identified a fourth category, termed 'disorganised attachment' in the childhood attachment literature and 'unresolved', unclassified' or 'fearful' attachment in the adult attachment literature. A disorganised attachment style is characterised by dissociative processes in response to threat (Main & Solomon, 1986; 1990) and a lack of coherent attachment strategies, involving a vacillation between approach and avoidance behaviours in relationships; for example, wanting intimacy with others, but fearing rejection and closeness (Bartholomew, 1997). This particular attachment pattern is hypothesised to result from childhood experiences where the attachment figure, a supposed source of safety, becomes a source of threat (Liotti, 2004). Most commonly, this paradoxical situation occurs when caregivers are the perpetrators of physical, sexual or emotional abuse (Lyons-Ruth & Jacobvitz, 1999), but it is also hypothesised that the development of a disorganised attachment pattern is influenced by more subtle (but frequent or pervasive) disruptions in parental attunement, possibly caused by a range of adverse conditions and circumstances (e.g., parental poor mental health, trauma and experiences of loss) (Cyr et al., 2010; Hesse & Main, 2006; Lyons-Ruth & Jacobvitz, 1999; Lyons-Ruth et al., 2005; Van IJzendoorn et al., 1995; 1999).

There is evidence of associations between earlier relational trauma and insecure attachment in people with psychosis (Berry et al., 2009; Mulligan & Lavender, 2010; Tait et al., 2004) and there is relatively consistent evidence that people with psychosis are more likely to report insecure attachment styles compared to non-clinical samples, with evidence of a predominance of avoidant attachment (Berry et al., 2008; Gumley, et al., 2014) or more recently disorganised attachment (Bucci et al., 2017). There are no studies directly comparing the proportion of different types of attachment in representative samples of people with and without psychosis. Rates of attachment on a self-report measure administered to a general population sample were: 59% secure, 11% anxious and 25% avoidant attachment (Mickelson et al., 1997). In a study using the Adult Attachment Interview (AAI) in a typical non-clinical adult sample of 584 non-clinical mothers, 58% were classified as secure, 24% as dismissing and 18% as preoccupied attachment (Van IJzendoorn & Bakermans-Kranenburg, 1996). In a study using the AAI in an early onset psychosis sample, MacBeth, Gumley, Schwannauer and Fisher (2011) report rates of 26.5% secure, 61.8% dismissing and 11.8% preoccupied attachment. In a large study using self-report measures with 588 people with psychosis, Bucci et al. (2017) report rates of 37% for secure, 20% for insecure-avoidant, 28% for insecure-anxious and 14% for disorganised attachment.

In examining the psychological mechanisms mediating the effects between trauma and psychosis, researchers have increasingly focused on specific psychotic experiences, such as paranoia and voices, and this is also true of the attachment and psychosis literatures. It has been argued that earlier interpersonal traumas increase vulnerability to both paranoia (Berry et al., 2008) and voice-hearing (Longden et al., 2012; Berry & Bucci, 2016) via disruptions in the attachment system. In a paper considering the possible psychological pathways linking early adversity to psychosis, Bentall et al. (2014) argued that attachment-threatening events might be more important in the pathways leading to paranoia than hallucinations. Empirical evidence to date has supported this proposal, with findings from both clinical and non-clinical studies demonstrating that anxious and avoidant attachment predict paranoia, but not hallucinations, after controlling for the co-variation between these two experiences (Pickering et al., 2008; Wickham et al., 2015). Similarly, anxious and avoidant attachment mediated the relationship between early adversity and paranoia, but not hallucinations, in a general population sample (Sitko et al., 2014). Associations between insecure attachment and paranoia make intuitive sense. Insecure attachment styles are associated with negative beliefs about the self and others, and avoidant attachment in particular is associated with avoidance of social relationships; these self and other beliefs and social withdrawal are fundamental to cognitive models of paranoia (Berry et al., 2007).

However, in contrast to the argument that attachment experiences are not involved in the development of voice-hearing, Berry & Bucci (2016) point out the robust associations between childhood abuse and voice-hearing (e.g., Read et al., 2005; Shevlin et al., 2007). They argue that experiences of childhood abuse where the perpetrator is a caregiver, or where the caregiver fails to appropriately support the victim, are also very likely to impact on the individual's attachment system. The authors present the Cognitive Attachment Model of Voices (CAV), which postulates that, in the context of early adversity, disorganised attachment might play a particularly important role in increasing vulnerability to voice-hearing. The CAV argues that disorganised attachment renders an individual more vulnerable to dissociate (either consciously or unconsciously) in response to ongoing abuse from caregivers or abuse in the context of later relationships, exacerbating the development of psychotic-like experiences, and voices in particular, in some individuals.

In support of hypothesised associations between attachment difficulties and dissociation, there is evidence of associations between retrospective reports of parental loss and later dissociation or absorption in offspring (Hesse & Van IJzendoorn, 1998; Liotti, 1992). Prospective, longitudinal studies have found similar results in terms of developmental pathways to dissociation (e.g., Dutra et al., 2009; Lyons-Ruth et al., 2006; Ogawa et al., 1997; Sroufe, 2005). For example, Ogawa et al. (1997) examined dissociative behaviours and their relationship to attachment organisation in 168 young adults at high risk of poor developmental outcomes due to poverty using a longitudinal design, which assessed traumatic life events, attachment quality, adaptive functioning and dissociative symptomatology at five time points, from birth to 19 years. In addition to age of onset, severity and chronicity of trauma, disorganised and avoidant attachment to parents was a significant predictor for scores on all the measures of dissociative phenomena. Surprisingly few studies have investigated associations between adult attachment and dissociation. One study investigated PTSD and dissociation in victimised female college students with and without a history of childhood abuse. They found that self-reported secure attachment style was negatively related to dissociation as measured by the Dissociative Experiences Scale (Bernstein & Putnam, 1986), and self-reported preoccupied (another term for anxious attachment) and fearful attachment were positively related to dissociation (Sandberg, 2010). When the effects of abuse and the four attachment scores were assessed in the same model, only fearful attachment had a unique contribution to dissociation. As argued below, fearful attachment is related to the concept of disorganised attachment and in particular taps into the approach-avoidant behaviour associated with this type of attachment pattern.

Despite relatively robust evidence of associations between dissociation and voice-hearing, and some evidence of associations between attachment difficulties and dissociation, there is a limited number of studies investigating associations between disorganised attachment and voice-hearing. One reason for the paucity of evidence is the lack of a suitable measure of disorganised attachment in adulthood. Studies of voice-hearing and attachment discussed above (e.g. Pickering et al., 2008; Sitko et al., 2014; Wickham et al., 2015) have measured attachment using self-report measures that include a fearful attachment subscale. The concept of fearful attachment taps into the vacillation between approach-avoidance behaviours in relationships that characterise disorganised attachment, but not the dissociative processes in response to threat that are also hypothesised to characterise the disorganised pattern of attachment. This concept is most closely assessed by the unresolved attachment pattern on the AAI (George et al., 1985). However, the AAI has only been used in a handful of psychosis studies which have had relatively small sample sizes (see Gumley et al., 2014, for a review), as the measure requires extensive training to use and is time-consuming to administer and score. A recent study by our research group has attempted to address the difficulty in measuring disorganised attachment by using latent profile analysis methods to derive a measure of disorganised attachment from a self-report measure of attachment assessing anxious and avoidant attachment styles (Bucci et al., 2017). In a sample of 588 participants with psychosis, we used scores on the anxious and avoidant subscales of the Psychosis Attachment Measure (PAM) (Berry et al., 2008), the most frequently used self-report attachment measure in psychosis research, to assign people to one of four attachment categories: secure, anxious, avoidant or disorganised. Participants in the secure category scored relatively low on all PAM items, participants in the anxious category scored relatively high on the PAM anxiety subscale items, participants in the avoidant category scored relatively high on the PAM avoidant subscale items, and participants in the disorganised category scored relatively highly on all PAM items. In line with our predictions from the CAV, we found that those reporting a trauma history – in particular, sexual and physical abuse – and more frequent positive psychotic symptoms, were assigned to a disorganised attachment class (Bucci et al., 2017).

Future research

The ideas presented in this chapter highlight a number of different foci for future research. First, studies should investigate the role of dissociation and disorganised attachment in explaining the association between early trauma and voices within a single model, preferably a serial mediation model (Hayes, 2013). Serial mediation is a statistical method that allows researchers to test the sequence of mediation effects. If the CAV is correct, we would expect to see that trauma would indirectly influence voice-hearing through the mediators of disorganised attachment and dissociation. Second, these studies need to investigate the role that commonly co-occurring symptoms, such as paranoia, play in explaining these relationships – and in particular associations between dissociation and other symptoms of psychosis. Third, as current evidence points to the fact that dissociation is a multi-faceted concept, studies need to tease out which particular aspects of dissociation are important in explaining any associations between trauma, attachment and voices. The Dissociative Experiences Scale (DES), which is the most commonly used measure of dissociation in the literature, does not provide an adequate assessment of the dissociative phenomenon of compartmentalisation. Compartmentalisation is defined in terms of dissociated memories, thoughts, flashbacks or emotional processes, and is arguably an important construct to consider in relation to hallucinations. Fourth, further research is needed to investigate associations between specific childhood adversities and attachment, including disorganised attachment, which is not well captured by self-report measures of attachment styles. As highlighted above, Bucci et al. (2017) describe using a simple self-report measure of attachment to derive a measure of disorganised attachment using latent class analysis, but arguably we need processes for more directly measuring disorganised attachment that are more feasible than the AAI to use in the context of large research studies. Fifth, there is a growing call to examine resilience factors within the context of trauma and psychosis. Secure attachment, which is shaped by biological, psychological and social influences, may be an important resilience factor that both influences the likelihood of experiencing dissociation in response to trauma and/or how adaptively people respond to psychosis symptoms once they develop. Indeed, evidence shows that secure attachment is a potentially important resilience factor in preventing the development of post-traumatic stress disorder following exposure to trauma (Woodhouse et al., 2015), suggesting it would be important to examine if these findings generalise to other trauma-related symptoms, such as dissociation and psychotic symptoms.

Finally, whilst our work provides potentially beneficial directions for supporting people with distressing voices, the clinical utility of attachment and dissociation-focused work in people with voices and other distressing psychotic experiences remains to be ascertained. A clearer mechanistic account of *how* attachment and dissociation increase one's propensity to develop voices would be beneficial to further strengthen the clinical and scientific rationale for such interventions. In parallel, the early stages of evaluation of the clinical efficacy of interventions with a direct focus on attachment and dissociation will benefit from the use of research designs that have the potential to clarify the exact mechanisms of action which lead to effective treatment; for example, carefully designed case series (e.g. Morley, 2007).

Clinical implications

The ideas presented here have a number of clinical implications, particularly for people with psychosis who also have complex, traumatic relational histories with caregivers, and who may be vulnerable to experiencing disorganised attachment patterns and associated dissociative processes in response to later threat. Trauma-focused interventions such as TF-CBT and EMDR are being increasingly evaluated as potential options for treating PTSD symptoms in those with psychosis. Whilst such interventions may prove beneficial for the treatment of 'straightforward' post-traumatic presentations, it is increasingly recognised that clients with complex trauma histories and related severe mental health needs may need interventions that are suitably adapted to account for the psychological consequences of complex trauma (e.g., Herman, 1992). As yet, there are no widely accepted or evidence-based guidelines for the management and treatment of psychological difficulties linked to complex trauma. However, clinicians have generally argued for the importance of using sequential approaches involving prolonged preparatory or stabilisation work (self-management of presenting difficulties, emotion-regulation and self-soothing, and promotion of safety and stability in the present) prior to the introduction of therapeutic work focusing on trauma and related difficulties (e.g., Herman, 1992; Linehan, 1993). Both service-user (ASCA, 2012) and professional (UKPTS, 2017) organisations have explicitly recommended that such stabilisation work includes adjustments to manage attachment issues and severe dissociative responses. Informed by the evidence reviewed in this chapter, clinicians could employ measures of attachment insecurity (e.g., the PAM) and dissociation (e.g., the DES) to augment the assessment of their clients' presenting difficulties and identify those who may need additional focus on attachment and dissociation, both at the outset and periodically throughout therapy.

A focus on attachment and dissociation emphasises the importance of so-called 'non-specific' factors within therapy and the power of the therapeutic relationship itself. In attachment terms, the stabilisation phase of therapy is key to developing a secure base akin to the idea of the caregiver acting as a secure base in infancy, thereby enabling the infant to explore the external world with the confidence that support and help is at hand if needed. Indeed, Bowlby (1988) conceptualised the therapeutic relationship as an attachment relationship and argued that effective psychotherapeutic intervention can provide an alternative interpersonal experience termed a 'corrective emotional experience', affording individuals the opportunity to develop a broader range of interpersonal behaviours. Therapists who display sensitivity, responsiveness, reliability and consistency are able to attune to their clients' emotional needs and offer a secure base in therapy. CBT therapies for psychosis traditionally advocate increased emphasis on engagement with this client group with early sessions dedicated to relationship building. However, in the case of those with disorganised attachment patterns, it is questionable whether there is sufficient time to achieve this goal within current CBT protocols for psychosis, or indeed the number of sessions typically delivered in National Health

Service settings within the UK. Indeed, we might predict that those with disorganised attachment are more likely to drop out of therapies, or if they do engage, make less therapeutic gains within the current service parameters. To provide effective therapy for this group, CBT for psychosis may in future need to develop a much greater focus on emotional-interpersonal factors (Liotti & Gumley, 2008).

In the context of an attachment-informed therapy for psychosis, once a 'secure base' has been established and the person is willing, individuals may feel more comfortable to explore and process the links between previous relationships and symptoms. A number of attachment-informed therapists have argued that the ultimate goal of therapy when working with traumatised people with disorganised attachment patterns is perhaps helping the person develop a narrative account of their experiences. This might involve a sequential process, starting with overcoming avoidance through imagery and later moving to a more objective distanced position (Holmes, 2001; Wallin, 2007; Van der Hart et al., 2006). In dissociation terms, this process ultimately helps individuals to integrate traumatic experiences and disassociated affect with other parts of their personality. For example, when working with earlier trauma, Van der Hart et al. (2006) suggest that the therapist must empathically explore all the client's conflicted feelings and beliefs related to perpetrators. We suggest that this approach of exploring the content of traumatic life experiences and sequelae would need to be carried out in addition to process-orientated approaches which address the person's relationship to distressing experience.

In addition to the above attachment-informed principles guiding the delivery of therapy, early stabilisation work might include specific intervention strategies for the management of dissociative responses. Although the added value of using strategies to counter dissociation in clients with distressing psychosis is yet to be evaluated, case studies (Larkin & Morrison, 2005; Newman-Taylor & Sambrook, 2013) and, more recently, small-scale trials (Farrelly et al., 2016) suggest that such work can be meaningfully integrated into psychological formulation and treatment plans for this client group. Such work could include cognitive-behavioural strategies to increase the controllability of dissociative responses, such as recognition and management of triggers as well as refocusing and grounding techniques (e.g., Kennerly, 1996, 2009). A range of 'third wave' CBT techniques for the promotion of alternative and potentially more adaptive emotion regulation abilities could similarly prove beneficial, such as distress tolerance skills and low arousal strategies (e.g., Linehan, 1993; McKay et al., 2012) or mindfulness training (Zerubavel & Messman-Moore, 2015).

In addition to an increased focus on stabilisation and the development of a secure base, we would argue that therapists working with people with disorganised attachment patterns need to explicitly consider the person's tendency to act in seemingly unpredictable ways within the therapeutic relationship and with others outside of therapy, including other mental health care workers, and acknowledge how this can worry, confuse or overwhelm others (Wallin, 2007). In this context, it is important that the therapist and other members of the mental health team remain concerned, but not become overwhelmed or frightened by, affect storms and shifting symptoms. With disorganised attachment patterns, the therapist must tolerate oscillation, for example missing sessions and drop-outs, and still proactively try to engage the person until they are ready. This may involve writing to or phoning the client following missed appointments. Therapists must also be especially mindful of repairing potentially frequent alliance ruptures (Wallin, 2007).

Conclusions

There is a growing call to understand the psychological mechanisms underpinning psychosis and apply this understanding to the development of psychological treatments. Here, we argue that the psychological mechanisms of dissociation and attachment might enhance current understanding. Further empirical work is needed to determine how these mechanisms interact with each other and to explain the trauma and psychosis link. Before this field can advance we need more sophisticated measures of the compartmentalisation aspect of dissociation and disorganised attachment. Nonetheless, on the basis of the evidence presented here, we suggest that there are sufficient grounds for exploring the concepts of dissociation and attachment within therapeutic work with those with psychosis and complex trauma histories.

References

Adults Surviving Childhood Abuse (2012). *Practice guidelines for treatment of complex trauma and trauma informed care and service delivery.* Kirribilli, Australia: ASCA.

Allen, J. G., Coyne, L. & Console, D. A. (1997). Dissociative detachment relates to psychotic symptoms and personality decompensation. *Comprehensive Psychiatry, 38*(6), 327–334.

Altman, H., Collins, M., & Mundy, P. (1997). Subclinical hallucinations and delusions in nonpsychotic adolescents. *Journal of Child Psychology and Psychiatry, 38*(4), 413–420.

American Psychiatric Association. (2013). *Diagnostic and statistical manual of mental disorders* (5th ed.). Arlington, VA: American Psychiatric Publishing.

Anketell, C., Dorahy, M. J., Shannon, M., Elder, R., Hamilton, G., Corry, M., MacSherry, A. & O'Rawe, B. (2010). An exploratory analysis of voice hearing in chronic PTSD: Potential associated mechanisms. *Journal of Trauma & Dissociation, 11*(1), 93–107.

Bartholomew, K. (1997). Adult attachment processes: Individual and couple perspectives. *Psychology and Psychotherapy: Theory, Research and Practice, 70*(3), 249–263.

Baldwin, P., Browne, D., Scully, P. J., Quinn, J. F., Morgan, M. G., Kinsella, A., Owens, J. M., Russell, V., O'Callaghan, E., & Waddington, J. L. (2005). Epidemiology of first-episode psychosis: Illustrating the challenges across diagnostic boundaries through the Cavan-Monaghan study at 8 years. *Schizophrenia Bulletin, 31,* 624–638.

Bentall, R. P. (1990). The illusion of reality: A review and integration of psychological research on hallucinations. *Psychological Bulletin, 107*(1), 82.

Bentall, R. P., de Sousa, P., Varese, F., Wickham, S., Sitko, K., Haarmans, M., & Read, J. (2014). From adversity to psychosis: Pathways and mechanisms from specific adversities to specific symptoms. *Social Psychiatry and Psychiatric Epidemiology, 49*(7), 1011–1022.

Bentall, R. & Varese, F. (2012). A level playing field? Are bio-genetic and psychosocial studies evaluated by the same standards? *Psychosis, 4*(3), 183–190.

Bentall, R. P. & Varese, F. (2013). Psychotic hallucinations. In F. Macpherson & D. Platchias (Eds.), *Hallucinatory experiences: Philosophical and psychological approaches.* Cambridge, MA: MIT Press.

Berenbaum, H., Thompson, R. J., Milanak, M. E., Boden, M. T. & Bredemeier, K. (2008). Psychological trauma and schizotypal personality disorder. *Journal of Abnormal Psychology, 117,* 502–519.

Bernstein, E. M. & Putnam, F. W. (1986). Development, reliability, and validity of a dissociation scale. *The Journal of Nervous and Mental Disease, 174*(12), 727–735.

Berry, K., Barrowclough, C. & Wearden, A. (2007). A review of the role of adult attachment style in psychosis: Unexplored issues and questions for further research. *Clinical Psychology Review, 27,* 458–475.

Berry, K., Barrowclough, C. & Wearden, A. (2008). Attachment theory: A framework for understanding symptoms and interpersonal relationships in psychosis. *Behaviour Research and Therapy, 46,* 1275–1282.

Berry, K., Barrowclough, C. & Wearden, A. (2009). Adult attachment, perceived earlier experiences of care giving and trauma in people with psychosis. *Journal of Mental Health, 18*(4), 280–287.

Berry, K. & Bucci, S. (2016). What does attachment theory tell us about working with distressing voices? *Psychosis, 8,* 60–71.

Berry, K., Barrowclough, C. & Wearden, A. (2008). Attachment theory: A framework for understanding symptoms and interpersonal relationships in psychosis. *Behaviour Research and Therapy, 46*(12), 1275–1282.

Bifulco, A., Moran, P. M., Ball, C. & Lillie, A. (2002). Adult attachment style. II: Its relationship to psychosocial depressive-vulnerability. *Social Psychiatry and Psychiatric Epidemiology, 37*(2), 60–67.

de Bont, P. A. J. M., van den Berg, D. P. G., van der Vleugel, B. M., de Roos, C., de Jongh, A., van der Gaag, M. & van Minnen, A. M. (2016). Prolonged exposure and EMDR for PTSD v. a PTSD waiting-list condition: Effects on symptoms of psychosis, depression and social functioning in patients with chronic psychotic disorders. *Psychological Medicine, 46*(11), 2411–2421.

Bowlby, J. (1969). *Attachment and Loss Vol. I.* London: Hogarth Press.

Bowlby, J. (1988). *A secure base: Clinical applications of attachment theory.* London: Routledge.

Brookwell, M. L., Bentall, R. P. & Varese, F. (2013). Externalizing biases and hallucinations in source monitoring, self-monitoring and signal detection studies: A meta-analytic review. *Psychological Medicine, 43*(12), 2465–2475.

Brown, R. J. (2006). Different types of 'dissociation' have different psychological mechanisms. *Journal of Trauma and Dissociation, 7*(4), 7–28.

Bucci, S., Emsley, R. & Berry, K. (2017). Attachment in psychosis: A latent profile analysis of attachment styles and association with symptoms in a large psychosis cohort. *Psychiatry Research, 247,* 243–249.

Cole, C. L., Newman-Taylor, K. & Kennedy, F. (2016). Dissociation mediates the relationship between childhood maltreatment and subclinical psychosis. *Journal of Trauma and Dissociation, 17*(5), 577–592.

Cutajar, M. C., Mullen, P. E., Ogloff, J. R. P., Thomas, S. D., Wells, D. L. & Spataro, J. (2010). Schizophrenia and other psychotic disorders in a cohort of sexually abused children. *Archives General Psychiatry, 67*(11), 1114–1119.

Cyr, C., Euser, E. M., Bakermans-Kranenburg, M. J. & Van IJzendoorn, M. H. (2010). Attachment security and disorganization in maltreating and high-risk families: A series of meta-analyses. *Development and Psychopathology, 22*(1), 87–108.

Dalenberg, C. J., Brand, B. L., Gleaves, D. H., Dorahy, M. J., Loewenstein, R. J., Cardena, E., Frewen, P.A., Carlson, E. B. & Spiegel, D. (2012). Evaluation of the evidence for the trauma and fantasy models of dissociation. *Psychological Bulletin, 138*(3), 550–588.

Dutra, L., Bureau, J. F., Holmes, B., Lyubchik, A. & Lyons-Ruth, K. (2009). Quality of early care and childhood trauma: A prospective study of developmental pathways to dissociation. *Journal of Nervous and Mental Disease, 197*(6), 383–390.

Evans, G. J., Reid, G., Preston, P., Palmier-Claus, J. & Sellwood, W. (2015). Trauma and psychosis: The mediating role of self-concept clarity and dissociation. *Psychiatry Research, 228*(3), 626–632.

Farrelly, A., Peters, E., Azis M., David, A. & Hunter, E. C. (2016). A brief CBT intervention for depersonalisation/derealisation in psychosis: Study protocol for a feasibility randomised controlled trial. *Pilot Feasibility Studies, 2*, 47.

Freyd, J. J. (2008). What juries don't know: Dissemination of research on victim response is essential for justice. *Trauma Psychology Newsletter, 3,* 15–18.

Geddes, G., Ehlers, A., & Freeman, D. (2016). Hallucinations in the months after a trauma: An investigation of the role of cognitive processing of a physical assault in the occurrence of hallucinatory experiences. *Psychiatry Research, 246,* 601–605.

George, C., Kaplan, N. & Main, M. (1985). *The Adult Attachment Interview.* Unpublished manuscript, University of California at Berkeley.

Goff, D. C., Brotman, A. W., Kindlon, D., Waites, M. & Amico, E. (1991). Self-reports of childhood abuse in chronically psychotic patients. *Psychiatry Research, 37*(1), 73–80.

Gómez, J. M., Kaehler, L. A. & Freyd, J. J. (2014). Are hallucinations related to betrayal trauma exposure? A three-study exploration. *Psychological Trauma: Theory, Research, Practice, and Policy, 6*(6), 675–682.

Granqvist, P., Mikulincer, M. & Shaver, P. R. (2010). Religion as attachment: Normative processes and individual differences. *Personality and Social Psychology Review, 14*(1), 49–59.

Gumley, A. I., Taylor, H. E. F., Schwannauer, M. & MacBeth, A. (2014). A systematic review of attachment and psychosis: Measurement, construct validity and outcomes. *Acta Psychiatrica Scandinavica, 129*(4), 257–274.

Hardy, A., Emsley, R., Freeman, D., Bebbington, P., Garety, P. A., Kuipers, E. E. & Fowler, D. (2016). Psychological mechanisms mediating effects between trauma and psychotic symptoms: The role of affect regulation, intrusive trauma memory, beliefs, and depression. *Schizophrenia Bulletin, 42*(1), 34–43.

Hayes, A. F. (2013). *Introduction to mediation, moderation, and conditional process analysis: A regression-based approach.* New York: Guilford Press.

Hazan, C. & Shaver, P. (1987). Romantic love conceptualized as an attachment process. *Journal of Personality and Social Psychology, 52*(3), 511.

Hesse, E. & Main, M. (2006). Frightened, threatening, and dissociative parental behavior in low-risk samples: Description, discussion, and interpretations. *Development and Psychopathology, 18*(02), 309–343.

Hesse, E. & Van IJzendoorn, M. H. (1998). Parental loss of close family members and propensities towards absorption in offspring. *Developmental Science, 1*(2), 299–305.

Herman, J. L. (1992). *Trauma and Recovery: The Aftermath of Violence--From Domestic Abuse to Political Terror.* New York: Basic Books.

Holmes, J. (2001). *Search for a secure base.* Hove (UK): Routledge.

Holmes, E. A., Brown, R. J., Mansell, W., Fearon, R. P., Hunter, E. C., Frasquilho, F. & Oakley, D. A. (2005). Are there two qualitatively distinct forms of dissociation? A review and some clinical implications. *Clinical Psychology Review, 25*(1), 1–23.

Hulette, A. C., Kaehler, L. A. & Freyd, J. J. (2011). Intergenerational associations between trauma and dissociation. *Journal of Family Violence, 26*, 217.

Kennerly, H. (1996). Cognitive therapy of dissociative symptoms associated with trauma. *British Journal of Clinical Psychology, 35*(3), 325–340.

Kennerly, F. (2009). *Overcoming childhood trauma.* London: Constable & Robinson.

Larkin, W., & Morrison, A. P. (2005). Relationships between trauma and psychosis: From theory to therapy. In W. Larkin & A. P. Morrison (Eds.), *Trauma and psychosis: New directions for theory and therapy* (pp. 259–282). London: Routledge.

Linehan, M. (1993). *Cognitive-behavioral treatment of borderline personality disorder.* New York: Guilford Press.

Liotti, G. (1992). Disorganized/disoriented attachment in the etiology of the dissociative disorders. *Dissociation: Progress in the dissociative disorders, 5*, 196–204.

Liotti, G. (2004). Trauma, dissociation, and disorganized attachment: Three strands of a single braid. *Psychotherapy: Theory, Research, Practice, Training, 41*(4), 472.

Liotti, G. & Gumley A. (2008). An attachment perspective on schizophrenia: The role of disorganized attachment, dissociation and mentalization. In A. Moskowitz, I. Schafer and M. Dorahy, (Eds.), *Psychosis, trauma and dissociation: Emerging perspectives on severe psychopathology.* London: Wiley. pp. 117–133.

Longden, E., Madill, A. & Waterman, M. G. (2012). Dissociation, trauma, and the role of lived experience: Toward a new conceptualization of voice hearing. *Psychological Bulletin, 138*(1), 28–76.

Longden, E., House, A. O. & Waterman, M. G. (2016). Associations between nonauditory hallucinations, dissociation, and childhood adversity in first-episode psychosis. *Journal of Trauma and Dissociation, 17*(5), 545–560.

Lyons-Ruth, K., Yellin, C., Melnick, S. & Atwood, G. (2005). Expanding the concept of unresolved mental states: Hostile/helpless states of mind on the Adult Attachment Interview are associated with disrupted mother–infant communication and infant disorganization. *Development and Psychopathology, 17*(01), 1–23.

Lyons-Ruth, K., Dutra, L., Schuder, M. R. & Bianchi, I. (2006). From infant attachment disorganization to adult dissociation: Relational adaptations or traumatic experiences? *The Psychiatric Clinics of North America, 29*(1), 63.

Lyons-Ruth, K. & Jacobvitz, D. (1999). Attachment disorganization. In J. Shaver, (Ed.), *Handbook of attachment. Theory, research and clinical implications.* London: Guilford Press. pp. 520–554.

MacBeth, A., Gumley, A., Schwannauer, M., & Fisher, R. (2011). Attachment states of mind, mentalization, and their correlates in a first-episode psychosis sample. *Psychology Psychotherapy: Theory, Research and Practice, 84*(1), 42–57.

Main, M. & Solomon, J. (1986). Discovery of an insecure-disorganized/disoriented attachment pattern. In T. Brazelton & M. Yogman, (Eds.), *Affective development in infancy.* Westport, USA: Ablex Publishing. pp. 95–124.

Main, M. & Solomon, J. (1990). Procedures for identifying infants as disorganized/disoriented during the Ainsworth Strange Situation. *Attachment in the preschool years: Theory, research, and intervention, 1*, 121–160.

Merckelbach, H. & Muris, P. (2001). The causal link between self-reported trauma and dissociation: A critical review. *Behaviour Research and Therapy, 39,* 245–254.

Mickelson, K. D., Kessler, R. C. & Shaver, P. R. (1997). Adult attachment in a nationally representative sample. *Journal of Personality and Social Psychology, 73*(5), 1092–1106.

Morley, S. (2007). Single case methodology in psychological therapy. In S. Lindsey & G. Powell, (Eds.), *The handbook of clinical adult psychology*, 3rd edn. London: Routledge. pp. 821–843.

Moskowitz, A. & Corstens, D. (2008). Auditory hallucinations: Psychotic symptom or dissociative experience? *Journal of Psychological Trauma, 6*(2–3), 35–63.

Moskowitz, A., Shafer, I. & Dorahy, M. J. (2009). *Psychosis, trauma and dissociation: Emerging perspectives on severe psychopathology.* Chichester: John Wiley & Sons.

Mulligan, A. & Lavender, T. (2010). An investigation into the relationship between attachment, gender and recovery from psychosis in a stable community-based sample. *Clinical Psychology and Psychotherapy, 17*(4), 269–284.

National Institute of Care Excellence (NICE) (2014). *NICE guidelines CG178 – Psychosis and schizophrenia in adults: Treatment and management.* London: National Institute for Health and Care Excellence.

Newman-Taylor, K. & Sambrook, S. (2013). The role of dissociation in psychosis. In F. Kennedy, H. Kennerley & D. Pearson, (Eds.), *Cognitive behavioural approaches to the understanding and treatment of dissociation.* Abingdon: Routledge. pp. 119–132.

O'Driscoll, C., Laing, J. & Mason, O. (2014). Cognitive emotion regulation strategies, alexithymia and dissociation in schizophrenia, a review and meta-analysis. *Clinical Psychology Review, 34*(6), 482–495.

Ogawa, J. R., Sroufe, L. A., Weinfield, N. S., Carlson, E. A. & Egeland, B. (1997). Development and the fragmented self: Longitudinal study of dissociative symptomatology in a nonclinical sample. *Development and Psychopathology, 9*(4), 855–879.

Perona-Garcelán, S., Carrascoso-López, F., García-Montes, J. M., Ductor-Recuerda, M. J., López Jiménez, A. M., Vallina-Fernández, O. & Gómez-Gómez, M. T. (2012a). Dissociative experiences as mediators between childhood trauma and auditory hallucinations. *Journal of Traumatic Stress, 25*(3), 323–329.

Perona-Garcelán, S., García-Montes, J. M., Ductor-Recuerda, M. J., Vallina-Fernández, O., Cuevas-Yust, C., Pérez-Álvarez, M., Salas-Azcona, R. & Gómez-Gómez, M. T. (2012b). Relationship of metacognition, absorption, and depersonalization in patients with auditory hallucinations. *British Journal of Clinical Psychology, 51*(1), 100–118.

Perona-Garcelán, S., García-Montes, J. M., Rodríguez-Testal, J. F., López-Jiménez, A. M., Ruiz-Veguilla, M., Ductor-Recuerda, M. J., Benítez-Hernández, M. M., Arias-Velarde, M. Á., Gómez-Gómez, M. T. & Pérez-Álvarez, M. (2014). Relationship between childhood trauma, mindfulness, and dissociation in subjects with and without hallucination proneness. *Journal of Trauma and Dissociation, 15*(1), 35–51.

Pickering, L., Simpson, J. & Bentall, R.P. (2008). Insecure attachment predicts proneness to paranoia but not hallucinations. *Personality and Individual Differences, 44*(5), 1212–1224.

Pilton, M., Varese, F., Berry, K. & Bucci, S. (2015). The relationship between dissociation and voices: A systematic literature review and meta-analysis. *Clinical Psychology Review, 40,* 138–155.

Read, J., Os, J. V., Morrison, A. P. & Ross, C. A. (2005). Childhood trauma, psychosis and schizophrenia: A literature review with theoretical and clinical implications. *Acta Psychiatrica Scandinavica, 112*(5), 330–350.

Read, J., Fink, P. J., Rudegeair, T., Felitti, V. & Whitfield, C. L. (2008). Child maltreatment and psychosis: A return to a genuinely integrated bio-psycho-social model. *Clinical Schizophrenia and Related Psychoses, 2*(3), 235–254.

Read, J. (2013). Childhood adversity and psychosis: From heresy to certainty. *Meanings of Madness Conference*, University College Cork, Ireland.

Read, J. & Gumley, A. (2008). Can attachment theory help explain the relationship between childhood adversity and psychosis? *Attachment: New Directions in Psychotherapy and Relational Psychoanalysis, 2*(1), 1–35.

Sandberg, D. A. (2010). Adult attachment as a predictor of posttraumatic stress and dissociation. *Journal of Trauma and Dissociation, 11*(3), 293–307.

Schäfer, I., Harfst, T., Aderhold, V., Briken, P., Lehmann, M., Moritz, S. & Naber, D. (2006). Childhood trauma and dissociation in female patients with schizophrenia spectrum disorders: An exploratory study. *Journal of Nervous and Mental Disease, 194*(2), 135–138.

Shevlin, M., Dorahy, M. J., & Adamson, G. (2007). Trauma and psychosis: An analysis of the National Comorbidity Survey. *American Journal of Psychiatry, 164*(1), 166–169.

Sin, J., Spain, D., Furuta, M., Murrells, T. & Norman, I. (2017). Psychological interventions for post-traumatic stress disorder (PTSD) in people with severe mental illness. *Cochrane Database of Systematic Review, Issue 1*. Art. No.: CD011464.

Sitko, K., Bentall, R. P., Shevlin, M., O'Sullivan, N. & Sellwood, W. (2014). Associations between specific psychotic symptoms and specific childhood adversities are mediated by attachment styles: An analysis of the National Comorbidity Survey. *Psychiatry Research, 217*(3), 202–209.

Sroufe, L. A. (2005). Attachment and development: A prospective, longitudinal study from birth to adulthood. *Attachment and Human Development, 7*(4), 349–367.

Steel, C. (2017) Psychological interventions for working with trauma and distressing voices: The future is in the past. *Frontiers in Psychology, 7*, 2035.

Tait, L., Birchwood, M. & Trower, P. (2004). Adapting to the challenge of psychosis: Personal resilience and the use of sealing-over (avoidant) coping strategies. *British Journal of Psychiatry, 185*, 410–415.

van den Berg, D. G., de Bont, P. M., van der Vleugel, B. M., de Roos, C., de Jongh, A., Van Minnen, A. & van der Gaag, M. (2015). Prolonged exposure vs. eye movement desensitization and reprocessing vs. waiting list for posttraumatic stress disorder in patients with a psychotic disorder: A randomized clinical trial. *JAMA Psychiatry, 72*(3), 259–267.

Van der Hart, O., Nijenhuis, E. R. & Steele, K. (2006). *The haunted self: Structural dissociation and the treatment of chronic traumatization*. New York: WW Norton & Company.

Van IJzendoorn, M. H. (1995). Adult attachment representations, parental responsiveness and infant attachment: A meta-analysis on the predictive validity of the Adult Attachment Interview. *Psychological Bulletin, 117*, 387–403.

Van IJzendoorn, M. H. & Bakermans-Kranenburg, M. J. (1996). Attachment representations in mothers, fathers, adolescents, and clinical groups: A meta-analytic search for normative data. *Journal of Consulting and Clinical Psychology, 64*(1), 8–21.

Van IJzendoorn, M. H. & Schuengel, C. (1996). The measurement of dissociation in normal and clinical populations: Meta-analytic validation of the Dissociative Experiences Scale (DES). *Clinical Psychology Review, 16*(5), 365–382.

Van IJzendoorn, M. H., Schuengel, C. & Bakerman-Kranenburg, M. J. (1999). Disorganized attachment in early childhood: Meta-analysis of precursors, concomitants, and sequelae. *Development and Psychopathology, 11*(2), 225–250.

van Os, J., Kenis, G. & Rutten, B. P. F. (2010). The environment and schizophrenia. *Nature, 468*(7321), 203–212.

Varese, F., Barkus, E. & Bentall, R.P. (2011). Dissociative and metacognitive factors in hallucination-proneness when controlling for comorbid symptoms. *Cognitive Neuropsychiatry, 16*(3), 193–217.

Varese, F., Barkus, E., & Bentall, R. P. (2012a). Dissociation mediates the relationship between childhood trauma and hallucination-proneness. *Psychological Medicine, 42*(5), 1025–1036.

Varese, F., Smeets, F., Drukker, M., Lieverse, R., Lataster, T., Viechtbauer, W. & Bentall, R. P. (2012b). Childhood adversities increase the risk of psychosis: A meta-analysis of patient-control, prospective-and cross-sectional cohort studies. *Schizophrenia Bulletin, 8*(4), 661–671.

Wallin, D. J. (2007). *Attachment in psychotherapy*. New York: Guilford Press.

Waters, F., Allen, P., Aleman, A., Fernyhough, C., Woodward, T. S., Badcock, J. C., Barkus, E., Johns, L., Varese, F., Menon, M., Vercammen, A. & Laroi, F. (2012). Auditory hallucinations in schizophrenia and nonschizophrenia populations: A review and integrated model of cognitive mechanisms. *Schizophrenia Bulletin, 38*(4), 683–693.

Whiffen, V. E., Judd, M. E. & Aube, J. A. (1999). Intimate relationships moderate the association between childhood sexual abuse and depression. *Journal of Interpersonal Violence, 14*(9), 940–954.

Wickham, S., Sitko, K. & Bentall, R. P. (2015). Insecure attachment is associated with paranoia but not hallucinations in psychotic patients: The mediating role of negative self-esteem. *Psychological Medicine, 45*(7), 1495–1507.

Williams, J., Varese, F., Berry, K. & Bucci, S. (under review). Psychological mediators of the relationship between childhood adversities and psychosis: A systematic review.

UK Psychological Trauma Society (2017). *Guidelines for the treatment and planning of services for complex post-traumatic stress disorder in adults.* Colchester (UK): UKPTS

Woodhouse, S., Ayers, S. & Field, A. P. (2015). The relationship between adult attachment style and post-traumatic stress symptoms: A meta-analysis. *Journal of Anxiety Disorders, 35,* 103–117.

Zerubavel, N. & Messman-Moore, T. L. (2015). Staying present: Incorporating mindfulness into therapy for dissociation. *Mindfulness, 6*(2), 303–314.

Part 2

SPECIFIC THERAPEUTIC APPROACHES

3

METACOGNITIVE TRAINING
Targeting cognitive biases

Ryan P. Balzan, Steffen Moritz and Brooke C. Schneider

The current version of the Diagnostic and Statistical Manual of Mental Disorders (DSM-5) defines *delusions* as 'fixed beliefs that are not amenable to change in light of conflicting evidence' (American Psychiatric Association, 2013, p. 87). Such a definition harks back to earlier conceptualisations that delusions are ultimately psychologically 'un-understandable' (Jaspers, 1913), and by implication resistant to rational counter-argument. Based on Jaspers' thinking, the field of psychiatry moved more towards treatment of the underlying neurochemistry believed to be responsible for these experiences. However, recent interest in adjunctive non-pharmacological treatments has brought an end to the 'psychological nihilism' era, and experiences like delusions are no longer considered psychologically un-understandable or even necessarily fixed (Kingdon & Turkington, 2008). Growing evidence normalises the anomalous experiences of individuals with psychosis, supporting the notion of a continuum of delusional thinking with 'clinical delusions' representing the severe end of the continuum (van Os & Reininghaus, 2016). For example, Freeman (2006) reported that 5–6% of the non-clinical population experience delusional thinking that causes non-clinically significant disruptions in functioning, while 10–15% of the non-clinical population may be identified as highly delusion-prone. As has been demonstrated in other chapters throughout this book, psychological approaches to these unusual experiences are now more focused on understanding the psychological processes that maintain them and relieving the distress they may cause.

Significant evidence indicates that Cognitive Behavioural Therapy for psychosis (CBTp) is effective in reducing the conviction and distress associated with delusional thinking (Turner et al., 2014; van der Gaag et al., 2014; Wykes et al., 2008). However, some authors have questioned whether CBTp is too broad an approach for specific experiences like delusions (Farhall & Thomas, 2013). Moreover, although individuals with psychosis tend to prefer psychotherapy to medications (McHugh et al., 2013), only a minority receives therapy beyond psycho-education. Access to treatment represents a significant barrier, in part due to the relatively low number of therapists with adequate training (Thomas, 2015).

Based partially on the aforementioned criticisms of CBTp, it has been suggested that interventions for delusional thinking should be targeting the cognitive and emotional processes theorised to be responsible for their formation and maintenance (Mehl et al., 2015). Metacognitive Training (MCT) for psychosis, a manualised group programme, represents one such intervention. MCT shares many of the key assumptions of CBTp (e.g., that delusional thinking reflects cognitive processes that can be modified), and clinical techniques (e.g., normalisation, Socratic discussion, reality testing), and is considered to be a variant of CBT. However, it focuses less on the content of the idiosyncratic beliefs than traditional CBT, and instead targets the underlying cognitive and social biases thought to underlie delusional beliefs and experiences (i.e., a less direct or 'backdoor' approach). Furthermore, MCT represents a 'low threshold' intervention and a variety of healthcare professionals can conduct the training. To improve dissemination, all materials are available for free via www.uke.de/mct and the programme has been translated into more than 30 languages.

Metacognitive Training (MCT)

Overview

The MCT programme is based on an extensive literature demonstrating that people who experience delusional thinking are more likely to exhibit several biased thinking and reasoning styles, relative to people without delusional ideation. These include:

- the Jumping to Conclusions (JTC) bias and a Bias Against Disconfirmatory Evidence (BADE) (for recent reviews and meta-analyses on these two biases, see Dudley et al., 2015; McLean et al., 2017);
- overconfidence in errors (for an overview, see Balzan, 2016a);
- biased monocausal and external attribution styles (see Merrin et al., 2007; Randjbar et al., 2011);
- theory of mind (ToM) deficits (see Brüne, 2005); and
- depressive cognitive schemata (see Moritz & Schneider, 2016).

The field is now even starting to work these biases into holistic theoretical models. For example, a recently published two-stage model brings together the JTC, BADE and overconfidence in errors biases, and posits that delusional thinking may be characterised by a lowered decision threshold that leads to a premature acceptance of hypotheses and the cessation of seeking counterevidence, reinforcing confidence in false hypotheses (Moritz et al., 2017).

Getting people to reflect on their 'thinking about thinking' (i.e., metacognition), particularly the cognitive distortions that might underlie usual experiences, has a number of benefits. One of the fundamental components of MCT is knowledge translation, or psycho-education, whereby people are informed of the latest empirical research linking cognitive biases to delusional thinking (metacognitive knowledge, according to Flavell, 1979). Cognitive biases are introduced as normal cognitive phenomena that everyone is susceptible to (in varying degrees), and MCT highlights that they may even contribute to the development of urban legends and conspiracy theories that are commonly held in the wider community. This psycho-education helps to normalise delusional thinking and reinforces the idea that it occurs along a continuum. To complete MCT people typically do not need to view their beliefs as symptoms, since individual delusional experiences are not the focus of therapy as they would be in traditional CBTp; in fact, by bringing cognitive biases to their attention, MCT actually helps to raise participants' awareness of the nature of their beliefs.

Furthermore, as MCT is administered in groups across a number of defined modules (available online at www.uke.de/mkt), it has the pragmatic benefit of allowing for wider dissemination than individualised therapy, by a broad range of mental health professionals (e.g., psychiatrists, clinical psychologists, mental health nurses, social workers, occupational therapists). The audio-visual format is also engaging for participants, which is important given that many people with psychosis experience difficulties with attention and memory (Fioravanti et al., 2012).

Another important component of MCT is demonstrating in sessions the cognitive and social biases linked to psychosis via exercises that target each bias individually (i.e., showing the bias 'at work'). This builds on the psycho-education presented to participants, as they can see first-hand in real-time that they are susceptible to a number of unhelpful thinking styles (metacognitive experiences, according to Flavell, 1979) and can begin to see that these biases may be contributing to their unusual experiences. Once participants have been informed about, and even experienced the biases in question, MCT then offers alternative thinking strategies, which may help participants to arrive at more appropriate inferences and thereby avoid the 'cognitive traps' that otherwise lead to delusional beliefs and experiences. Fundamentally, participants are encouraged to reflect on three key questions: 'What is the available evidence?', 'Are there alternative ways of thinking about this', and 'Am I over-reacting to the current situation?' Building upon the metacognitive model of Asher Koriat which emphasises the importance of confidence (e.g., Koriat et al., 1999), MCT aims to plant the 'seeds of doubt' within participants, thereby encouraging critical reflection, and ultimately reducing the severity of delusional ideas and their (possible) repercussions.

What follows is a brief overview of the material covered across the MCT group programme, which encompasses the six cognitive and social biases the programme targets (i.e., Jumping to Conclusions, Bias Against Disconfirmatory Evidence, overconfidence in errors, attribution biases, theory of mind deficits, and depressive cognitive schemata); for each, we will highlight the three core components of MCT (psycho-education, exercises that elicit the bias, and alternative thinking strategies). Finally, as people with psychosis experience stigmatisation and suffer from low self-esteem, two new MCT modules that deal with these issues have recently been incorporated into the programme, and these will also be summarised.

Jumping to Conclusions (JTC)

It is well established that people with delusional tendencies often exhibit a JTC bias (Dudley et al., 2015; McLean et al., 2017; Ross et al., 2015; So et al., 2016). This bias is characterised by the tendency to make 'short-circuit' decisions on the basis of limited evidence – a process that may foster and maintain delusional beliefs and experiences. For example, crackling noises over a phone line might lead someone to jump to the conclusion that their phone has been 'bugged' and support the belief that they are being monitored by intelligence agents. So frequent is this bias in people with psychosis that the MCT programme dedicates two modules to JTC.

In both modules, the pros (e.g., saving time) and cons (e.g., less reliable judgement, high probability of errors) of jumping to conclusions are discussed across a range of situations; for example, trivial decisions like buying a particular brand of yoghurt from a range of different options, through to complex social situations where the consequences of hasty decisions can be dramatic (e.g., souring a friendship). In an effort to normalise delusional beliefs and thinking styles, participants are invited to discuss the potential role that JTC might play in the development and maintenance of urban legends and conspiracy beliefs. These beliefs are like delusions, as they are based on very little or selective evidence (e.g., the Beatles' *Abbey Road* album cover has been used as 'evidence' to support the conspiracy belief that Paul McCartney died in 1966 and was replaced by a lookalike double, given that Paul is barefoot and is smoking with his right hand in the picture despite being rumoured to be left-handed). By getting participants to understand that JTC affects all people (not only those experiencing delusions), we aim to reduce the stigma associated with psychosis.

Both modules demonstrate the bias at work across a number of exercises. One of these exercises shows participants a series of partial images, which over time, are eventually revealed to show a completed picture. For each partial image, participants are asked if they have enough evidence to guess what the picture represents; as shown in Figure 3.1, the first series of images is ambiguous, and may represent any number of objects (shirt, old tent), but it eventually becomes obvious the image is actually of a girl. In this way, participants learn to avoid making hasty decisions ('it is an old shirt') and that delaying decisions improves accuracy. In another exercise, participants are presented with two-way visual illusions that simultaneously represent two different images (e.g., the 'rabbit-duck' illusion) and are encouraged to observe both images. This task demonstrates that hasty decisions do not always lead to errors, but that they might not capture 'the big picture'. The final task type presents participants with paintings, of which they are asked to guess the correct title from four possible options. For the majority of

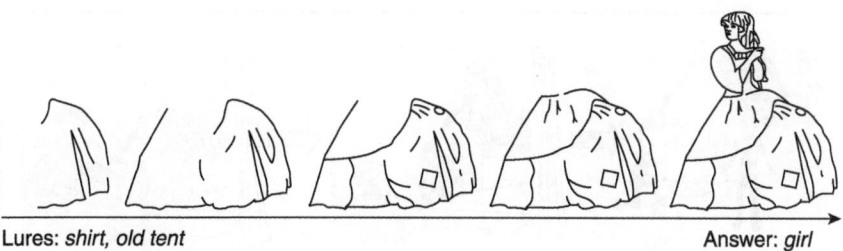

Lures: *shirt, old tent*   Answer: *girl*

Figure 3.1 'Girl' stimuli set for 'fragmentation exercise' in the JTC module

Source: https://clinical-neuropsychology.de/metacognitive_training

these paintings, participants have to really study the finer details of the scene for clues and discuss as a group what the correct answer might be. This again encourages participants to resist making hasty decisions and reinforces that intensive evidence accumulation and exchanging views with others can work better than committing quickly.

Changing beliefs: Bias Against Disconfirmatory Evidence (BADE)

It is part of human nature to cling onto our first impressions or beliefs, despite being presented with counter-evidence or rational counter argument, particularly if we have maintained this belief for some time. The tendency to not consider or to down-play the importance of disconfirmatory evidence is part of a broader bias, usually referred to as the *confirmation bias*, and has been studied extensively within the general population (Oswald & Grosjean, 2004). However, the tendency to fail to integrate counter-evidence into pre-existing beliefs is particularly exaggerated in people with delusional thinking styles (for a recent meta-analysis on BADE, see McLean et al., 2017), and it may be one of the central mechanisms that could account for why these beliefs are maintained in the face of overwhelming counter-evidence. Indeed, the idea that delusional thinking styles are 'fixed' remains one of their defining characteristics (American Psychiatric Association, 2013), and is one of the reasons why they can be so difficult to treat with traditional cognitive-behavioural techniques (i.e., considering the evidence for and against a particular belief).

This module introduces participants to the BADE concept by considering reasons why we might cling to beliefs (e.g., eases decision-making) but also highlights the disadvantages of doing so (i.e., social consequences such as prejudice and overgeneralisation). Historical and case examples are given illustrating how an unwillingness to revise opinions and beliefs can lead to serious problems, or even disastrous events (e.g., the belief that *Titanic* was 'unsinkable' led to dismissal of early warnings that the ship was in trouble), which reinforces the idea

Interpretations

1) The boy is happy because he was finally adopted = **lure**
2) The parents praise their son for reporting a fire, so it was put out in time = **true**
3) The boy received a good mark at school = **lure**
4) The boy set a fire without getting caught

Figure 3.2 Example of a 'BADE exercise' (picture order is 3, 2, 1)

Source: https://clinical-neuropsychology.de/metacognitive_training

that BADE is a common human tendency ('to err is human'), thereby reducing self-stigma.

The main exercise in this module consists of a series of three pictures depicting events from one scenario, but shown in reverse order, whereby the last scene is shown first. Therefore, the picture sequence gradually disambiguates a scenario (see Figure 3.2). For each picture, participants are asked to gauge the plausibility of four different interpretations. One of these interpretations is the 'true' answer, but this is often only evident after all three pictures are presented; two of the other interpretations are therefore lures, which seem correct on presentation of the first picture, but are eventually shown to be implausible after the third picture. Complementary to the exercises in the JTC module, the learning objective is to search for more information before making a decision (resist hasty decisions), and to integrate any disconfirmatory evidence that is encountered (i.e., 'events sometimes turn out very differently than originally expected, and that we should always consider different interpretations and adjust our beliefs accordingly').

Overall, the programme reinforces the notion 'to err is human', and that we must be prepared for the possibility of error. Recognising the potential influence of the biases (JTC, BADE, etc.) in the decision-making process helps to plant to 'seeds of doubt' and reduce conviction in delusional thinking frameworks.

Overconfidence in errors

There is growing evidence that people with psychosis are overconfident in errors and slightly underconfident in correct responses, particularly when it comes to false memory errors (i.e., remembering things that have not occurred); for a recent review, see Balzan, 2016a. This mechanism may play a crucial role in raising the level of conviction necessary to form and maintain delusional thinking; that is, attaching high confidence to the accuracy of erroneous memories or perceptions. For example, 'I'm very confident my neighbour was staring angrily at me this morning' may trigger a strong conviction in a fixed false belief such as, 'I am under surveillance and my life is in danger'. By contrast, people without psychosis are more likely to attach 'non-trustworthy' tags to these memories. In fact, decreasing overconfidence in errors may be one of the mechanisms of change evoked by antipsychotic agents (Andreou, et al., 2014).

Given the evidence that overconfidence in errors is particularly strong for memory errors, this module begins by highlighting the fallibility of memory in general (i.e., all people are prone to forgetting and adding to information that was not originally present), and offers strategies to improve memory (e.g., mnemonics; incorporating multiple senses during encoding). However, the emphasis is on reducing confidence in vague memories, which is achieved by demonstrating how easy it is to elicit false memories. Participants are instructed to look at pictures of complex scenes carefully and to try and memorise each item (see Figure 3.3 for

Figure 3.3 'Pool scene' from the memory/overconfidence module; people often falsely recall items (e.g., towels; sunhat) with high confidence despite them not being depicted in the picture

Source: https://clinical-neuropsychology.de/metacognitive_training

an example). Each picture is followed by a recognition task in which participants have to decide whether an item was displayed (e.g., were towels present?), before revealing the items that were not actually there in the original picture (e.g., towels, sunhats). Participants thereby quickly learn how fallible memory can be and are encouraged to doubt non-vivid memories, particularly in social situations when incorrectly insisting that something happened may result in interpersonal conflict.

Attributional style

Research has shown that people with psychosis tend to provide one-sided mono-causal explanations for complex social events (Kinderman & Bentall, 1997; Randjbar et al., 2011), despite the fact that such events are typically the result of multiple simultaneous factors. Importantly, one-sided attributions, such as blaming others (individuals or organisations) for negative events, can reinforce the notion that the outside world is dangerous or threatening, which can further fuel delusional thinking (e.g., the mafia is solely responsible for my problems). This module there-fore addresses the social consequences of different attributional styles (e.g., blaming others for failure may lead to interpersonal tensions). After addressing these conse-quences, participants are encouraged to brainstorm multiple explanations for specific social events (e.g., 'people laugh while you are speaking at a party'). The learning objective here is that there are always a number of different possible expla-nations (e.g., self, others, circumstances) that should be considered even if only one explanation seems valid at first, which may help to overcome the tendency to rely on monocausal attribution biases. For example, if for the scenario 'people laugh while you are speaking at a party', participants were to give a negative one-sided explanation (e.g., 'they are obviously making fun of me'), we would encourage them to consider alternative explanations: 'I didn't notice that I had accidentally said something funny and actually made a good joke' (self); 'one of the other people had just made a joke that I didn't hear' (others); 'it is a party and everyone is in a festive mood and laughing at every opportunity' (circumstance). Not only does this foster the idea that multiple factors contribute to the outcome of a single event (i.e., self, others, circumstances), but it also works to reduce paranoia by highlight-ing that it is not always justified to put the blame for negative events onto others. The module also includes a section on auditory hallucinations; typically, these experiences are (mis)attributed to other persons (e.g., implanted chip) or powers (e.g., mind-reading), but participants are invited to consider other explanations (e.g., 'self-generated, external stresses make me more sensitive to this experience').

Theory of mind deficits

Theory of mind (ToM) is a construct that represents the ability to accurately infer the mental states (e.g., thoughts, perspectives, beliefs) of others, but this complex social skill can be underdeveloped in people with psychosis (e.g., Brüne, 2005). Consequently, people with psychosis may place unwarranted emphasis on particular facial expressions or body language without considering the wider context, or they may misinterpret the intention of others in social interactions, especially when these interpretations are biased by negative moods (e.g., 'everybody is against me'). Such misapprehension, in conjunction with a tendency to make hasty decisions, may reinforce delusional (particularly persecutory) ideas. For example, the 'pensive therapist' may be misinterpreted as the 'hostile therapist', who does not actually want the client to improve. Indeed, it is pointed out that many misunderstandings and conflicts with others arise simply because people incorrectly guess what is on others' minds.

MCT dedicates two modules to ToM, which both include a variety of exercises to improve social cognitive skills and attenuate overconfidence. One exercise aims to demonstrate the diversity of cues for social cognition, and how an overreliance on a particular cue (e.g., facial expressions, attire) may lead to errors (e.g., a 'shady' looking person is revealed to be a well-respected doctor). Another task shows participants cropped images that depict facial expressions or gestures that are highly suggestive of a particular interpretation (e.g., 'man receives bad news'), but changes when extra contextual information is provided (e.g., 'street musician').

These exercises highlight that while facial expressions are very important for the understanding of the inner feelings of a person, they can often lead to false conclusions. Therefore, consistent with the other modules, we stress that additional information (e.g., the situation and/or prior knowledge about that person) should always be considered before facial expressions or body language can be interpreted as a direct reflection of the person's state of mind. Another exercise is similar to those presented in the BADE module (see Figure 3.2), where scenes of social events are presented in reverse sequential order, such that the final picture in the sequence (which has the least contextual information) is displayed first and the necessary contextual information to correctly deduce the scene is not revealed until the end. This teaches participants the need to delay decisions, consider multiple perspectives simultaneously, and evaluate the available contextual information to accurately interpret complex social situations (note overlap with JTC, BADE, and attribution modules).

Depressed mood

Given that more than half of people with psychosis symptoms also experience symptoms consistent with affective disturbances such as depression (Buckley et al., 2009), this module focuses on the cognitive biases (or depressive schemata) and dysfunctional coping strategies that underlie depressive symptoms. In this way, we again aim to normalise these symptoms and experiences, and highlight that this way of thinking can ultimately be altered. Drawing from CBT approaches, biases and dysfunctional coping strategies covered include:

- overgeneralisation (i.e., the tendency to generalise negative events to all current or future situations);
- selective perception (narrowing attention to negative aspects of an event);

- the denial of positive feedback but uncritical acceptance of negative feedback;
- catastrophic thinking;
- thought suppression; and
- magnification and minimisation (i.e., maximise positive attributes of others while minimising one's own).

Simple techniques to raise depressed mood are also covered; for example, writing down positive things that have occurred on that day and reflecting on these, and behavioural activation.

Self-esteem and stigma

Many people with psychosis will also experience low self-esteem. This may be driven by several factors; for example, the symptoms themselves (e.g., persecution, paranoia), or the stigma and shame of having a diagnosis of psychosis. Studies suggest people attach greater priority to the treatment of emotional problems like low self-esteem than the so-called positive symptoms of psychosis (Moritz et al., 2016). Furthermore, the improvement of low self-esteem may also help to improve feelings of paranoia or persecution (Freeman & Garety, 2014). Therefore, two new modules dealing with low self-esteem and stigma have recently been added to the MCT programme. Ultimately, the modules aim to raise self-esteem and reduce the impact of stigma by getting participants to:

- focus on their strengths over their apparent weaknesses (e.g., keeping a 'joy diary');
- address rumination from their 'inner critic';
- become more aware that having mental health difficulties does not equate to being unable to accomplish meaningful and valuable things;
- observing the rates of mental illness and frequency of psychotic symptoms (which are much higher than most people think); and
- learning how to effectively communicate one's mental health difficulties to others (describing the experience of delusions and hallucinations to others, rather than sharing a potentially misunderstood label such as 'schizophrenia').

Efficacy

There have now been several clinical trials investigating the feasibility and effectiveness of group-based MCT since its inception. The earlier trials were predominantly focused on feasibility, and suggested that MCT was superior to a control condition on usefulness to daily life, participant engagement, and subjective effectiveness (Gawęda et al., 2009; Moritz & Woodward, 2007). Low powered or non-randomised clinical trials that followed also suggested that MCT may lead to reduced delusional severity, improved social functioning, insight and subjective quality of life, and led to more optimal performance on cognitive bias tasks, relative to treatment-as-usual (e.g., Balzan, et al., 2014; Moritz, Kerstan, et al., 2011). More recently, a large assessor-blind randomised controlled trial involving a sample of 150 people with a diagnosis of psychosis experiencing active delusions was carried out (Moritz et al., 2014; Moritz et al., 2013); MCT was compared to cognitive remediation (16 sessions each with assessments at baseline, four weeks, six months, and three years later). Relative to the active controls receiving cognitive remediation, MCT participants experienced significantly reduced delusions on multiple scales at all post-treatment time points, including three-years post-treatment. Importantly, significant group differences at the three-year follow-up were also found on measures of self-esteem and quality of life, which did not distinguish groups at earlier assessment points. Taken together, these results suggest that MCT exerts sustained effects on the reduction of delusions over and above the effects of antipsychotic medication. Finally, a recent meta-analysis on all existing MCT trials concluded that the programme exerts a significant small to moderate effect on delusional thinking and positive symptoms (Eichner & Berna, 2016), which has been corroborated recently (Liu, Tang, Hung, Tsai, & Lin, in press). However, it should be noted that not all trials have resulted in significant improvements for MCT (van Oosterhout et al., 2014). This suggests that the group-based approach may not be appropriate for all individuals, particularly those with acute delusions or high levels of paranoia who might not cope well with being in a group setting (Moritz et al. 2016).

Individualised Metacognitive Training (MCT+)

Both CBTp and MCT have been shown to be effective treatments for people experiencing delusional thinking, but both also appear to have their limitations; CBTp may not be targeting the specific cognitive biases underlying delusions, while group-based MCT may not be indicated when delusions are particularly resistant or severe, or when group settings are inappropriate. Accordingly, Individualised Metacognitive Training (or MCT+) was developed to maximise the efficiency, yet minimise the potential limitations, of both MCT and CBTp. This hybrid programme combines the focus on cognitive biases of group MCT with elements of individual CBTp; this allows therapists to simultaneously focus on the underlying cognitive biases while tailoring the content to the client's specific beliefs and needs. In this way, MCT+ may be a more effective treatment than either MCT or CBTp used in isolation.

MCT+ covers the same six cognitive and social biases as the original group programme (i.e., JTC, BADE, overconfidence, attributions, theory of mind deficits, and depressive schemata). It uses many of the same exercises outlined above, but also borrows a lot of the core techniques from CBTp. One of these is conducting a comprehensive psychological assessment that incorporates a detailed background history as well as current symptoms; from this, MCT+ therapists can work collaboratively with participants in creating a case formulation that is then referred to across sessions. Case formulations, a defining component of CBT (Kuyken et al.,

2009), help participants to see the origins of their symptoms, as well as the connections between thoughts, feelings and behaviours that may be maintaining these symptoms; we particularly emphasise the role of cognitive biases in these formulations, which provides the basis and rationale for the programme. Due to the individualised format of MCT+, we can go into a person's delusional thinking framework in much more depth than in the original group-programme and employ standard CBT techniques to raise the client's awareness of implausible content in their beliefs, such as evaluating the evidence for and against them. The individualised approach also allows for a greater range of therapeutic strategies, such as:

- establishing therapy goals (e.g., reducing paranoia in public spaces, improving social skills);
- use of role-plays (e.g., viewing beliefs as though an outsider; 'what would you say if a friend told you that?');
- reality testing and confronting avoidance and safety behaviours (e.g., not going into crowded shopping centres, wearing dark sunglasses in public);
- Socratic discussion (i.e., therapist taking the position of a naïve questioner to generate pros, cons and consequences of a particular viewpoint or behaviour); and
- involving trusted relatives and friends to aid in the process of the therapy (e.g., relatives can help to recognise the early warning signs of relapse).

MCT+ dedicates an entire module to relapse prevention, which focuses on coping strategies for stress. For instance, we discuss how stress may, in extreme cases, lead to a relapse, and how managing stress and monitoring early warning symptoms may prevent relapse from occurring.

However, it is important to note that these CBTp techniques are utilised within the framework of cognitive biases: the bias in question, rather than the individual delusion, is the starting point for discussion. For example, when evaluating the evidence for a client's beliefs, we would encourage the client to consider how the Jumping to Conclusions bias or a bias against disconfirmatory evidence can influence people to look for evidence in a particular way, and stop people from seeing alternative explanations. We believe this is a gentler, less direct approach than traditional CBTp that, over time, plants and nurtures the 'seeds of doubt' and may foster a stronger therapeutic alliance. Moreover, MCT+, much like the original programme, employs many real-world examples, audio-visual material (including videos) and illustrative exercises, which most clients find engaging and entertaining.

Efficacy

Evidence for MCT+ is still emerging, and adequately powered randomised controlled trials are still being conducted. However, a number of case studies and preliminary clinical trials have been published which are worth mentioning here.

One of the first published trials randomised 48 participants to a hybrid of group MCT plus individualised MCT+, or cognitive remediation as the control condition (Moritz, Vitzthum et al., 2011). Participants in the MCT/MCT+ group showed significantly greater improvement on delusion severity, delusional conviction and lower susceptibility to JTC; a single case study using the same hybrid approach also showed a substantial symptom reduction after four weeks of combined therapy (Vitzthum et al., 2014). Another case report, based on two individuals with active delusions who received four weeks of MCT+ alone (without concurrent antipsychotic medication) also showed substantial reduction in delusional severity, improved clinical insight into their symptoms and reduced vulnerability to cognitive biases (Balzan & Galletly, 2015). The most comprehensive trial to date randomised 92 people with current or past delusions to 12 (twice-weekly) sessions of either MCT+ or a control intervention (Andreou et al., 2017). At the initial six-week follow-up, participants who had received MCT+ had significantly lower delusion severity and higher levels of self-reflectiveness (medium effect size). Although differences were no longer significant at six-month follow-up, the authors noted methodological limitations that may have contributed to this (e.g., lower attendance rates in the control group; lower baseline delusion severity in the MCT+ group) and the MCT+ programme has since been updated and expanded. We are currently conducting a trial on the newest version of MCT+ (Schneider et al., 2016) and, clearly, more trials are required before any firm conclusions can be drawn about its efficacy. Nevertheless, given that MCT+ is based on two evidence-based treatment programmes for delusional thinking, it has the potential to be an effective treatment option, particularly for those who might not be suited to group programmes (e.g., due to elevated social anxiety or paranoia) or those who might find traditional CBTp too confrontational. It is also worth noting that there is another individualised 'Reasoning Training' therapy programme which therapists may wish to use in conjunction with MCT+, given that it similarly focuses on data gathering and belief inflexibility biases; it has also been shown to be effective in reducing susceptibility to these biases and to delusional conviction (Ross et al., 2011).

Conclusions

Over the last two decades, we have seen increasing attention paid to psychological treatments for psychosis, particularly CBTp. Concurrently, there has been a refinement of our understanding of the cognitive mechanisms that lead to the development and maintenance of experiences and beliefs that may reflect delusional thinking. Both group MCT and its individual MCT+ counterpart have combined these two streams of development into a comprehensive treatment for delusional thinking, and there is growing evidence to suggest this approach is effective. However, we still have more work ahead of us, as there are many unanswered questions left to address. These include, but are not limited to, the efficacy of MCT/MCT+ for people with first episode or early onset psychosis (who might particularly benefit from the less confrontational, yet engaging, approach of MCT/ MCT+), and whether we can further improve efficacy of the programme by combining it with other psychological treatments such as cognitive remediation (Balzan, 2016b). Indeed, the end of the 'psychological nihilism' era has led to many exciting developments in the field, which include the development of MCT for delusional thinking. Ultimately, we hope that this body of work is able to continue benefitting individuals who experience distress from these experiences and beliefs.

References

American Psychiatric Association. (2013). *Diagnostic and statistical manual of mental disorders* (5th ed.). Arlington, VA: American Psychiatric Publishing.

Andreou, C., Moritz, S., Veith, K., Veckenstedt, R., & Naber, D. (2014). Dopaminergic modulation of probabilistic reasoning and overconfidence in errors: A double-blind study. *Schizophrenia Bulletin, 40*, 558–565.

Andreou, C., Wittekind, C., Fieker, M., Heitz, U., Veckenstedt, R., Bohn, F., & Moritz, S. (2017). Individualized metacognitive therapy for delusions: A randomized controlled rater-blind study. *Journal of Behavior Therapy and Experimental Psychiatry, 56*, 144–151.

Balzan, R. P. (2016a). Overconfidence in psychosis: The foundation of delusional conviction? *Cogent Psychology, 3*, 1135855.

Balzan, R. P. (2016b). Re: Can cognitive remediation improve subsequent response to low-intensity Cognitive Behaviour Therapy for psychosis in people with schizophrenia? *Australian & New Zealand Journal of Psychiatry, 51*, 190–191.

Balzan, R. P., Delfabbro, P. H., Galletly, C., & Woodward, T. S. (2014). Metacognitive training for patients with schizophrenia: Preliminary evidence for a targeted, single-module programme. *Australian & New Zealand Journal of Psychiatry, 48*, 1126–1136.

Balzan, R. P., & Galletly, C. (2015). Metacognitive Therapy (MCT+) in patients with psychosis not receiving antipsychotic medication: A case study. *Frontiers in Psychology, 6*.

Brüne, M. (2005). 'Theory of mind' in schizophrenia: A review of the literature. *Schizophrenia Bulletin, 31*, 21–42.

Buckley, P. F., Miller, B. J., Lehrer, D. S., & Castle, D. J. (2009). Psychiatric comorbidities and schizophrenia. *Schizophrenia Bulletin, 35*, 383–402.

Dudley, R., Taylor, P., Wickham, S., & Hutton, P. (2015). Psychosis, delusions and the 'Jumping to Conclusions' reasoning bias: A systematic review and meta-analysis. *Schizophrenia Bulletin, 42*, 652–665.

Eichner, C., & Berna, F. (2016). Acceptance and efficacy of Metacognitive Training (MCT) on positive symptoms and delusions in patients with schizophrenia: A meta-analysis taking into account important moderators. *Schizophrenia Bulletin, 42*, 952–962.

Farhall, J., & Thomas, N. (2013). Cognitive and behavioural therapies for psychosis. *Australian & New Zealand Journal of Psychiatry, 47*, 508–511.

Fioravanti, M., Bianchi, V., & Cinti, M. (2012). Cognitive deficits in schizophrenia: An updated metanalysis of the scientific evidence. *BMC Psychiatry, 12*, 1–20.

Flavell, J. H. (1979). Metacognition and cognitive monitoring: A new area of cognitive-development inquiry. *American Psychologist, 34*, 906–911.

Freeman, D. (2006). Delusions in the non-clinical population. *Current Psychiatry Reports, 8*, 191–204.

Freeman, D., & Garety, P. (2014). Advances in understanding and treating persecutory delusions: A review. *Social Psychiatry and Psychiatric Epidemiology, 49*, 1179–1189.

Gawęda, Ł., Moritz, S., & Kokoszka, A. (2009). The metacognitive training for schizophrenia patients: Description of method and experiences from clinical practice. *Psychiatria Polska, 43*, 683–692.

Jaspers, K. (1913). *Allgemeine Psychopathologie. Ein Leitfaden für Studierende, Ärzte und Psychologen.* Berlin: J. Springer.

Kennedy, J. L., Altar, C. A., Taylor, D. L., Degtiar, I., & Hornberger, J. C. (2014). The social and economic burden of treatment-resistant schizophrenia: A systematic literature review. *International Clinical Psychopharmacology, 29*(2), 63–76.

Kinderman, P., & Bentall, R. P. (1997). Causal attributions in paranoia and depression: Internal, personal, and situational attributions for negative events. *Journal of Abnormal Psychology, 106*, 341–345.

Kingdon, D., & Turkington, D. (2008). *Cognitive therapy of schizophrenia.* New York: Guildford Press.

Koriat, A., & Levy-Sadot, R. (1999). Processes underlying metacognitive judgments: Information-based and experience-based monitoring of one's own knowledge. In S. Chaiken, & Y. Trope (Eds.). Dual process theories in social psychology (pp. 483–502). New York: Guilford.

Kuyken, W., Padesky, C. A., & Dudley, R. (2009). *Collaborative case conceptualization: Working effectively with clients in Cognitive-Behavioral Therapy.* New York: Guilford Press.

Liu, Y. C., Tang, C. C., Hung, T. T., Tsai, P. C., & Lin, M. F. (in press). The Efficacy of Metacognitive Training for Delusions in Patients With Schizophrenia: A Meta-Analysis of Randomized Controlled Trials Informs Evidence-Based Practice. *Worldviews on Evidence-Based Nursing.*

McHugh, R. K., Whitton, S. W., Peckham, A. D., Welge, J. A., & Otto, M. W. (2013). Patient preference for psychological vs. pharmacological treatment of psychiatric disorders: A meta-analytic review. *The Journal of Clinical Psychiatry, 74*(6), 595–602.

McLean, B. F., Mattiske, J. K., & Balzan, R. P. (2017). Association of the jumping to conclusions and evidence integration biases with delusions in psychosis: A detailed meta-analytic approach. *Schizophrenia Bulletin, 43*, 344–354.

Mehl, S., Werner, D., & Lincoln, T. M. (2015). Does Cognitive Behavior Therapy for psychosis (CBTp) show a sustainable effect on delusions? A meta-analysis. *Frontiers in Psychology, 6*, 1450.

Merrin, J., Kinderman, P., & Bentall, R. P. (2007). 'Jumping to conclusions' and attributional style in persecutory delusions. *Cognitive Therapy and Research, 31*, 741–758.

Moritz, S., Berna, F., Jaeger, S., Westermann, S., & Nagel, M. (2017). The customer is always right? Subjective target symptoms and treatment preferences in patients with psychosis. *European Archives of Psychiatry and Clinical Neuroscience, 267*, 335–339.

Moritz, S., Kerstan, A., Veckenstedt, R., Randjbar, S., Vitzthum, F., Schmidt, C., Heise, M., & Woodward, T. S. (2011). Further evidence for the efficacy of a metacognitive group training in schizophrenia. *Behaviour Research and Therapy, 49*(3), 151–157.

Moritz, S., Pfuhl, G., Lüdtke, T., Menon, M., Balzan, R. P., & Andreou, C. (2017). A two stage account of the positive symptoms of psychosis: Highlighting the role of lowered decision thresholds. *Journal of Behavior Therapy and Experimental Psychiatry, 56*, 12–20.

Moritz, S., & Schneider, B. C. (2016). From the incomprehensible to the partially understood. An update on cognitive bias research and metacognitive training in schizophrenia psychosis. *Current Treatment Options in Psychiatry, 3*, 83–98.

Moritz, S., Veckenstedt, R., Andreou, C., & et al. (2014). Sustained and 'sleeper' effects of group metacognitive training for schizophrenia: A randomized clinical trial. *JAMA Psychiatry, 71*, 1103–1111.

Moritz, S., Veckenstedt, R., Bohn, F., Hottenrott, B., Scheu, F., Randjbar, S., . . . Roesch-Ely, D. (2013). Complementary group Metacognitive Training (MCT) reduces delusional ideation in schizophrenia. *Schizophrenia Research, 151*, 61–69.

Moritz, S., Vitzthum, F., Randjbar, S., Veckenstedt, R., & Woodward, T. S. (2011). Antipsychotic treatment beyond antipsychotics: Metacognitive intervention for schizophrenia patients improves delusional symptoms. *Psychological Medicine, 41*, 1823–1832.

Moritz, S., Werner, D., Menon, M., Balzan, R. P., & Woodward, T. S. (2016). Jumping to negative conclusions – a case of study-gathering bias? *Psychological Medicine, 46*, 59–61.

Moritz, S., & Woodward, T. S. (2007). Metacognitive training for schizophrenia patients (MCT): A pilot study on feasibility, treatment adherence, and subjective efficacy. *German Journal of Psychiatry, 10*, 69–78.

Oswald, M. E., & Grosjean, S. (2004). Confirmation bias. In R. F. Pohl (Ed.), *Cognitive illusions: A handbook on fallacies and biases in thinking, judgement and memory* (pp. 79–96). East Sussex: Psychology Press.

Randjbar, S., Veckenstedt, R., Vitzthum, F., Hottenrott, B., & Moritz, S. (2011). Attributional biases in paranoid schizophrenia: Further evidence for a decreased sense of self-causation in paranoia. *Psychosis, 3*, 74–85.

Ross, K., Freeman, D., Dunn, G., & Garety, P. A. (2011). A randomized experimental investigation of reasoning training for people with delusions. *Schizophrenia Bulletin, 37*, 324–333.

Ross, R. M., McKay, R., Coltheart, M., & Langdon, R. (2015). Jumping to conclusions about the beads task? A meta-analysis of delusional ideation and data-gathering. *Schizophrenia Bulletin, 41*, 1183–1191.

Schneider, B. C., Brüne, M., Bohn, F., Veckenstedt, R., Kolbeck, K., Krieger, E., . . . Moritz, S. (2016). Investigating the efficacy of an individualized metacognitive therapy program (MCT+) for psychosis: Study protocol of a multi-center randomized controlled trial. *BMC Psychiatry, 16*(1), 51.

So, S., Siu, N., Wong, H., Chan, W., & Garety, P. (2016). 'Jumping to conclusions' data-gathering bias in psychosis and other psychiatric disorders — Two meta-analyses of comparisons between patients and healthy individuals. *Clinical Psychology Review, 45*, 151–167.

Thomas, N. (2015). What's really wrong with cognitive behavioural therapy for psychosis? *Frontiers in Psychology, 6.*

Turner, D., van der Gaag, M., Karyotaki, E., & Cuijpers, P. (2014). Psychological interventions for psychosis: A meta-analysis of comparative outcome studies. *American Journal of Psychiatry, 171*, 523–538.

van der Gaag, M., Valmaggia, L. R., & Smit, F. (2014). The effects of individually tailored formulation-based cognitive behavioural therapy in auditory hallucinations and delusions: A meta-analysis. *Schizophrenia Research, 156*, 30–37.

van Oosterhout, B., Krabbendam, L., de Boer, K., Ferwerda, J., van der Helm, M., Stant, A. D., & van der Gaag, M. (2014). Metacognitive group training for schizophrenia spectrum patients with delusions: A randomized controlled trial. *Psychological Medicine, 44,* 3025–3035.

van Os, J., & Reininghaus, U. (2016). Psychosis as a transdiagnostic and extended phenotype in the general population. *World Psychiatry, 15*(2), 118–124.

Vitzthum, F. B., Veckenstedt, R., & Moritz, S. (2014). Individualized Metacognitive Therapy program for patients with psychosis (MCT+): Introduction of a novel approach for psychotic symptoms. *Behavioural and Cognitive Psychotherapy, 42*(01), 105–110.

Wykes, T., Steel, C., Everitt, B., & Tarrier, N. (2008). Cognitive Behavior Therapy for schizophrenia: Effect sizes, clinical models, and methodological rigor. *Schizophrenia Bulletin, 34*(3), 523–537.

4

MINDFULNESS IN CBT
FOR PSYCHOSIS

Katherine Newman-Taylor and Nicola Abba

Introduction

Over the last three decades mindfulness has been adopted and adapted from spiritual traditions for use in secular health settings, particularly in the UK and the US, as a means of alleviating suffering. The aim is to foster a *decentered awareness* of internal experience, such as pain, thoughts and images, and respond with a compassionate curiosity rather than habitual patterns of rumination and avoidance that maintain distress. In this way, we may learn to live well with difficult thoughts and feelings, and ourselves, and engage more fully in our lives (Kabat-Zinn, 1990, 2013; Segal et al., 2002; Teasdale & Chaskalson, 2011a, 2011b; Williams 2008).

Mindfulness is incorporated in a number of process-based cognitive behavioural therapies that benefit people with psychosis, including Person Based Cognitive Therapy (PBCT) (Chadwick, 2006), Acceptance and Commitment Therapy (ACT) (Hayes et al., 1999; Morris et al., 2013) and Compassion Focused Therapy (CFT) (Gilbert, 2009; Gumley et al., 2010). Interestingly, hypothesised mechanisms of change for the role of mindfulness are similar across these approaches, as well as when incorporated into more traditional CBT for psychosis (Newman-Taylor & Abba, 2015).

As psychologists and cognitive behavioural therapists, we use mindfulness when indicated by psychological formulation of the cognitive, behavioural and affective processes involved in the development and maintenance of a person's distress (following Teasdale et al., 2003). In this chapter we outline current cognitive theory on mechanisms of therapeutic change, and the implications for responding mindfully to psychosis. We then describe the practicalities of introducing and teaching mindfulness in the context of CBT for psychosis.

There are limits to how fully we can understand mindfulness as an experiential skill by reading chapters and attending talks. For those interested, we recommend commencing a personal practice. Additionally, we have sought to illustrate the use of mindfulness with a series of quotes. We hope this gives a rich sense of what it might be like to be 'lost in psychosis', as well as moments of stillness and acceptance of psychosis and the self.

Current cognitive theory and mechanisms of change

CBT aims to support people's recovery by working collaboratively to understand the development and maintenance of distressing psychosis and enable people to make changes on the basis of this formulation, in line with their goals and aspirations.

Early accounts of CBT suggest that therapeutic change may be achieved by addressing both cognitive content (our appraisals of ourselves and others) and process (how we tend to interpret information) (Beck, 1976; Beck et al., 1979). More recently, in their work on mechanisms of change in depression, Teasdale, Williams and colleagues have placed greater emphasis on process than content of thought. These authors argue that an inability to step back or *decenter* from transient internal experience constitutes a key vulnerability to mental ill-health, and that cognitive therapies, including Mindfulness Based Cognitive Therapy (MBCT) and traditional CBT, effect change by fostering a decentered awareness of thoughts and feelings as *events of the mind* rather than necessarily accurate representations of the self or the world (Kuyken et al., 2010; Teasdale, 1999; Teasdale et al., 1995, 2000, 2002).

It is important to note that decentering involves an accepting, non-judgemental stance towards our experience and ourselves. In learning to recognise and disengage from habitual patterns such as avoidance and rumination, we develop '. . . the capacity to take a present-focused, non-judgmental stance in regards to thoughts and feelings, and accept them' (Fresco et al., 2007, p. 448).

We can expand this explanation of decentered awareness to conceptualise *doing* and *being* modes of mind (Segal et al., 2002; Williams, 2008, 2013). These describe processing patterns that incorporate thinking, feeling, behavioural urges and physical sensations that are linked and shift together. When we are in a *doing mode of mind*, we engage in automatic discrepancy-based processing (recognising a mismatch between current and desired states; for example, the difference between being fearful and desiring to be unafraid), assume that thoughts and feelings necessarily reflect reality, and strive to avoid unwanted internal experience, thereby increasing distress. In a *being mode* we attend to present moment experience, intentionally turn towards difficult thoughts and feelings, and allow these to come and go as transient mental events. A *doing* mode of mind leaves us vulnerable to recurrent episodes of distress whereas a *being* mode of mind, which may be cultivated through mindfulness as well as cognitive and other therapies, reduces the likelihood of mental ill-health (cf. Wells & Matthews, 1996).

Key psychological processes in mindfulness for psychosis

If cognitive therapies are effective insofar as they enable people to develop a decentred awareness or being mode of mind in relation to difficult internal experience, we can hypothesise that CBT and mindfulness for psychosis may effect change by facilitating a decentred awareness or being mode of mind in relation to psychotic experience. That is, people may learn to allow voices, paranoid thoughts and images to come and go without the struggle that exacerbates distress; instead adopting a compassionate curiosity towards these experiences and their meaning in relation to self.

Certainly, our clinical work suggests that people often respond to psychotic experience in ways that inadvertently increase distress. Unpleasant voices, paranoia and images can be experienced as intolerable and trigger strategies such as avoidance and rumination (Chadwick et al, 2005; Morrison & Wells, 2007). Just as people with depression or anxiety can get stuck in these habitual patterns, people with psychosis can become entangled in understandable but unhelpful reactions, characteristic of a doing mode of mind, which maintain distress and may increase the likelihood of relapse (Austin et al., 2015; Newman-Taylor et al., 2009a; Sellers et al., 2016; Sellers, 2017).

A grounded theory of mindful responding to psychosis provides evidence both of the processes maintaining distress, and of contrasting factors cultivated through mindfulness (Abba et al., 2008). Grounded theory is a systematic method of analysing qualitative data, such as people's descriptions of their internal experience, leading to the construction of a broader conceptual understanding or theory. This grounded theory was derived from accounts of people who had been referred to their local city-based psychology service and attended a rolling mindfulness group (see Chadwick et al., 2005). The first 16 people who completed the group were invited to take part in the study. All met group criteria for distressing psychosis and all had been prescribed medication. All reported paranoia, 11 heard voices and five experienced other hallucinations. Thirteen people had received a diagnosis of paranoid schizophrenia, two of psychotic depression and one of psychotic episode. Ten people were engaged with local community mental health teams, one was an acute in-patient at the time of the group, and five attended from 24-hour rehabilitation hostels.

The grounded theory identified people's key concern as the tyrannical relationship with psychosis. In response, a three-stage process emerged in which people redefined their relationship with psychosis through mindfulness practice: (1) centering, (2) allowing voices, thoughts and images to come and go, and (3) acceptance. Centering involved present moment awareness and being open to psychotic experience, in contrast to a sense of being lost in psychosis. Allowing voices, thoughts and images to come and go incorporated an intentional turning towards these experiences, in contrast to attempts to avoid or change them; for example through cognitive avoidance, rumination, worry or confrontation. The third stage combined acceptance of the direct experience of psychosis and the self, in contrast to judgements (typically condemnation) of both.

These aspects of the tyrannical relationship with psychosis, and the contrasting stages of mindful responding, bear clear similarities to the doing and being modes of mind as these might be applied to psychosis. For utility in clinical practice these can be described more simply, as shown in Figure 4.1.

While there is an implicit development in mindful responding from being open to psychotic experience, through letting come and go, to acceptance – the grounded theory does not assume a linear progression through distinct stages.

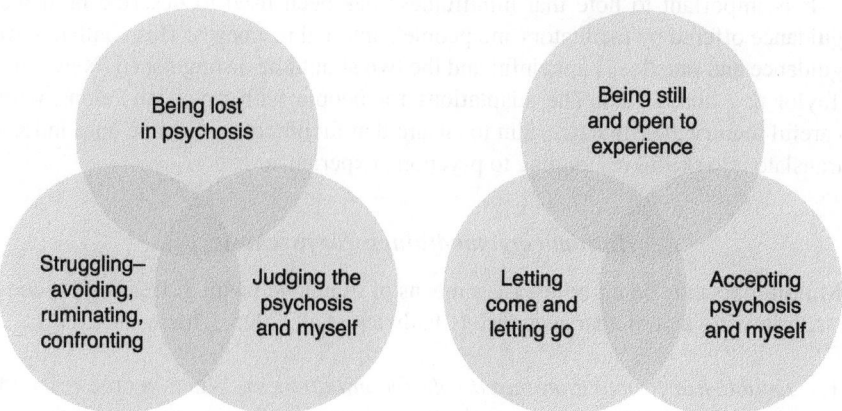

Figure 4.1 Mindful and unmindful relationship to psychosis

Indeed, the quotes below indicate a fluidity of experience, and moments of each rather than stability of any particular state.

The therapist's task, then, is to facilitate mindful responding to distressing psychosis if this is likely to be useful and acceptable to the person. This work assumes and is rooted in an interpersonally effective therapeutic relationship:

> What I found helpful was that you didn't give up on me when I'd given up on you. I felt at one stage I wasn't going to come anymore and I had to force myself to come at times when I might not have done and you were so supportive when I got here. You hadn't given up on me.

Mindfulness in practice

Adaptations for people with distressing psychosis

Clinicians have been understandably cautious about teaching mindfulness to people with psychosis. In addition to the small number of studies suggesting that some intensive meditation practices may trigger psychosis (e.g., Kuijpers et al., 2007; Lu & Pierre, 2007; Naveen & Telles, 2003; Sethi & Bhargava, 2003), clinicians may fear that allowing voices and paranoid thoughts 'free rein' could exacerbate rather than alleviate distress.

Helpfully, Chadwick (2006) identifies the key issue as 'how mindfulness can safely and therapeutically be introduced to people with distressing psychosis' (p. 81). Practitioners from traditional and third wave Cognitive Behavioural Therapies emphasise particular adaptations, including grounding prompts, short sessions of up to about ten minutes, and frequent facilitation (Chadwick, 2006; 2014; Chadwick et al., 2005; Thomas et al., 2013).

It is important to note that mindfulness has been used to describe both the guidance offered by facilitators and people's internal responses. This conflation of guidance and practice is unhelpful and the two should be distinguished (Newman-Taylor & Abba, 2015). The adaptations for people with psychosis, along with careful inquiry after practice, aim to ensure that facilitators' guidance does indeed translate into skilful responding to psychotic experience.

Introducing mindfulness for psychosis

Mindfulness may be introduced as a means of living well with distressing psychosis, following a particular sequence (Chadwick et al., 2005; Chadwick, 2006):

1   *Establish a formulation-based role for mindfulness.* When people respond to psychosis with strategies such as avoidance, rumination, worry, confrontation and judgement, and these strategies exacerbate rather than ameliorate distress, mindfulness may be a valuable alternative. In CBT for psychosis, we use behavioural approaches to address overt avoidance and safety behaviours; encourage reflection on, and reconsideration of distressing appraisals; and introduce mindfulness as a means of disengaging from judgement and habitual processing patterns, in line with the person's goals (as illustrated by the example in Figure 4.2).

2   *Explain the rationale.* Mindfulness is discussed in relation to the person's direct experience. Using guided discovery, we explore the impact of psychosis, current coping strategies and the effect of these. The overlapping circles, in Figure 4.2, may be useful here. We name the common urge to struggle with psychosis (which often brings short-term relief) and to condemn oneself. Mindful responding can then be drawn out as a possible alternative; e.g., 'What might it be like if you were able to let these voices come and go, to live without this exhausting battle?' – again using the overlapping circles if helpful.

3   *Carry out a short practice and check understanding.* We use mindfulness of the breath repeatedly so people can learn to master one particular approach. A brief three to five-minute version of the standard eight to ten-minute practice is used. Following this, we elicit any moments of decentered awareness when the person was able to observe familiar patterns of struggle and judgement, and any moments of stillness in contrast to the usual sense of being lost in psychosis. This allows the person to make an informed choice about whether to pursue mindfulness.

4   *Agree plans for regular practice (at least six to eight sessions).* This may be through further individual sessions in the context of CBT for psychosis, or in a group setting. Subsequent sessions combine guided mindfulness and inquiry after practice. These focus on particular aspects of mindful relating in turn: (1) being still and anchoring attention on the breath, (2i) letting go (2ii) letting come, and (3) acceptance of psychosis and self.

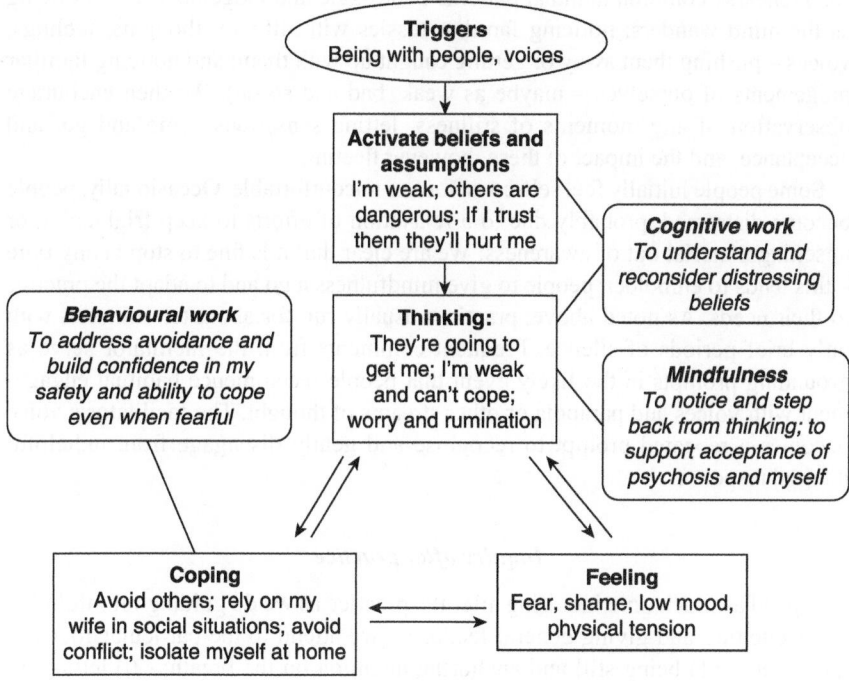

Figure 4.2 Formulation-based rationale for mindfulness (details have been changed to preserve anonymity)

Guiding practice

We always start by guiding people to ground awareness in the body and breath, attending to physical sensations such as the floor solid beneath our feet and the rise and fall of the abdomen with the breath. People are invited to close their eyes if willing to do so. We practise alongside and usually close our eyes too. We note that the intention is not to breathe in any particular way but to allow the attention to settle on the sensations of the breath where these are most salient, such as the tips of the nostrils or the abdomen. We encourage people to notice the sensations, thoughts, images and voices as these arise in conscious awareness, and then notice as they pass.

It can be helpful to name internal events as these arise and pass ('worry' or 'voices'). This facilitates a decentered awareness of sensations as transient mental events, rather than necessarily accurate reflections of self or the world ('just worry' or 'just a voice') (following Teasdale, 1999; Teasdale et al., 1995; 2000; Williams, 2008).

Sessions focusing on specific aspects of mindfulness (being still and anchoring attention on the breath; letting go and letting come; acceptance of psychosis and self) rehearse common habitual patterns of struggle and judgement (e.g., noticing as the mind wanders; noticing familiar tussles with difficult thoughts, feelings, voices – pushing them away or getting caught up with them; and noticing familiar judgements of ourselves – maybe as weak, bad and so on). We then encourage observation of any moments of stillness, letting sensations come and go, and acceptance, and the impact of these, however fleeting.

Some people initially feel self-conscious or uncomfortable. Occasionally, people become distressed, probably due to a relaxation of efforts to keep frightening or upsetting material out of awareness. We are clear that it is fine to stop at any time – this tends to embolden people to give mindfulness a go and to adapt the practice to their needs. As noted above, practices usually run for about ten minutes, with only brief periods of silence. Frequent comments from the facilitator serve as grounding prompts in the likely event that people recommence habitual engagement with voices and paranoia or other streams of thought. The facilitator's voice becomes a repeated prompt to recognise and gently disengage from unhelpful internal responses.

Inquiry after practice

We spend as much time inquiring after the practice as we do guiding mindfulness. After eliciting and giving general feedback, we attend to the particular focus of the session: (1) being still and anchoring attention on the breath; (2i) letting go (2ii) letting come; and (3) acceptance of psychosis and self. We are interested in moments when the person was able to notice familiar patterns of understandable but unhelpful responding, and any contrasting moments of stillness, letting come and go, and acceptance. The person is encouraged to explore the impact of these habitual responses and any instances of mindful responding.

It is important to be clear that *accepting* voices and thoughts does not mean we agree with the voices or internal judgements, nor suggest passivity in the face of perceived oppression. We are attending to moments of acceptance that 'right now, I'm hearing a voice screaming at me' or 'here I am judging myself to be useless, worthless scum' or 'I'm having the thought that they think I'm a paedophile' and noticing the impact.

We provide audio recordings of guided practice and teach the *three-minute breathing space* (Segal, et al., 2002), and are interested in examples of people's use of these between sessions.

When incorporating mindfulness into CBT for psychosis, clinical decision points arise when we need to judge whether it is likely to be most useful to focus on content or process. Rick described an enduring fear that 'they're going to get me' and struggled to leave the house. At times it was useful to attend to the content, inviting a reconsideration of this belief on the basis of his formulation, for example, 'Rick, is it useful at this point to recall where these fears come from?' and encouraging a behavioural approach to test whether it was safe for Rick to go out, even when feeling anxious. At other times it was useful to focus on the process; for example, 'and what is it like when this fear takes hold . . . are there any moments when you can let this familiar fear come and go without reacting . . . and what is this like?' Later in therapy, it can be valuable to come to joint decisions about whether to focus on the content or process of thought.

Recognising and disengaging from the tyrannical relationship with psychosis

We hope the material to this point explains when mindfulness may be useful to people with psychosis, and how this can be introduced. We have described how we guide practice and have outlined a broad framework for inquiry. The inquiry after practice is essential in encouraging people to reflect on moments when they recognise and choose to disengage from habitual responses, and the impact on both psychosis and the self. This learning can then be incorporated into further practice.

Of course, all this is easier said than done! In this section we use clinical examples from Abba, Chadwick & Stevenson (2008) to illustrate people's experiences of distressing psychosis and skilful responses. This is in order to give clinicians a sense of what to listen for when inquiring about people's practice, and how to facilitate mindful responding.

'Being lost in psychosis' or 'being still and open to experience'

Intrusive voices, thoughts and images typically initiate a doing mode of mind, characterised by struggle and judgement. These reactions and associated distress follow on quickly from the intrusions and often appear indistinguishable. The sense of being lost in psychosis can be overwhelming:

> They've got a hold over you, these voices. They will make you very angry, they will make you distressed, angry, you can even start crying. It won't let you go, it just won't let you lie there and rest, they're always at you, they're at you 24 hours of the bloody day. You would have thought, oh just hearing a sound could be, could make you want to die, but it can, they're very severe voices.

In this first stage, we are inviting people to be still and open to experience. This is extremely difficult. In threat situations, we are hard-wired to respond in ways that increase our likelihood of survival in the event of physical danger. So we are asking people to do the opposite of what their minds and bodies are urging them to do. We reflect on this and ask if, in the face of this recurrent threat, they are able to respond differently for a moment and see what this might be like.

We have found that many are struck by the contrast to more familiar agitation or restlessness: 'A lot of the time I was very agitated and therefore I couldn't concentrate and I couldn't really stay. I had to go out of the room a lot of the time.'

Mindfulness practice involves slowing down, being still: 'You're static. To me my normal state of affairs is I'm moving all the time, I'm running away or I'm scared . . . this mindfulness thing . . . it's just a few minutes' release and peace from that and it's the first time where I stop moving.' Similarly, '. . . when I'm having real problems with thoughts and images . . . it's difficult at times to use it . . . but when I have been able to do that it's just been really calming.'

In addition to slowing down, this stage involves a *choiceless awareness* of whatever comes to mind – whether sounds, bodily sensations, voices, thoughts or images. This can be learnt through a gentle persistence in returning attention to the body and breath, and other present moment experience, knowing that the mind will wander and wander again.

We can facilitate this stillness and broadening of awareness with prompts to: (1) ground awareness in the body and breath, (2) concentrate gently on what is present, and (3) reconnect with the present moment each time the mind wanders. By anchoring attention in the body and breath, we are in a more a stable position to begin to develop the ability to attend not just to *what* is present, but *whatever* is present – a choiceless awareness.

The nature of the mind is such that our attention rarely settles for long. The flow of concentration from the body and breath, to whatever comes to mind, and back to the breath, is emphasised in both guidance and inquiry. We note how we typically cycle through this process of grounding and opening attention many times when practising mindfulness; for example, 'Each time your mind wanders, just notice this, and when you're ready gently bring your attention back, reconnecting with the sensations of your breath as these are right now.' This is extended in the inquiry; for example, 'Did you notice your mind wandering . . . and when you noticed this, what did you do . . . were you able gently to bring your attention back to your breathing . . . and what was it like to do that . . . and then what happened?' With regular practice, people learn the value of patiently and repeatedly returning to the breath, as our group participants noted: 'So you just do it again . . . just concentrate on a tingle in your hands or whatever, then go for the breathing again.' Similarly:

> As long as you've got something to concentrate on, i.e. your breathing, it helps in a way, there's not so many distractions. Your mind's like a spotlight, it can move around all over the place, if you've got something you can just focus on, like your breathing, then it does help, it stops your mind wandering so much. If you find it wandering you just draw a natural breath.

'Struggling' or 'letting come and letting go'

Distressing internal experience elicits struggle. This may be through suppression, rumination and confrontation. For example, 'I lose my temper sometimes. That can happen. Your emotions, you start drawing them all in, you get that whirlpool effect which drags you down.' These struggles can become violent: 'After 20 minutes you're going to be screaming, breaking windows, throwing your shoes against the wall, banging your fists against the wall' and 'distressfully leaping about in the space, reacting, reacting'.

In this second stage, we are suggesting that people let go of attempts to control or change their experience and instead simply be with the voices, thoughts and images, in the moment each is present. Similar to the choiceless awareness of the first stage, this is a *non-reaction*. Again, we are asking people to do the opposite of habitual and possibly hard-wired responses. Our group participants described this as having to: 'unlearn your responses to these thoughts and feelings' and 'when you get the voices . . . let the voices happen . . . How can I put it? If you've got voices controlling you, try and just let it and then you'll find out that it didn't control you after all. It's just a voice', and 'you don't have to try too hard. The trick is to not try in a way'.

This stage involves an intentional turning towards, rather than away from, voices, thoughts and images. In the guidance and inquiry, we suggest bringing the focus of awareness fully to each passing sensation and ask people to notice when the mind is caught up in familiar patterns of struggle. For example, 'Where is the mind now? Maybe caught up in worries, judgements or trying to push thoughts, feelings, voices out of mind?' In addition to noting the mind has wandered and returning awareness to the breath (as emphasised in stage one), we invite a greater familiarity with these *habits of mind*, attending to particular patterns of thought, and naming these if the person finds this useful (for example, 'arguing', 'analysing' or 'shouting back') before letting these go and returning attention to the breath once more.

Simply noticing these patterns is valuable: '. . . just sort of get fed up with the same old pattern, you know, I've been here before, struggling, trying to work them out, fighting'. This can also prompt alternative responses: 'I'm aware when I lock on to one of these thoughts or ideas or images or whatever has come into my head, when I lock on one of them and I start following it, I realise I'm doing it and . . . whoa, back, refocus' and 'at the end of a thought I'll go back to the breathing'.

If we can catch ourselves in the act of reacting, we have in this moment briefly stepped out of the reaction. We then have a choice whether to return to habitual patterns of struggle or bring our full awareness to the passing events of the mind in the absence of reaction: 'You get a thought coming in and it's a case of down tools' and 'your mind goes round and round in circles, not really getting anywhere. Letting go helps, you avoid getting into some ritual that goes on longer than the actual thought or image itself.' 'If they come you just let them go and they're not there and you're not fighting with them and you're not struggling with them.'

This can be hard: 'I still find it difficult not to be enticed by some of the images and thoughts and voices that come into my head.' However, practise can ease distress: 'Letting go of voices and the meaning of what they're saying' and 'it's a way of trying to, not get the thoughts to go away but to stop worrying about them and the anxiety about them.'

'Judging' or 'accepting psychosis and myself'

Psychosis can reflect and form the basis for narrow, fixed and condemnatory self-definition. When people believe they are abnormal, worthless or useless, and spend much of their time each day struggling with voices, streams of thought and images that reflect and reinforce these beliefs, it is hard to separate transient internal experience from the self. Mindfulness can foster this distinction, as described by one of our group members: 'If I'm judging the thoughts I have, I can judge myself as good or bad . . . if I'm not judging it makes me feel better about myself'.

In this third stage we pay increasing attention to psychotic experience as transient events of the mind that can be accepted as part of, but not necessarily defining, the self. A key message is 'I am more than my psychosis'. It is important to check that people remain clear about what is being accepted – the presence of voices, thoughts and so on, rather than earlier meanings, judgements and sub-jugated relationship to the psychosis or others. People have described this as: 'Accept my thoughts, my images, my voices as they come and not follow one off on a thread, not follow one, just to be neutral and accept it, accept it as it comes.' Similarly, 'You use the mindfulness and manage to put it to one side, wouldn't say manage to get rid of it completely but you accept it then let it go for that moment. As you go on and on, the moments get longer and longer which hopefully will make you feel better and better as you get more experience of the process' and 'no bad or good feelings, just feelings – makes it more manageable, less scary, overwhelming'.

Non-judgement of self may follow non-judgement of experience: 'Accept it's there, don't judge it. I'm not a bad person because of it' and 'I've thought that basically that I'm not wrong, that I'm quite acceptable' and 'realising you have an internal critic that isn't exactly you'. Linked to this comes a growing self-efficacy when people feel more in control of their lives as they relinquish attempts to control the mind: '. . . it will deflate. You know this big thing that comes in with lots of bluster, if you do that it will deflate down and deflate to this tiny little thing . . . it's just a load of hot air and bluster.' 'You don't lose your mind to them.'

> When I'm accepting everything the way it's meant to be at that particular moment in time, then things are OK, and I feel OK, but if I'm doing the opposite, if I'm not accepting things, if I'm judging things – I don't like this and I don't like that and I wish I wasn't here, I wish I was there – I've got that uneasiness, that dis-ease. I feel OK about myself and I'm accepting everything the way it's meant to be in that particular moment. And that's what I think mindfulness is, it's that particular moment.

Summary and conclusions

Current cognitive theory suggests that cognitive therapies and mindfulness are effective through facilitating a *decentred* awareness or *being mode of mind* in relation to psychotic experience. Learning to allow voices, paranoid thoughts and images to come to mind, and then pass without struggle and judgement, reduces distress and enables people to live well with their psychosis and themselves.

The emerging research suggests that with particular adaptations, mindfulness can be safely and therapeutically introduced to people with distressing psychosis (Chadwick et al., 2005; 2009; Ellett, 2013; Newman-Taylor et al., 2009b), and when incorporated in Mindfulness Based Cognitive Therapy (Langer et al., 2012), Person Based Cognitive Therapy (Dannahy et al., 2011) and ACT (Bach & Hayes, 2002; Bach et al., 2012; Gaudiano & Herbert, 2006; Shawyer et al., 2012; White et al., 2011). Attentional Training, in which people are taught to focus, switch and divide attention between different sounds and spatial locations (Hatashita-Wong & Silverstein, 2003; Valmaggia et al., 2007; Wells, 1990) and mindfulness for 'negative symptoms' of psychosis (Johnson et al., 2011) also show promise.

While this literature allows a cautious optimism, further work is needed to strengthen the evidence base (Khoury et al., 2013) and examine mechanisms of change (Chadwick, 2014). Specifically, we need to determine whether mindfulness effects change through facilitating a decentered awareness or being mode of mind in relation to psychosis and the self, as cognitive theory would suggest. We know that psychotic experience is often accompanied by intense emotion, such as fear, low mood, anger and shame, and that this in turn forcefully directs our internal resources, initiating a doing mode of mind – probably for good evolutionary reasons. Learning to recognise and disengage from these habitual responses is no mean feat, and yet the accumulation of many moments of mindful responding yields an understanding that we do not need to be defined by our internal experience, psychosis or otherwise, or by narrow and condemnatory constructions of self.

Process-based approaches, as described in this book, may be particularly valuable to people with compelling voices and paranoia that echo a rigidly defined and flawed sense of themselves. When people judge themselves by their psychosis (judgements that are often reinforced socially and systemically through stigma and the organisation of our institutions), we seek to support an acceptance of the complexity of internal experience and the self. Mindfulness in the context of CBT is one way to facilitate this recovery and thereby enable people to live more fully, as they choose.

Acknowledgement

We would like to recognise the courage and determination of all the people with distressing psychosis who have helped us understand how mindfulness may be useful. We would also to thank Professor Paul Chadwick who helped develop many of these ideas. The quotes in this chapter are taken from material gathered for the grounded theory of mindful responding to psychosis (Abba et al., 2008). Those previously published are reproduced here in line with copyright and permissions guidance.

References

All URLs accessed March 2018.

Abba, N., Chadwick, P., & Stevenson, C. (2008). Responding mindfully to distressing psychosis: A grounded theory analysis. *Psychotherapy Research, 18(1)*, 77–87. doi: dx.doi.org/10.1080/10503300701367992

Austin, S. F., Mors, O., Nordentoft, M., Hjorthøj, C. R., Secher, R. G., Hesse, M., . . . & Wells, A. (2015). Schizophrenia and metacognition: An investigation of course of illness and metacognitive beliefs within a first episode psychosis. *Cognitive Therapy and Research, 39*(1), 61–69.

Bach, P., & Hayes, S. C. (2002). The use of acceptance and commitment therapy to prevent the rehospitalization of psychotic patients: A randomized controlled trial. *Journal of Consulting and Clinical Psychology, 70(5)*, 1129. doi: dx.doi.org/10.1037/0022-006X.70.5.1129

Bach, P., Hayes, S. C., & Gallop, R. (2012). Long-term effects of brief acceptance and commitment therapy for psychosis. *Behavior Modification, 36(2)*, 165–181. doi: dx.doi.org/10.1177/0145445511427193

Beck, A. T. (1976). *Cognitive therapy and the emotional disorders*. Oxford: International Universities Press.

Beck, A.T., Rush, A.J., Shaw, B.F., & Emery, G. (1979). *Cognitive therapy of depression*. New York: Guilford Press.

Chadwick, P. (2006). *Person Based Cognitive Therapy for distressing psychosis*. Chichester: Wiley.

Chadwick, P., Newman-Taylor, K., & Abba, N. (2005). Mindfulness groups for people with psychosis. *Behavioural and Cognitive Psychotherapy, 33*(3), 351–359. doi: dx.doi.org/10.1017/S1352465805002158

Chadwick, P. (2014). Mindfulness for psychosis. *British Journal of Psychiatry, 204*(5), 333–334.

Dannahy, L., Hayward, M., Strauss, C., Turton, W., Harding, E., & Chadwick, P. (2011). Group Person Based Cognitive Therapy for distressing voices: Pilot data from nine groups. *Journal of Behavior Therapy and Experimental Psychiatry, 42(1)*, 111–116. doi: dx.doi.org/10.1016/j.jbtep.2010.07.006

Ellett, L. (2013). Mindfulness for paranoid beliefs: Evidence from two case studies. *Behavioural and Cognitive Psychotherapy, 41*(2), 238–243.

Fresco, D. M., Segal, Z. V., Buis, T., & Kennedy, S. (2007). Relationship of post-treatment decentering and cognitive reactivity to relapse in major depression. *Journal of Consulting and Clinical Psychology, 75*(3), 447.

Gaudiano, B. A., & Herbert, J. D. (2006). Acute treatment of inpatients with psychotic symptoms using Acceptance and Commitment Therapy: Pilot results. *Behaviour Research and Therapy, 44*(3), 415–437.

Gilbert, P. (2009). Introducing compassion focussed therapy. *Advances in Psychiatric Treatment, 15*, 199–208.

Gumley, A., Braehler, C., Laithwaite, H., MacBeth, A., & Gilbert, P. (2010). A compassion focused model of recovery after psychosis. *International Journal of Cognitive Therapy*, *3*(2), 186–201.

Hatashita-Wong, M., & Silverstein, S. M. (2003). Coping with voices: Selective attention training for persistent auditory hallucinations in treatment refractory schizophrenia. *Psychiatry, 66*(3), 255–261.

Hayes, S. C., Stroshal, K., & Wilson, K.G. (1999). *Acceptance and Commitment Therapy: An experiential approach to behavior change.* New York: Guildford Press.

Johnson, D. P., Penn, D. L., Fredrickson, B. L., Kring, A. M., Meyer, P. S., Catalino, L. I., & Brantley, M. (2011). A pilot study of loving-kindness meditation for the negative symptoms of schizophrenia. *Schizophrenia Research, 129(2)*, 137–140. doi: dx.doi.org/10.1016/j.schres.2011.02.015

Kabat-Zinn, J. (1990). *Full catastrophe living: Using the wisdom of your body and mind in everyday life.* New York: Delacorte.

Kabat-Zinn, J. (2013). *Full catastrophe living, revised edition: How to cope with stress, pain and illness using mindfulness meditation.* London: Hachette.

Khoury, B., Lecomte, T., Gaudiano, B. A., & Paquin, K. (2013). Mindfulness interventions for psychosis: A meta-analysis. *Schizophrenia Research, 150*(1), 176–184.

Kuijpers, H. J. H., van der Heijden, F. M. M. A., Tuinier, S., & Verhoeven, W. M. A. (2007). Meditation-induced psychosis. *Psychopathology, 40*(6), 461–464. doi: dx.doi.org/10.1159/000108125

Kuyken, W., Watkins, E., Holden, E., White, K., Taylor, R. S., Byford, S., Evans, A., Radford, S., Teasdale, J. D., & Dalgleish, T. (2010). How does mindfulness-based cognitive therapy work? *Behaviour Research and Therapy, 48*(11), 1105–1112.

Langer, Á. I., Cangas, A. J., Salcedo, E., & Fuentes, B. (2012). Applying mindfulness therapy in a group of psychotic individuals: A controlled study. *Behavioural and Cognitive Psychotherapy, 40(*01), 105–109.

Lu, J. S., & Pierre, J. M. (2007). Psychotic episode associated with Bikram yoga. *American Journal of Psychiatry, 164*(11), 1761–1761.

Morris, E. M., Johns, L. C., & Oliver, J. E. (Eds.) (2013). *Acceptance and commitment therapy and mindfulness for psychosis.* Chichester: John Wiley & Sons.

Morrison, A. P., & Wells, A. (2007). Relationships between worry, psychotic experiences and emotional distress in patients with schizophrenia spectrum diagnoses and comparisons with anxious and non-patient groups. *Behaviour Research and Therapy, 45*(7), 1593–1600.

Naveen, K. V., & Telles, S. (2003). Sensory perception during sleep and meditation: Common features and differences. *Perceptual and Motor Skills, 96*(3), 810–811. doi: dx.doi.org/10.2466/pms.2003.96.3.810

Newman-Taylor, K., Graves, A., & Stopa, L. (2009a). Strategic cognition in paranoia: The use of thought control strategies in a non-clinical population. *Behavioural and Cognitive Psychotherapy, 37,* 25–38.

Newman-Taylor, K., Harper, S., & Chadwick, P. (2009b). Impact of mindfulness on cognition and affect in voice hearing: Evidence from two case studies. *Behavioural and Cognitive Psychotherapy, 37*(4), 397–402. doi: dx.doi.org/10.1017/S135246580999018X

Newman-Taylor, K. & Abba, N. (2015). Mindfulness meditation in CBT for psychosis. In B. A. Gaudiano (Ed.), *Incorporating acceptance and mindfulness into the treatment of psychosis: Current trends and future directions.* Oxford: OUP.

Segal, Z. V., Williams, J. M. G., & Teasdale, J. D. (2002) *Mindfulness based cognitive therapy for depression: A new approach to relapse prevention.* New York: Guilford Press.

Sellers, R., Gawęda, Ł., Wells, A., & Morrison, A. P. (2016). The role of unhelpful metacognitive beliefs in psychosis: Relationships with positive symptoms and negative affect. *Psychiatry Research, 246,* 401–406.

Sellers, R., Varese, F., Wells, A., & Morrison, A. P. (2017). A meta-analysis of metacognitive beliefs as implicated in the self-regulatory executive function model in clinical psychosis. *Schizophrenia Research, 179,* 75–84.

Sethi, S., & Bhargava, S. C. (2003). Relationship of meditation and psychosis: Case studies. *Australian & New Zealand Journal of Psychiatry, 37*(3), 382–382. doi: dx.doi. org/10.1046/j.1440-1614.2003.11721.x

Shawyer, F., Farhall, J., Mackinnon, A., Trauer, T., Sims, E., Ratcliff, K., . . . & Copolov, D. (2012). A randomised controlled trial of acceptance-based cognitive behavioural therapy for command hallucinations in psychotic disorders. *Behaviour Research and Therapy, 50*(2), 110–121.

Teasdale, J. D., Segal, Z., & Williams, J. M. G. (1995). How does cognitive therapy prevent depressive relapse and why should attentional control (mindfulness) training help? *Behaviour Research and Therapy, 33*(1), 25–39. doi: dx.doi.org/10.1016/0005-7967(94) E0011-7

Teasdale, J. D. (1999). Metacognition, mindfulness and the modification of mood disorders. *Clinical Psychology and Psychotherapy, 6*(2), 146–155. doi: dx.doi.org/10.1002/ (SICI)1099-0879(199905)6:2<146::AID-CPP195>3.0.CO;2-E

Teasdale, J. D., Segal, Z. V., Williams, J. M. G., Ridgeway, V. A., Soulsby, J. M., & Lau, M. A. (2000). Prevention of relapse / recurrence in major depression by Mindfulness Based Cognitive Therapy. *Journal of Consulting and Clinical Psychology, 68*(4), 615. doi: dx.doi.org/10.1037/0022-006X.68.4.615

Teasdale, J. D., Moore, R. G., Hayhurst, H., Pope, M., Williams, S., Segal, Z. V. (2002). Metacognitive awareness and prevention of relapse in depression: Empirical evidence. *Journal of Consulting and Clinical Psychology, 70*(2), 275–287.

Teasdale, J. D., Segal, Z. V., & Williams, J. M. G. (2003). Mindfulness training and problem formulation. *Clinical Psychology: Science and Practice, 10*(2), 157–160.

Teasdale, J. D., & Chaskalson, M. (2011a). How does mindfulness transform suffering? II: The nature and origins of dukkha. *Contemporary Buddhism, 12*(01), 89–102.

Teasdale, J. D., & Chaskalson, M. (2011b). How does mindfulness transform suffering? I: the transformation of dukkha. *Contemporary Buddhism, 12*(01), 103–124.

Thomas, N., Morris, E. M., Shawyer, F., & Farhall, J. (2013). Acceptance and commitment therapy for voices, 95–111. In E. M. Morris, L. C. Johns, & J. E. Oliver (Eds.), *Acceptance and commitment therapy and mindfulness for psychosis.* Chichester: John Wiley & Sons.

Valmaggia, L. R., Bouman, T. K., & Schuurman, L. (2007). Attention training with auditory hallucinations: A case study. *Cognitive and Behavioural Practice, 14*(2), 127–133. doi: dx.doi.org/10.1016/j.cbpra.2006.01.009

Wells, A. (1990). Panic disorder in association with relaxation-induced anxiety: An attentional training approach to treatment. *Behaviour Therapy, 21*, 273–280.

Wells, A., & Matthews, G. (1996). Modelling cognition in emotional disorder: The S-REF model. *Behaviour Research and Therapy, 34*(11), 881–888.

White, R., Gumley, A., McTaggart, J., Rattrie, L., McConville, D., Cleare, S., & Mitchell, G. (2011). A feasibility study of Acceptance and Commitment Therapy for emotional dysfunction following psychosis. *Behaviour Research and Therapy, 49*(12), 901–907. doi: dx.doi.org/10.1016/j.brat.2011.09.003

Williams, J. M. G. (2008). Mindfulness, depression and modes of mind. *Cognitive Therapy and Research, 32*(6), 721–733.

Williams, J. M. G. (2013). Personal communication.

5

ACCEPTANCE AND COMMITMENT THERAPY

Eric M. J. Morris

Acceptance and Commitment Therapy (ACT) is the approach most clearly linked with the term 'third wave'. Steven Hayes, an originator of ACT, first used the term third wave (Hayes, 2004) to identify a set of commonalities across newer CBT approaches, which are focused on strengthening trans-diagnostic processes of change through acceptance, mindfulness and action based on personal values. These concerns are central to the ACT approach, helping people to develop a different relationship with their experiences, and to engage in actions and choices based on chosen life directions (personal values).

ACT is a psychological therapy concerned with a central question: How do we help people to pursue what matters to them in life, in the face of the myriad ways to suffer? Further, how do we help people to not just survive life's vicissitudes, but thrive?

ACT is a cognitive behavioural therapy that aims to promote quality of life, functioning and personal effectiveness. The ACT model integrates processes of change (principally acceptance, mindfulness and values-based action) to increase psychological flexibility. Psychological flexibility is the ability to more fully contact the present moment as a conscious human being and, depending on the opportunities of the current situation, skilfully engage in actions guided by personal values (Hayes et al., 1999). Psychological flexibility is a set of interrelated skills that have been associated with a wide range of improvements in wellbeing, quality of life and personal effectiveness (Kashdan & Rottenberg, 2010; Levin et al., 2012).

The effectiveness of ACT has been studied in over 200 randomised controlled trials, across a wide range of problems and disorders including: chronic pain, anxiety, depression, alcohol and substance misuse, workplace stress, epilepsy and diabetes. Compared to treatment as usual (or no therapy) ACT has been found to show moderate to large effects, comparable to other cognitive behavioural therapies (A-Tjak et al., 2015; Öst, 2014). Studies of ACT have demonstrated that changes in psychological flexibility during therapy relate to improvements in outcome (e.g., Ruiz, 2012; Vowles et al., 2014). This work has been extended to evaluations of interventions which help people with psychosis (e.g., Bach & Hayes, 2002; Johns et al., 2016; Shawyer et al., 2012; White et al., 2011).

ACT fosters behaviours that encourage psychological flexibility. These behaviours are developed in therapy and then further strengthened through out-of-session activities. The behaviours ACT promotes are talked about in terms of Open skills, Aware skills and Engaged skills (Hayes et al., 2013). Open skills are about taking a stance of willingness (active acceptance) towards inner experiences, from a position of non-judgement of these experiences. Aware skills are about connecting with the present moment and having a flexible perspective on one's own experiences (by being the container of your experiences, for example). Engaged skills are about clarifying and connecting with personal values and acting flexibly to persist or change in line with those values, based on the current situation. The ACT model provides ways to strengthen these skills, using an experiential learning approach: sessions typically involve the use of metaphor, exploration of the pragmatics of client actions, and practising exercises to increase the ability to be present, open to experience, and connect with personal values. As ACT is a behaviour therapy, it includes the full range of empirically-based change strategies available, such as exposure, behavioural activation, problem-solving and skills development. It is this combination of behavioural methods with a focus on cognition from a contextual perspective (see below), combining both the 'old and new' in behaviour therapy, that makes ACT a third wave therapy.

How ACT was developed

ACT was first developed in the early 1980s, emerging out of clinical behaviour analysis, a radical behavioural approach to therapy. The findings of experimental studies of rule governance conducted by Steven Hayes and colleagues informed the development of a therapeutic model. They demonstrated that when human behaviour is guided by rules, this can result in an insensitivity to environmental changes, making it harder for people to learn from direct experience (Zettle & Hayes, 1986). Hayes considered this as potentially important from a clinical perspective, observing that for many problems and disorders people engage in repetitive and unhelpful actions, even when their experience suggests that those responses do not work. Hayes theorised that the presence of rules (socially generated or self-derived) contribute to this inflexibility in people's responses to their problems.

The radical behavioural background to ACT is distinctive and important. ACT is based on a philosophy of science, and a different set of theoretical assumptions from many other cognitive behavioural therapies. Its background is Contextual Behavioural Science (CBS) (Hayes et al., 2012), which aims to develop a behavioural science that can adequately cohere across the range of human experience and activity, and link with empirically-derived principles of learning. The purpose of CBS is to develop a science that explores the prediction and influence of behaviour with precision, scope and depth (Hayes et al., 2012). Behaviour is anything a whole organism does, considered in the context of both the historical and current environment. The goal of CBS is to understand behaviour in context, so we can find better ways to influence it. CBS has a philosophical link with pragmatism, and a stance towards truth that is about successful working (functional contextualism: Hayes et al., 1999). What is considered 'true' is what advances a previously-stated goal. Contextualists are interested in changing the world, rather than just explaining it; they are interested in identifying potentially modifiable features of the environment to influence behaviour (Wilson, 2001). This means explanations about behaviour are not considered complete unless they consider the current and historical context in which actions occur.

ACT is theoretically consistent with operant learning principles (i.e., learning through consequences such as rewards and punishments). In the development of CBT, understanding the behaviour of adults using models based on operant learning was largely abandoned when cognitive models were adopted in mainstream CBT practice (e.g., Seligman, 1970). ACT is based on a fully behavioural account of human language and cognition, called Relational Frame Theory (RFT) (Hayes et al., 2001). RFT is a behavioural account of how human actions can be influenced by arbitrary sense-making based on derived understandings; that is, understanding not based on direct, personal experience. The nature of language allows humans to learn in ways that do not involve direct experience. The things people learn can then be easily carried from one situation to another, making us somewhat immune to changes in the environment. This is an advantage, and it offers an easy way for people to learn how to avoid dangers and to benefit from others' experiences. However, there are also disadvantages: people can learn to be fearful of things, even when this response is unhelpful and unwarranted; also, they may fail to learn from experience, making the same unhelpful responses across time. In addition, they may be influenced by a coherent (but unworkable) story about themselves, or because certain coping strategies have been suggested as the 'right' thing to do (social pressure rather than pragmatism). There is a lot more to RFT which is beyond the scope of this chapter (see Barnes-Holmes et al. (2004) for an overview of a RFT understanding of clinical problems).

We can consider the development of ACT as a response to the centrality of cognitive models in clinical psychology. Radical behaviourists rejected mental causation for behaviour (for a discussion see Torneke et al., 2010), but historically were challenged when they tried to extend verbal learning principles into the field of psychological therapy (Cullen, 2008). The empirical and conceptual work of RFT provides a progressive direction for a coherent science of human behaviour (Hayes et al., 2012). RFT is receiving increasing empirical support as a basic science account of language, with many studies demonstrating support for RFT principles in areas of understanding analogy, metaphor, perspective-taking, and the generalisation of stimulus functions such as fear and avoidance (for an overview see Barnes-Holmes et al., 2015).

The implications of a contextual way of understanding and influencing behaviour

The contextual approach influences how ACT therapists work with experiences such as thoughts, beliefs, voices, urges and feelings. The ACT therapist explores how internal experiences act as barriers to taking *values-based action* and helps the client to develop more flexible responses to these experiences, to enable greater choice about actions. The ACT therapist focuses on contexts where language reinforces unhelpful responses to experiences, and promotes learning from experience, so more flexible and effective actions are established. This experiential approach involves the therapist speaking with the purpose of shaping psychologically flexible client responses.

The ACT therapist focuses on language processes, helping the client to notice and respond flexibly to both their experiences and how their mind appraises them. The therapist encourages the client to develop a greater awareness of language as a tool to achieve aims, clarifying when certain types of thoughts and meaning are useful (based on the aim of engaging in values-based action), and when they are not. For example, the therapist may explore occasions and situations when certain self-narratives and labels are useful to the client, and when they are not. In situations where these narratives are less useful, the ACT therapist helps the client to respond flexibly, by practising noticing of the *process* by which language shapes experience (using mindfulness, metaphors and exercises to develop an observing perspective to feelings and thoughts).

A key aspect is helping the client to construct and connect with abstract sources of purpose and meaning to motivate behaviour change (Villatte et al., 2015). Personal values function as inexhaustible reinforcers based on language processes; a form of 'fighting fire with fire' by enabling the client to base their behaviour on a purpose identified by them, rather than relying on extrinsic motivators. For some clients, this may involve exploring sources of meaning that have not been attended to due to struggle with, or engulfment by, difficult experiences. This can involve reconnecting with qualities of action that mattered in the past. An example may be a person choosing to return to acting in caring ways towards others, even while holding suspicions about their intentions, because to them it matters to act in an open and generous way. For other clients, it may be about constructing new purposes, and choosing to 'try out' different behaviours to see what they are like. An example here may be a person who has not previously used their spare time to care for and nurture themselves (tending in the past to put others' needs ahead of their own), but now choses to do so. In both cases, the client is encouraged to notice what it is like to be engaged in values-based actions and make comparisons with occasions when their behaviour is about controlling, avoiding or being entangled with experiences. The client is encouraged to trust their own experience about what works, and to use skills in mindfulness and acceptance to be open and aware of the feelings, thoughts and unusual experiences that may arise when acting on values.

Understanding how people respond to unusual and anomalous experiences: acts in context

The ACT model identifies factors associated with unusual experiences and psychosis that appear to contribute to greater distress and disability. The model suggests the following processes contribute to greater struggle with, and engulfment by, experiences:

- Experiential avoidance
- Cognitive fusion (responding to the literal content of experiences)
- Limited or restricted contact with the present moment
- Rigid and narrow perspective-taking
- Disconnection from personal values
- Lack of persistence and flexibility in choices and actions; avoidance-based actions

These unhelpful processes are involved in a wide variety of human problems and can be considered a set of general vulnerability factors for poor wellbeing, suffering and disability, including psychosis (Kashdan & Rottenberg, 2010; Morris et al., 2013). In relation to psychosis, it has been demonstrated that people who are more distressed and have poorer quality of life, tend to respond to unusual experiences in psychologically inflexible ways (Morris et al., 2014; Varese et al., 2016).

The following example is a constructed vignette, based on clinical interactions with various people.

> Ben is a 40-year-old unemployed man living in social housing. He is single and in limited contact with his elderly parents, due to disagreements. Over a long period, Ben has been distressed by hearing voices that criticise him and command him to hurt himself. He believes these voices are caused by demonic forces, punishing him for mistakes he made when a teenager (being involved in petty crime), and are intending to destroy him.
>
> Ben is fearful of hearing commands from the voices, particularly those to hurt others. While he has never acted on commands to hurt others, he has tried to appease the voices by sometimes acting on less harmful commands, such as denying himself enjoyable activities (e.g., watching football on the TV or going for walks to the local park). Sometimes Ben tries to anticipate what may anger the voices and makes choices to limit his enjoyment 'just in case'. This usually means switching off the TV or radio halfway through a football game, or isolating himself, as he thinks the voices do not want him to have friends. Ben frequently describes feeling sad and lonely and is pessimistic about the future as he worries that the voices may harm him and succeed in ruining his life. Ben reports

he spends a lot of time ruminating on how he is being punished by voices. Ben states that if he had a free choice (i.e., if he could be sure of resisting the voices' commands or if the voices left him alone) he would like to have a job. He would also like to have friends and a better relationship with his family.

Ben has been prescribed anti-psychotic medication. He finds that the voices are less frequent and intense when he takes medication; he also worries less. However, he finds when taking medication, he feels sluggish, lacks motivation, and that his thinking is not as sharp. Ben is also receiving support from a community mental health nurse, with whom he has a good relationship.

Ben knows that other people do not believe he is being tortured by demonic forces; he has been told by health professionals that he has been diagnosed with a psychotic illness. Ben was admitted to a psychiatric hospital several times when he was younger. He was still living with his parents at the time and he describes these admissions as very stressful, with lots of family arguments. Ben sometimes thinks mental illness could be an explanation for his problems, although he finds it hard to understand how his mind creates voices that seem to know things he doesn't. He describes his voices as very powerful, knowledgeable and in control of his life.

Understanding Ben's problems using the ACT model

ACT provides ways of conceptualising how Ben may be entangled with his experiences.

Ben responds to his voices in ways suggesting *cognitive fusion*: responding to the voices from a position of subjugation and acting on the belief he is being punished. Ben also engages in various choices and actions that serve the purpose of *experiential avoidance*: he does things to limit contact with voices and other experiences, such as isolating himself, switching off the radio and acting on lesser commands to appease the voices.

A further thing that contributes to the struggle for Ben is his *limited contact with the present moment*. His attention is dominated by scanning for threats (in the form of voice commands), by rumination and by worry about the future (which he assumes will be negative: another threatening experience). Ben's connection with chosen life directions (*values*) is limited by how he responds to the voices. His actions are dominated by efforts to avoid triggering the voices and their effects on his life.

This example provides a useful way of understanding how *psychological inflexibility* may play a role in the maintenance of Ben's distress and entanglement with his experiences. The ACT model considers that some responses to unusual experiences can be *unworkable*: that is, they reduce the opportunity for the person to engage in actions based on chosen life directions (values). This personal cost is explored with the client by looking at the short- and long-term effects of specific ways of coping, and what valued actions are possible. The ACT therapist would engage with Ben by carefully validating and understanding his efforts to cope, and also help him develop a new relationship with the voices through connecting with values, practising mindfulness and active acceptance (letting go of struggling with what cannot be controlled and being open to experiences from an observing perspective). I will use Ben's example later in the chapter to illustrate how the ACT may be done in practice.

Empirical studies of the ACT processes and interventions

There have been two major strands of empirical study informing the ACT approach to helping people with psychosis.

One area of investigation concerns whether *psychological inflexibility* is associated with greater distress and disability in the context of auditory hallucinations, paranoia and delusional thinking. This research draws upon what is already understood about responses to these experiences. Several responses to unusual experiences have been consistently found to be unhelpful in terms of long-term functioning, such as engaging in avoidance, suppression, or using them as guides for actions when these actions are self-defeating or destructive. These responses are seen across a range of unwanted or entangling inner experiences, which involve efforts to try to suppress experience, or to avoid an experience being triggered, and can lead to patterns of responding with personal cost (Gross, 2002; Hayes et al., 1996; Wegner & Zanakos, 1994). As with other problems where an experience is not easily controlled or limited, active acceptance can be a workable response to voice hearing (e.g., Farhall & Gehrke, 1997). This way of responding has been associated with more equal and less distressing relationships between the voice hearer and their voices (Morris et al., 2014; Varese et al., 2016). Similarly, acceptance can also buffer distress associated with delusional thinking over time (Oliver et al., 2012) and with paranoia (Udachina et al., 2009; Udachina et al., 2014).

A second area of investigation has concerned efficacy: thus far ACT has shown promise as a psychological therapy for people recovering from psychosis. People with psychosis who have engaged in ACT have demonstrated improvements in a variety of outcomes, such as lower rehospitalisation rates (Bach & Hayes, 2002; Gaudiano & Herbert, 2006), reductions in depression following an episode of psychosis (White et al., 2011), less compliance with command hallucinations (Shawyer et al., 2012) and greater wellbeing and quality of life (Johns et al., 2016).

Over time there has been a trend towards greater methodological rigour in randomised controlled trials of ACT for psychosis, with estimates of intervention effects becoming more modest compared to the early studies, which were less rigorous and may have inflated those intervention effects. In addition, ACT for psychosis research has been influenced by wider changes of focus in CBT research, such as developing more targeted interventions (focusing on one symptom, rather than trying to be a 'one size fits all approach' – see Thomas, 2015), and having an explicit focus on improving wellbeing. Finally, since ACT is a mindfulness-based intervention, it has been included in meta-analyses of these approaches. Khoury et al. (2013) found mindfulness-based interventions for people with psychosis are showing promise as approaches to reducing distress and negative symptoms.

The therapeutic relationship

I am human, and nothing of that which is human is alien to me.
Terence, Roman playwright, 195–159 BC

The ACT therapeutic relationship is characterised by warmth, acceptance and genuineness. The ACT stance is that the therapist and client are in the same predicament when it comes to the ways language can amplify suffering, by encouraging us to struggle or be guided by our inner experiences. ACT very much takes an approach of common humanity, considering the same, normal processes are as likely to affect the therapist, as they are the client.

This is not to say that the client's experiences of suffering are trivialised or minimised. It is recognised that some people have more than their fair share of challenging life experiences. These can then contribute to forms of psychological inflexibility, which make sense as historically-formed ways of coping with difficult situations. For example, someone who experienced childhood maltreatment who then, as an adult, struggles with connection and intimacy due to persisting mistrust and fear of vulnerability.

It is recognised that the client is the expert of their experiencing. Because ACT relies on the client's own descriptions of their inner experiences and identification of the purposes of their actions, it is essential to avoid any suggestion the client is 'wrong'. The client's perspective on the lived experience of their life helps us to understand the workability of their actions, whether driven by responding to inner experiences or by pursuing values.

Both the ACT therapist and the client may hold unhelpful beliefs about people who describe unusual experiences and/or engage in 'incoherent talk' (speech that is hard to follow, due to leaps in logic or idiosyncrasies of language). It is useful for the ACT therapist to be sensitive to the ways people can be stigmatised and excluded, and how personal biases about the social acceptability of those with psychosis may be a result of enculturation (including media representations of serious mental disorder) and the therapist's own learning history. An understanding of RFT helps to clarify that the presence of these biases is not necessarily a problem, because the ACT therapist can promote valued living by using their psychological flexibility skills to observe these thoughts and find ways to respond in the moment to the client. In addition, if the therapist does not have lived experience of psychosis, skills in perspective-taking may help the therapist to understand how the client feels, by connecting with the shared experience of being human (feeling, thinking, choosing, valuing).

The ACT approach is to treat people as intact and whole. As the processes that lead to human suffering are considered normal (due to the way language works – see Torneke, 2010), then, in a fundamental way, the client and therapist are 'in the same boat', in tackling the challenge of living guided by values in the face of unwanted, puzzling and entangling experiences.

This acceptance of people and the situations they are in – as complete human beings, not broken or different – is essential to ACT. The 'Two Mountains' metaphor (Hayes et al., 1999) illustrates a way of describing the ACT therapeutic relationship. This is how this was introduced to Ben in his sessions:

> Ben, what we do in the sessions may be like this: imagine there are two mountains, two Mountains of Life. Each of us is climbing our own mountain. I can look over from my mountain and see you climbing yours. You know what it is like to be climbing your mountain: what it feels like to be holding on to the side of the mountain, the way the rocks feel as you climb, the feel of the weather as you make this journey. The way the sun feels while climbing, what it is like when it is misty or rainy. Ben, you know what it is like to be climbing your mountain of life: you are the expert on your experience of living. What I can bring as your therapist is a *perspective*, what I see from my mountain, looking over at yours . . . I can bring what I observe and share this, but you are the one who knows what it is like to be climbing your mountain.

Hopefully, what the ACT therapist brings to the therapeutic relationship are various perspectives useful to the client, including the pragmatic approach ACT presents. The client brings perspectives from their lived experience of making choices, along with what it is like to be 'the person behind their eyes', the 'experiencer' of their life as lived.

How the therapeutic relationship is developed

Typically, in engaging people recovering from psychosis in ACT, the therapist displays flexibility and openness, presenting the approach in a straightforward way. This means the therapist provides information about ACT and what to expect, so the client can make an informed decision about whether to participate.

The ACT therapist describes how sessions will involve several elements: discussing issues and concerns; trying out experiential exercises; sharing what the client made of the exercises; and making plans to engage in activities between sessions. The ACT therapist will explain how sessions are collaborative in nature (perhaps by describing the 'Two Mountains' metaphor), and that there are likely to be times when 'things will be stirred up', especially if sessions are about important life directions. It is essential to convey the expectation that sessions may involve discomfort and vulnerability, as the therapist does not want to surprise the client when inviting them to notice and practise willingness towards previously-avoided content and experiences.

ACT has a directive style: the therapist encourages the client to become more connected with the present moment, to notice and practise non-judgement towards inner experiences, and to persist with values-based actions. Sessions may be challenging at times, with the therapist coaching the client to respond in ways that may be unfamiliar (such as using active acceptance). Throughout, the ACT therapist is carefully promoting the client's ability to choose in each situation whether they want to practise openness towards experience.

A common early point of exploration is the client's own experience of the *work-ability* of their actions, considering the experiences they have, and their personal values. This is explored by encouraging the client to reflect on the short- and long-term costs of their ways of coping with psychotic and emotional experiences. Typically, the therapist and client explore what choices and actions would be ideal, if the client felt they had a free choice to respond to the life circumstances before them. Clients who can identify a discrepancy between the outcome of their current actions, and how they would like their life to be, may benefit from ACT.

> Ben and the therapist explored how he had been coping with the voices, what Ben intended by his choices and the effects of this coping. The therapist invited Ben to consider coping in terms of what mattered to him (rather than what the voices wanted). Ben described being 'imprisoned' by his fear of the voices and not doing what he desired, which would be connecting with others and in some way contributing. The therapist carefully encouraged Ben to connect and 'make room' in the moment for his hurt about missed opportunities. Ben was also gently guided to notice that the voices had failed in controlling what mattered to him, despite years of threats: 'Perhaps our work is about building on what matters [values], exploring ways to act and finding different ways to respond to voices?' Ben reflected that in an important way, the voices could never win, because he still cared. While it hurt, there was hope too.

Importantly here the therapist validates the client's responses to their history and current circumstances, but also helps them take a new perspective. The ACT therapist expresses the desire to help the client strengthen skills that will enable them to take actions that will work better over the long-term.

Adapting ACT to be a useful therapy for people with psychosis

The functional model underpinning ACT means therapy is adapted to the needs of the client, rather than being a 'one size fits all' approach. As ACT is a model, rather than a set of techniques, it means a variety of strategies can be used to foster psychological flexibility, depending on the client's strengths, learning history and circumstances. In other words, it is a formulation-driven approach.

In my experience, training ACT therapists to work effectively with people recovering from psychosis is about helping them to respond in flexible and open ways. An important feature of ACT is the style of the therapy sessions. Given that the experiences of people with psychosis can be pathologised, invalidated and stigmatised, it is important to conduct ACT in ways that foster recovery. The following principles are important:

Appreciation – of the whole person, living in their current environment, with the history they have.

Connection – with the shared experience of being human, including the common struggle with living a meaningful life, in the face of experiences that invite struggle.

Addition – of willingness and valuing to coping, rather than seeking to fix people. Presenting the ACT skills as potential additional useful ways to expand your life, to be judged by the client's own experience of workability, rather than the therapist's expertise.

Construction – of a life worth living, today. Choosing values to create life meaning and purpose, rather than focus on long-term goals which are dependent on changes in the client's experiences or circumstances. Using active acceptance to find purpose today and to set a direction in the moment, as a form of personal liberation.

Specific adaptations of ACT for people with psychosis

There are several adaptations that can make ACT an engaging approach for people with psychosis. These adaptations are about helping to make the approach easier to understand and remember, particularly for people who may have limited attention, be preoccupied, or have cognitive difficulties, which make learning more challenging.

Repetition and using a clear session structure

This will make the experience predictable and memorable. ACT works best when the client is regularly exposed to the key messages about psychological flexibility skills. Also, because some clients may have low tolerance for uncertainty, or be concerned about being controlled or manipulated (especially those with trauma histories or suspicious thinking), the therapist makes the session predictable in terms of structure, describing experiential exercises ahead of time and being open about their intentions (based on personal values), which helps to engage clients.

Using briefer and more 'talky' mindfulness exercises

This aspect of ACT has been informed by broader mindfulness and psychosis literature (Chadwick et al., 2009; Dannahy et al., 2011). Various exercises have been adapted to make them briefer, with fewer pauses, to help clients follow instructions by providing more anchors and grounding (such as being able to follow the therapist's voice during the exercise). By approaching mindfulness as a set of functional processes (Hayes & Shenk, 2004) rather than as formal practices (such as requiring lengthy periods of meditation), there are more options for engaging people who may have difficulty due to their mental states (or medication side effects), enabling them to take part in exercises to strengthen their skills in noticing and non-judgemental awareness. This approach also emphasises the use of mindfulness in everyday life, by finding ways to bring noticing as a quality of awareness to a broad range of activities (Morris et al., 2013).

Using a central metaphor to foster learning

Compared to the usual way ACT is done, it can be helpful to reduce the number and complexity of the metaphors being presented. One way is to use a central metaphor, which then functions as a scaffold for the activities, exercises and briefer metaphors utilised in the intervention. This central metaphor is designed to be memorable, captures the essence of the problems with workability the client describes and is repeated throughout the sessions. An example of a central metaphor used in ACT for psychosis sessions is the 'Passengers on the Bus' exercise (Morris et al., 2013; described below).

'Physicalising' exercises

To make the experiential style of ACT impactful and memorable, many exercises and metaphors are acted out, or made more tangible by using drawings and props. The intention is to show how we can respond to the same experience in a variety of ways. A classic example is the acting out of the 'Passengers on the Bus' metaphor. Here the client is the driver of their Bus of Life, with the capacity to steer it in valued directions, while various passengers who are along for the ride – feelings, sensations, thoughts, urges, voices – try to guide the direction the bus driver goes in, or encourage a struggle in some way.

> The therapist asked Ben to imagine he was the driver of his bus, noticing which 'passengers' had been travelling with him. Ben identified his passengers – worries, anxiety, loneliness and the voices. Ben and the therapist then discussed the ways he coped with these passengers, how he drove his bus in certain directions to try to limit how noisy they got. Ben said that while he had been driving carefully, over time he did not feel like he was travelling anywhere important to him. While his life seemed to be about making sure nothing bad happened, nothing good happened either. Carefully, and over a number of sessions, the therapist asked Ben to consider where he would like to go, if he could choose, having noticed and tried to 'make room for passengers' (active acceptance of experiences

through mindfulness). Ben wanted to take the direction of contributing to others, by working or volunteering. Although he experienced trepidation about the prospect, he also wondered what might be possible if his life didn't have to be given over to controlling voices.

In ACT groups we may act out this metaphor, encouraging one client to be the driver of their bus, while other group participants act as passengers, trying out various ways in which the driver copes with their experiences and exploring the workability of these responses in the light of the driver's chosen valued directions.

Values: constructed and discovered

The ACT therapist strengthens the idea of life as a 'work in progress', by helping the client to explore possible actions and chosen life directions, even when this is may be uncertain, messy and unfinished. We ask clients to consider what they would choose as a meaningful life, starting from this moment forward. We would argue this is consistent with a recovery focus (see below).

Moving forwards can include making mistakes, learning from experience and trying things out.

> The therapist encouraged Ben to approach his chosen life directions like 'trying on a set of clothes' . . . 'You can try on a piece of clothing for a day, to see what it is like to wear it, what responses you get from the world . . . And you can easily put it back on the rack and try something else.' Without the pressure to 'get it right' or make a long-term commitment, Ben felt freer to explore what mattered to him . . . it had been a long time. He tried out several directions, taking actions between the sessions, noticing his experiences and sharing these with the therapist, to discuss what he discovered so far.

This quality of valuing, the freedom to choose without needing to justify choices, or be locked into a heavy commitment about what you choose, is an essential feature of ACT. Many people find this liberating, particularly in contrast to struggling with experiences and the idea you need to be in control in the face of unusual perceptions, self-critical thoughts, disturbing urges, etc.

The ACT therapist is also sensitive to the possibility that the client may not have had the opportunity to reflect on their personal values in this way before, or not for many years due to struggling with, or engulfment by, experiences. Because many clients have a history of invalidation, trauma and exclusion their values may have become hidden or unclear to them. Similarly, if the first episode of psychosis occurred when the client was young, the psychosis may have disrupted the developmental tasks of identity formation.

Along with the task of establishing valued directions, is that of reinforcing small steps towards taking action. Recovery from psychosis is a challenging business. The ACT therapist wants to promote the client's persistence and flexibility in making choices and taking actions over the course of moments, days, months. The style is of encouragement to the client of any efforts they make to pursue valued directions in their life.

Finally, therapist self-disclosure is used to bring qualities of common humanity, and to model present moment and flexible responses to experiences. After engaging in experiential exercises with the client, the therapist typically discloses their own internal responses and noticing and may share their own experience of struggling as they have tried to live consistently with their values. The key to using self-disclosure in ACT is that it is about teaching the client greater psychological flexibility (Westrup, 2014). Connection regarding the shared challenge of living according to values may strengthen the therapeutic relationship.

ACT is recovery-orientated

It can be argued that ACT provides an evidence-based way of doing therapy consistent with recovery principles.

Personal recovery has been defined as 'a deeply personal, unique process of changing one's attitudes, values, feelings, goals, skills and/or roles . . . a way of living a satisfying, hopeful and contributing life even with the limitations caused by illness' (Anthony, 1993).

There are a number of ways in which ACT is consistent with a personal recovery approach. We can consider ACT in terms of the Connectedness, Hope, Identity, Meaning and Empowerment (CHIME) framework, which describes the processes involved in recovery (as described by Leamy et al., 2011 in the first systematic review and narrative synthesis of personal recovery).

Connectedness – the pro-social approach of ACT orientates us towards connection with others, whether that be through our relationships, our roles, our striving to make a contribution, and/or recognising that as humans, we all struggle and suffer.

Hope – hope is an active stance we can take towards our world: ACT promotes choices and actions focused on active engagement with life, rather than resignation or entanglement in unhelpful self-stories. The ACT approach is to acknowledge feelings may come and go; our hopeful actions are a way to change our world.

Identity (the re-establishment of a positive identity) – ACT encourages contact with self as awareness, noticing the process by which our minds create stories about ourselves. Instead of being entangled in the mind's judge-ments, we observe whether they are useful for our chosen life directions. A 'flexible identity' in pursuit of values-based action is promoted, rather than self-consistency.

Meaning and purpose (finding meaning in life) – life's pain can be dignified if it is a part of doing the things that are important to us. Through acting on personal values, contact with meaning is increased.

Empowerment (encouraging self-management) – in ACT we help people to be 'response-able'; in other words, to act on their values rather than their fear, through developing an open, compassionate stance towards their own experiences and themselves. People can be empowered by being encouraged to learn from their experiences.

Supporting personal recovery involves strengthening psychological flexibility in pursuit of a life of purpose and meaning. This means supporting the *process* of personal recovery: different people make different choices about what matters to them.

Discussion of critical perspectives

The third wave of CBT, ACT and contextual behavioural science

ACT presents an integrative model and extends the boundaries of CBT, providing a contemporary model of behaviour therapy informed by a contextual understanding of how language shapes experience. The difference between the second and third waves of CBT is not simply emphasis: it is about a reconnection with learning principles considered to have been superseded by cognitive models (Seligman, 1970; Hayes et al., 2012), and a reinvigorated understanding of the process of psychotherapy from a radical behavioural perspective (Cullen, 2008). There is debate about whether this link with functional contextualism is important (e.g., Hofmann & Asmundson, 2008), and some suggest that there is nothing distinctive about ACT as a model that is not already dealt with in traditional CBT. Certainly, at the level of technique in the past 10 years, mainstream CBT has absorbed mindfulness, active acceptance and an emphasis on values. While these techniques may be integrated into cognitive models, the functional and contextual stance to thinking and feeling, along with the clarity about philosophy of science has not (yet) (see Hayes & Hofmann, 2017).

Is there room in the ACT approach for people to find meaning in their experiences?

A criticism of ACT is that the focus on accepting experiences could be a sophisticated form of ignoring experience, rather than learning from it, or indeed finding deep meaning and value in the experience. A common source of this concern comes from those with lived experience of voice hearing, who suggest the most effective way of relating to voices is to befriend them and find meaning within them. This way of responding to the voice hearing experience is not inconsistent with ACT; however, ACT emphasises personal choice and preference rather than achievement of a process goal. So, it may be that for some people who are recovering from psychosis, finding the 'silver lining' within their experiences is useful and part of a valued direction, while for others, choosing to focus instead on different values may be more useful.

Conclusion

ACT as a psychological therapy is about liberation. ACT promotes skills to exercise personal choice and freedom over what you want to do with your experiences. The key is liberation from aversive control, so that you can choose what your life is about. Personal meaning, spirituality and connecting with the function of your experiences is very much consistent with contextual approaches to psychological therapy. It can be argued that this liberation stance is part of the heritage of a radical behavioural perspective to influencing behaviour.

References

All URLs accessed March 2018.

Anthony, W. A. (1993). Recovery from mental illness: The guiding vision of the mental health service system in the 1990s. *Psychosocial Rehabilitation Journal, 16*(4), 11.

A-Tjak, J. G. L., Davis, M. L., Morina, N., Powers, M. B., Smits, J. A. J., & Emmelkamp, P. M. G. (2015). A meta-analysis of the efficacy of Acceptance and Commitment Therapy for clinically relevant mental and physical health problems. *Psychotherapy and Psychosomatics, 84*(1), 30–36. doi.org/10.1159/000365764

Bach, P., & Hayes, S. C. (2002). The use of Acceptance and Commitment Therapy to prevent the rehospitalization of psychotic patients: A randomized controlled trial. *Journal of Consulting and Clinical Psychology, 70*(5), 1129–1139. doi.org/10.1037//0022-006X.70.5.1129

Barnes-Holmes, Y., Kavanagh, D., & Murphy, C. (2015). Relational Frame Theory. *The Wiley Handbook of Contextual Behavioral Science*, 115–128.

Barnes-Holmes, Y., Barnes-Holmes, D., Mchugh, L., & Hayes, S. C. (2004). Relational Frame Theory: Some implications for understanding and treating human psychopathology. *International Journal of Psychology and Psychological Therapy, 4*(2).

Chadwick, P., Hughes, S., Russell, D., Russell, I., & Dagnan, D. (2009). Mindfulness groups for distressing voices and paranoia: A replication and randomized feasibility trial. *Behavioural and Cognitive Psychotherapy, 37*(4), 403. doi.org/10.1017/S1352465809990166

Cullen, C. (2008). Acceptance and Commitment Therapy (ACT): A third wave behaviour therapy. *Behavioural and Cognitive Psychotherapy, 36*(6), 667. doi.org/10.1017/S1352465808004797

Dannahy, L., Hayward, M., Strauss, C., Turton, W., Harding, E., & Chadwick, P. (2011). Group person-based cognitive therapy for distressing voices: Pilot data from nine groups. *Journal of Behavior Therapy and Experimental Psychiatry, 42*(1), 111–116. doi.org/10.1016/j.jbtep.2010.07.006

Farhall, J., & Gehrke, M. (1997). Coping with hallucinations: Exploring stress and coping framework. *The British Journal of Clinical Psychology / the British Psychological Society, 36 (Pt 2)*, 259–261.

Gaudiano, B. A., & Herbert, J. D. (2006). Acute treatment of inpatients with psychotic symptoms using Acceptance and Commitment Therapy: Pilot results. *Behaviour Research and Therapy, 44*(3), 415–437. doi.org/10.1016/j.brat.2005.02.007

Gross, J. J. (2002). Emotion regulation: Affective, cognitive, and social consequences. *Psychophysiology, 39*(3), 281–291.

Hayes, S. C. (2004). Acceptance and Commitment Therapy, Relational Frame Theory, and the third wave of behavioral and cognitive therapies. *Behavior Therapy, 35*, 639–665.

Hayes, S. C., Barnes-Holmes, D., & Roche, B. (Eds.) (2001). Relational frame theory: A post-Skinnerian account of human language and cognition. New York: Springer Science & Business Media.

Hayes, S. C., Barnes-Holmes, D., & Wilson, K. G. (2012). Contextual behavioral science: Creating a science more adequate to the challenge of the human condition. *Journal of Contextual Behavioral Science, 1*(1–2), 1–16. doi.org/10.1016/j.jcbs.2012.09.004

Hayes, S. C., & Hofmann, S. G. (2017). The third wave of cognitive behavioral therapy and the rise of process-based care. *World Psychiatry, 16*(3), 245–246.

Hayes, S. C., Levin, M. E., Plumb-Vilardaga, J., Villatte, J. L., & Pistorello, J. (2013). Acceptance and Commitment Therapy and contextual behavioral science: Examining the progress of a distinctive model of behavioral and cognitive therapy. *Behavior Therapy, 44*(2), 180–198. doi.org/10.1016/j.beth.2009.08.002

Hayes, S. C., & Shenk, C. (2004). Operationalizing mindfulness without unnecessary attachments. *Clinical Psychology: Science and Practice, 11*(3), 249–254.

Hayes, S. C., Strosahl, K. D., & Wilson, K. G. (1999). Acceptance and Commitment Therapy: An experiential approach to behavior change. New York: Guildford Press.

Hayes, S. C., Wilson, K. G., Gifford, E. V, Follette, V. M., & Strosahl, K. (1996). Experimental avoidance and behavioral disorders: A functional dimensional approach to diagnosis and treatment. *Journal of Consulting and Clinical Psychology, 64*(6), 1152–1168. doi.org/10.1037/0022-006X.64.6.1152

Hofmann, S. G., & Asmundson, G. J. G. (2008). Acceptance and mindfulness-based therapy: New wave or old hat? *Clinical Psychology Review, 28*(1), 1–16. doi.org/10.1016/j.cpr.2007.09.003

Johns, L. C., Oliver, J. E., Khondoker, M., Byrne, M., Jolley, S., Wykes, T., . . . Morris, E. M. J. (2016). The feasibility and acceptability of a brief Acceptance and Commitment Therapy (ACT) group intervention for people with psychosis: The 'ACT for life' study. *Journal of Behavior Therapy and Experimental Psychiatry, 50*, 257–263. doi.org/10.1016/j.jbtep.2015.10.001

Kashdan, T. B., & Rottenberg, J. (2010). Psychological flexibility as a fundamental aspect of health. *Clinical Psychology Review, 30*(7), 865–878. doi.org/10.1016/j.cpr.2010.03.001

Khoury, B., Lecomte, T., Gaudiano, B. A., & Paquin, K. (2013). Mindfulness interventions for psychosis: A meta-analysis. *Schizophrenia Research, 150*(1), 176–184.

Leamy, M., Le Boutillier, C., Bird, V. J., Davidson, L., Williams, J., & Slade, M. (2011). What does recovery mean in practice? A qualitative analysis of international recovery-oriented practice guidance. *Psychiatric Services.*

Levin, M. E., Hildebrandt, M. J., Lillis, J., & Hayes, S. C. (2012). The impact of treatment components suggested by the Psychological Flexibility Model: A meta-analysis of laboratory-based component studies. *Behavior Therapy, 43*(4), 741–756. doi.org/10. 1016/j.beth.2012.05.003

Morris, E. M. J., Garety, P., & Peters, E. (2014). Psychological flexibility and nonjudgemental acceptance in voice hearers: relationships with omnipotence and distress. *Australian and New Zealand Journal of Psychiatry, 48*(12), 1150–1162. doi.org/10.1177/0004867 414535671

Morris, E. M. J., Johns, L. C., & Oliver, J. E. (2013). *Acceptance and Commitment Therapy and mindfulness for psychosis.* Hoboken, NJ: John Wiley & Sons.

Oliver, J. E., O'Connor, J. A., Jose, P. E., McLachlan, K., & Peters, E. (2012). The impact of negative schemas, mood and psychological flexibility on delusional ideation–mediating and moderating effects. *Psychosis, 4*(1), 6–18.

Öst, L.-G. (2014). The efficacy of Acceptance and Commitment Therapy: An updated systematic review and meta-analysis. *Behaviour Research and Therapy, 61*, 105–121. doi.org/10.1016/j.brat.2014.07.018

Ruiz, F. J. (2012). Acceptance and Commitment Therapy versus traditional cognitive behavioral therapy: A systematic review and meta-analysis of current empirical evidence. *International Journal of Psychology and Psychological Therapy, 12*(3), 333–357.

Seligman, M. E. P. (1970). On the generality of the laws of learning. *Psychological Review, 77*(5), 406–418. doi.org/10.1037/h0029790

Shawyer, F., Farhall, J., Mackinnon, A., Trauer, T., Sims, E., Ratcliff, K., . . . Copolov, D. (2012). A randomised controlled trial of acceptance-based cognitive behavioural therapy for command hallucinations in psychotic disorders. *Behaviour Research and Therapy, 50*(2), 110–121. doi.org/10.1016/j.brat.2011.11.007

Thomas, N. (2015). What's really wrong with cognitive behavioral therapy for psychosis? *Frontiers in Psychology, 6*, 323.

Torneke, N. (2010). Learning RFT: An introduction to relational frame theory and its clinical application. Oakland, CA: New Harbinger Publications.

Torneke, N., Barnes-Holmes, D., & Hayes, S. (2010). Learning RFT. misc, Oakland: New Harbinger Publications.

Udachina, A., Thewissen, V., Myin-Germeys, I., Fitzpatrick, S., O'Kane, A., & Bentall, R. P. (2009). Understanding the relationships between self-esteem, experiential avoidance, and paranoia. *The Journal of Nervous and Mental Disease, 197*(9), 661–668. doi. org/10.1097/NMD.0b013e3181b3b2ef

Udachina, A., Varese, F., Myin-Germeys, I., & Bentall, R. P. (2014). The role of experiential avoidance in paranoid delusions: An experience sampling study. *British Journal of Clinical Psychology, 53*(4), 422–432. doi.org/10.1111/bjc.12054

Varese, F., Morrison, A. P., Beck, R., Heffernan, S., Law, H., & Bentall, R. P. (2016). Experiential avoidance and appraisals of voices as predictors of voice-related distress. *British Journal of Clinical Psychology.* doi.org/10.1111/bjc.12102

Villatte, M., Villatte, J., & Hayes, S. (2015). *Mastering the clinical conversation: Language as intervention.* New York: Guildford Press.

Vowles, K. E., Witkiewitz, K., Sowden, G., & Ashworth, J. (2014). Acceptance and commitment therapy for chronic pain: Evidence of mediation and clinically significant change following an abbreviated interdisciplinary program of rehabilitation. *The Journal of Pain, 15*(1), 101–113. doi.org/10.1016/j.jpain.2013.10.002

Wegner, D. M., & Zanakos, S. (1994). Chronic thought suppression. *Journal of Personality, 62*(4), 616–640. doi.org/10.1111/j.1467-6494.1994.tb00311.x

White, R., Gumley, A., McTaggart, J., Rattrie, L., McConville, D., Cleare, S., & Mitchell, G. (2011). A feasibility study of Acceptance and Commitment Therapy for emotional dysfunction following psychosis. *Behaviour Research and Therapy*, *49*(12), 901–907. doi.org/10.1016/j.brat.2011.09.003

Wilson, K. G. (2001). Some notes on theoretical constructs types and validation from a contextual behavioral perspective – Wilson.pdf, *1*, 205–215.

Zettle, R. D., & Hayes, S. C. (1986). Dysfunctional control by client verbal behavior: The context of reason-giving. *The Analysis of Verbal Behavior*, *4*, 30–38.

6

COMPASSION-FOCUSED THERAPY FOR RELATING TO VOICES

Charles Heriot-Maitland and Gerrard Russell

Compassion-Focused Therapy (CFT) is not a distinct school of therapy, but more a framework for focusing interventions that span across (and have emerged from) multiple different therapy traditions and approaches. In this respect CFT is a process-driven, rather than technique-driven, approach. The process unfolds to create certain contexts and conditions for an individual that will facilitate their mind's natural adaptive, healing and problem-solving processes. So, essentially, CFT aims to create the conditions within a person's environment, body and mind that will give them the best chance of working with, and integrating, distressing emotions and experiences. The CFT claim is that whatever threat-related intervention is required in therapy (e.g., addressing a fear, trauma, avoided emotion, behaviour), this will be more successful having first created these 'optimum' physiological and motivational conditions.

The particular conditions that CFT aims to foster are those of *safeness* and *compassion*. As we will discover in this chapter, safeness physiology and compassionate mentality are mutually supportive. In the same way that compassionate intentions and actions will support experiences of social safeness, affiliation and connection, the body experience of social safeness will also support the types of mental states that are conducive to compassion (e.g., mentalising, empathy, etc.).

A bio-psycho-social approach

CFT is very much a bio-psycho-social approach, in the true (intended) sense of the term, in that all three (biological, psychological and social) aspects of safeness and compassion are regarded as having fundamental and equal importance and are enlisted in therapy to support each other and the overall process. At the biological level, CFT utilises a range of practices to directly stimulate safeness physiology, (e.g., exercises with soothing breathing, grounding, body posture, facial expression and voice tone). At the psychological level, CFT aims to activate these systems through exercises with attention, memory and imagery, as well as cultivate

98

compassionate motives through mentalising and cognitive exercises, such as writing letters, diaries and logs.

There is also a significant behavioural component to CFT, which importantly carries the key processes of safeness and compassion out into the social sphere. This often takes the form of exercises that encourage giving and receiving compassion, as well as noticing and engaging with pro-social behaviour. Wherever possible, there will be efforts to identify and establish safe, supportive relationships, networks and social interactions. Particularly in psychosis, when people often experience stigma and isolation in relation to their experiences, the establishment of safe, validating inter-personal contexts will play a key role in the recovery process.

A scientific approach to the brain

CFT is a trans-diagnostic approach as it is based on a science of the brain, rather than a science of any particular 'pathology' or any particular treatment. This means that with CFT, we are starting from a different premise to that of most approaches to mental health, that is, the premise of normality. This means that in therapy we approach an individual with a consideration of their 'normal' evolved brain, and how this brain has been operating and adapting to the different conditions, relationships and environments of their life. So, we are primarily interested in finding out which bio-psycho-social experiences have occurred and, as a result, which brain systems have been activated and sensitised, and which have not.

An important model universally employed in CFT across all mental health problems and diagnoses, is to formulate brain systems as the '3 circles model' – or more formally, the three types of affect regulation system (Gilbert et al., 2009). This model, which is directly drawn (and simplified) from neuroscientific studies of emotion (Depue & Morrone-Strupinsky, 2005; Panksepp, 1998), distinguishes three main emotion systems, each with different evolutionary functions: (i) threat and self-protection; (ii) drive and resource-seeking; and (iii) soothing and affiliation. Mapping out the activation, balance, and interplay of these three systems, both historically (i.e., in response to earlier life experiences), and in day-to-day life, is key in formulating the development and maintenance of mental health problems. In CFT terms, most, if not all, mental health symptoms and diagnoses can be seen as a set of strategies used to manage the threat system, often in the absence of sufficient resources in the soothing system to internally regulate the threat.

A CFT approach to psychosis

The experiences reported by people with psychosis, such as voices and threat beliefs, as well as other associated phenomena (e.g., behavioural, attentional and information processing routines) can be understood, in CFT terms, as normal products of an overstimulated threat system, coupled with insufficient internal resources to soothe or regulate this system. What this means, at the physiological level, is that the entire brain-body system that has evolved to process and respond to threats, is being constantly stimulated. And the more this system gets activated (e.g., over a lifetime), the more sensitised it becomes. As if this weren't problematic enough, psychosis-related diagnoses like 'schizophrenia' carry severe social stigma, and many of those diagnosed will internalise this stigma to experience shame. This brings an additional layer of threat linked to one's social position. CFT is particularly well-suited to address these key threat-based processes in psychosis because the approach is specifically designed to regulate threat by building feelings of safeness and by cultivating compassion for self and others.

In CFT for psychosis, we would first of all aim to establish *internal* and *external* experiences of social safeness. The *internal* experiences come through practices such as grounding, posture and soothing breathing, which activate the (threat-calming) parasympathetic system. The *external* experiences will come through building relationships and social interactions that feel safe, validating and understanding. This starts with the therapeutic relationship itself, but crucially aims to extend into wider relationships with friends, family, networks, etc. We know from attachment theory that a secure base within affiliative connections is the ideal kind of platform we need to start developing the confidence and courage to explore our experiences.

The next key aim of CFT for psychosis is to then start gradually developing the compassionate mentalities and qualities that will be required to do the intervention work: essentially, building the resources required to experience and integrate the threat system in a safe way. In CFT, we help a person to cultivate these resources by developing a compassionate self-identity: the *compassionate self*. Through the therapy process, the compassionate self becomes the holder or container for all the various motives, qualities, skills, postures, tones, etc., that are being practised. So, over time, the compassionate self not only becomes the organiser of a person's mind, body and behaviour, but also becomes the orchestrator of a rebalancing of their three systems. Again, using the language of attachment theory, the compassionate self acts as an inner secure base and safe haven – a place (in the mind) from which to come and go back to when relating to one's internal world of emotions and experiences, as well as the external world.

Psycho-educational material is woven into the therapy, which helps people to develop self-compassionate wisdom and understanding about the evolutionary and neuroscientific functioning of the brain (Gilbert, 2014, 2015). In CFT, psycho-education aims to establish a de-shaming ('it's not our fault') understanding of how tricky our brains can be: due to evolutionary design, they naturally and inevitably cause problems for us. It is particularly helpful for someone experiencing paranoia, for instance, to understand the evolutionary bias of the threat system, which operates for our survival on a 'better safe than sorry' basis, and therefore potentially has bias towards detecting and over-estimating danger. Also, very relevant for people with psychosis-related difficulties is education about *dissociation* as a natural and adaptive process to protect them from becoming overwhelmed by distressing experiences, seen in CFT as the brain's threat-protection mechanism.

The five key stages of a CFT intervention can be summarised as follows:

Stage 1) Establishing safeness and connection.
Stage 2) Learning about evolved brains, emotional systems and multiple selves.
Stage 3) Developing a shared formulation.
Stage 4) Cultivating/deepening the compassionate self.
Stage 5) Directing compassion to others, self, dissociated parts/voices.

The fifth stage is where all the preparation and training of the other four stages are directly applied in the form of interventions with the threat system. In CFT, we refer to this as *directing the compassionate self* or *putting the compassionate self to work*. As mentioned in the opening paragraph of this chapter, these interventions can take many forms (e.g., imagery, chair work, letter-writing, behavioural activation, etc.), but crucially in CFT, all are tied together by first engaging compassion motives.

An episode of Compassion-Focused Therapy

To illustrate the approach, one of the authors (GR) will share his personal experience of a six-month (25-session) course of CFT with the other author (CHM) as his therapist. The issues that Gerry was struggling with at the beginning of therapy were paranoia and voices. The goal of therapy, however, was to come off medication so that he could bring some 'life' back into his existence. He had lost his social spark, his sex drive, his chirpy personality. The medication had deadened his creative flair and pretty much everything else that was enjoyable. His voices were suppressed by anti-psychotics, but at a cost. Gerry was fully aware that coming off medication might involve a risk of his voices returning; a risk he was willing to take.

My difficulties and my route into CFT

I (GR) began to hear voices for no reason; they were menacing, threatening and violent voices. They intimated me most of the day and night. Two of these groups of thugs were the Voodoo Gang and The Gangster Gang.

The Voodoo Gang wanted to cut off my head and eat my brains to give them my so-called powers. I was like a third party listening in to their conversations about me, and they knew when I was listening in. Everywhere I went they would be in my mind threatening to murder me. They followed me in the streets and tried to break into my flat. It came to the point where I was so paranoid I blocked all the doors so I could stay safe and slept with a hammer by my bedside to protect me and my wife.

The Gangster Gang wanted to bury me alive as they believed I had read their minds and knew where their gold bullion stash was hidden. They had assassins hired to follow me to work and I drove home crazy ways to get away from them.

I was at war with these voices. I wanted to destroy them and eliminate them by psychic means. I had an astral knife fight with the gangster one night. I was in his bedroom and we were stabbing each other. I could feel the pain of the dagger entering my flesh. Lots of different frightening paranoid scenarios continued to assail me at this time. I prayed very hard to stop these voices, but the intensity only got worse. They decided that if they could not catch me they would harm/kidnap my wife as they knew where she worked late at night. I was trapped and the only way to save her was for me to commit suicide because then they would leave her alone, so I hanged myself with wire from the ceiling of my flat. Luckily the wire extended and I passed out on the floor. I then went into my front room and exposed two live wires, wrapped them around my finger and turned on the switch. I was blown across the room.

I needed help badly so the next day I drove to hospital and signed myself in. When I was in hospital I was given many drugs but could not handle them. They made me a zombie, then I tried another one and I felt different. I was released from hospital and spent 10 years taking these drugs, but I was not the same dynamic person I had always been. I tried many times to give them up, but the voices always returned. The drugs have a long-term effect, one of which is the loss of libido. I wasn't warned about this, but in hindsight I had no other choices at the time. I was willing to try anything to get back to my normal self. My doctor sent me to the mental health team, who mentioned I could try therapy. I was put on a two-month waiting list, during which time I got a letter offering me a new therapy called Compassion-Focused Therapy, which was in its trial period.

Gerry's background

Gerry explained to his therapist (CHM) that he was always full of curiosity as a child. He grew up in a religious family in Belfast, and remembers incessantly asking his Auntie, 'Where is God? Is he there? Is he behind the sofa? Is he up the chimney?'. Belfast in the 1960s and 1970s was rife with religious intolerance. If you were found to be of the wrong religion (either Catholic or Protestant), you would be beaten up. It was normal for Gerry and other school children to be put on the spot by bullies demanding they recite the Lord's Prayer. This was to identify whether or not they were to be beaten up: 'People seemed to like fighting.' Gerry didn't tell his parents though; he didn't want to bother them as they were working flat out, doing their best to provide for the family.

Gerry has always had a creative talent. At school he achieved academically, was good at music and he won prizes for poetry and creative writing. He remembers the jealousy of other children when collecting prizes at school assembly. He started writing songs, and from the age of 15, he was playing in bands as the lead guitarist and singer. He enjoyed being 'the star' and in the spotlight, loving the attention (especially from women); however, there was a considerable downside, too: it made him a target. Not only was there this fearful sense of others' jealously, that people would resent him because of his talent, but there was also a very real threat of becoming a *literal* target. In the early 1970s, concert halls and venues were bombing targets in Belfast, and Gerry had heard stories of bombs exploding in fire escapes killing people trying to escape. There was also a famous incident at the time of a popular Irish band being murdered in their tour bus after a gig. One time, Gerry's band was playing in a packed Roman Catholic hall and, while they were on stage, there was a phone call to the venue saying there was a bomb inside. Having a talent was a threat for Gerry. 'Just look at John Lennon,' he said.

The Catholic hall incident was one catalyst for Gerry to leave Belfast for London, where he found a buzzing music scene; the life of 'sex, drugs and rock 'n roll'. It was a psychedelic period, and almost inevitably for a creative musician like Gerry, he was using hallucinogenic drugs and mind expansion/transcendence techniques. He was very interested in astral travel and practised meditations with the aim of leaving his body. Drugs supported these journeys into the extremes of consciousness and gave him new insights, which of course satisfied that existential curiosity he'd always had growing up. One time, when he was 42 years-old, Gerry left his body completely and was in a mystical state for about six months. He refers to this as his 'Kundalini experience' as this captures the sensation he felt of a burning serum/energy running up his spine and into his brain. This profoundly intense and prolonged experience lead him to believe that he was someone special, maybe Jesus. Perhaps this special gift which allowed him to move in spatial relationship to thoughts in the minds of himself and others, and to read the minds of others, could be put to good use in the world. One particularly positive use would be sharing his ability to read minds so that dishonest people would be revealed to others, which would ultimately enhance the spread of love in the world.

However, although this was a special gift and important role, there was once again the flip-side: special talent was dangerous. There would be those who would target Gerry for this. And people can be pretty cruel and ruthless when you're on the wrong side of them. These experiences, talents and special roles were therefore things that Gerry had to hide.

Starting therapy

In Gerry's therapy one of the initial aims was to establish a bodily experience of safeness through the practice of grounding, changes to posture and soothing breathing, all of which can activate the (threat-calming) parasympathetic system. In CFT, this lays the foundation for then developing the compassionate mentalities and qualities that are required to do the intervention work. This corresponds to Stage 1 in the summary overview (above). To cultivate 'internal' social safeness, Gerry started a regular practice of breathing, grounding and imagery exercises, both in and out of sessions. To cultivate 'external' social safeness, Gerry started planning social activities with his friends and tried to gradually increase opportunities for social engagement and connection. For him, this often took the form of attending public events and talks held by foreign embassies in central London. We particularly spent time in therapy trying to identify which of the people in his social network were best suited to which type of social experience; for example, if some were better for fun and pleasure, and others were better for emotional sharing and discussing anomalous experiences (mind-reading, voice-hearing, etc.). We explored online resources and communities, too; for example, Intervoice, the international hearing-voices community (www.intervoiceonline.org). Again, the rationale here was to foster interpersonal experiences of social safeness, connection and validation.

In the early sessions, we also started to explore the CFT psycho-educational material around evolved tricky brains, emotional systems and multiple selves (corresponding to Stage 2 in the summary overview). Kirby & Gilbert (2017) provide a detailed, up-to-date overview of how 'tricky brain' psycho-education is typically presented in CFT. For Gerry, this laid some important normalising and de-shaming foundations. We mapped out the interactions of 'old-brain' (i.e., older evolutionary functions such as basic motives, emotions and behaviours) and 'new-brain' (i.e., newer brain functions and competencies such as imagination, planning and self-monitoring), showing how these old brain–new brain interactions result in the brain getting caught in 'loops'. Gerry was learning to become a mindful observer of his own mind, with its typical daily loops and patterns, as well as linking this to a physiological awareness of his own three systems (threat, drive and soothing) and how these were balanced in his daily life.

The concept of multiple selves was introduced early on, and thereafter became embedded into the therapy language; for example, Gerry would readily exchange phrases like, 'I am feeling anxious' with 'there's my anxious self' or 'my anxious self has come online'. This brought a relational framework to the therapy process, preparing Gerry for thinking about his relationship with his self and his emotions. This greatly helped with Gerry's awareness of *how* he was relating to himself, (e.g., whether his self-to-self relationship was critical or supportive). It also introduced the possibility of more choice in the matter, and the potential for intentionally cultivating a style of self-relating that was more caring and compassionate.

Compassionate Mind Training and developing
Gerry's compassionate self

Compassionate Mind Training (CMT) and the process of building a compassionate self continued throughout therapy, from start to finish (this relates to Stage 4 in the summary overview). With Gerry, as with all CFT clients, it was important to really draw out his own intuitive wisdom about compassion, and his own existing compassionate qualities and skills. This was aided by guided discovery of compassionate memories and scenarios, as well as through regular validation from the therapist: 'Ah, that's your compassionate wisdom right there, Gerry! That's fantastic, that's your compassionate self!'

This was very reinforcing for Gerry, and he really started to value his compassionate self. The therapy also involved a variety of exercises, some of which are briefly summarised below.

Attention training and mindfulness practice

Gerry practised attention training to become more aware of his old–new brain loops. He developed mindful awareness, which he referred to as his 'view from the balcony'. This helped him to start using his attention as a skill or tool to intentionally move away from unhelpful (threat-based) loops, but also to move towards more helpful and compassionate loops and patterns.

Grounding and body posture

Gerry practised noticing and cultivating experiences of safeness, stability and groundedness in his body. He practised experimenting with certain body postures and movements to support these experiences: for example, he found that more confident, upright and expansive postures were more supportive of his wise, compassionate self; in contrast to more inward and tighter body postures, which were more familiar and associated with his anxious self.

Breathing practice

Gerry practised slowing down his breathing rhythm, whilst paying attention to any sensations of slowing down in the body. He found that slowing the breathing rhythm, and practising smooth and even breaths, gave him feelings of calmness and groundedness, which was very helpful for steadying and anchoring himself when dealing with strong threat-based emotions.

Facial expression and voice tone

Gerry experimented with different kinds of facial expressions and voice tones in order to identify those that most supported his compassionate intentions and motives. In particular, when working with his self-monitoring (meta-cognitive) thoughts, he noticed that although sometimes the content of his thoughts was sensible and logical, the emotional tone was quite patronising and critical, with the consequence of stimulating his threat system. He therefore practised shifting to self-monitoring with a more friendly, warm, supportive tone.

Practices with memory and imagery

Gerry practised focusing on images and sensory memories of safeness and compassion, which directly stimulated associated physiology and emotion. One particular 'safe place' image Gerry used was linked to his memory of walking into a Cathedral and becoming immersed in the sense of quietness and peacefulness. He also developed an image of an ideal compassionate other, and an ideal compassionate self, and practised focusing on the warmth within his relationships using these images, (i.e., the flow of both giving and receiving compassion).

Fears, blocks and resistances to compassion

An important part of CFT is working with the barriers to compassion, many of which are outlined in the *Fears of Compassion Scales* (Gilbert et al., 2011). For Gerry, there were particular fears concerning receiving compassion from others. The imagery practices were helpful in identifying these fears; for example, he noticed that when imagining being open to the compassion of another, his threat system was triggered. This was helpful information from his threat system, in that it identified fears that could then be worked with in therapy by firstly bringing compassionate wisdom, validation and understanding to the fear (and its causes), and secondly developing a compassionate action plan; for example, a graded exposure plan to build tolerance and to desensitise the fear.

Developing a compassionate self

Gerry's compassionate self acted as a container for all the various practices, postures, qualities, skills, motives, etc., outlined above. Gerry could then cultivate his compassionate self as an imagined self-identity and focus on each of the particular qualities that this self would need in order to address some of the struggles he faced. The therapist would ask, 'What would your compassionate self ideally be like to deal with this difficulty? Even if you feel that you can't do it, what qualities would your ideal compassionate self be drawing on to be able to do this?'

One of key challenges facing Gerry was how to tolerate his hostile voices, how to manage his fears of being harmed by them, and how to move towards being less distressed/debilitated by them. Gerry highlighted the compassionate self qualities of strength and wisdom as important here; strength and courage to stand up to the voices and tolerate their attacks, and wisdom to understand what's driving them and to determine the best way forward.

Exploring possible functions of voices

Having spent time in therapy creating the conditions for safeness and compassion, and establishing the 'secure base' embodied as his compassion self, Gerry was able to courageously embark on a guided discovery of the possible meanings and functions of his voices. In relation to the stages previously outlined, this was partly Stage 3 (formulating), but importantly, doing so from a wise, compassionate stance (i.e., Stage 5). We developed a calm curiosity towards them and what drives the voices, wondering what they represented emotionally for Gerry. The two main lines of functional exploration that emerged were: (i) Voices as representing a fear; and (ii) Voices as protective against a fear.

(i) Voices as representing a fear

This line of exploration was initiated by asking Gerry to consider what would happen if he actually gave the voices what they wanted, 'Suppose you just gave the voices your mind-reading talents? How would you feel then? What would the fear be?'

This helped Gerry to explore whether the voices might represent his own fear of being robbed of these special talents and whether, underneath that, there might be a fear of being a 'nobody' without these talents (i.e., people not interested in him, being isolated, lonely, etc.).

We were also continuously trying to make emotional links back to Gerry's own personal life (events, relationships and experiences) with questions like, 'Are there any other times in your life when people have tried to steal from you? Are there times when people have tried to stop you from having, or resented you for having, special talents and gifts? Are there times when people have really admired and valued you for your talents?'

As noted in Gerry's background, there were clear occasions when Gerry did experience the danger of having talents (jealousy at school; threats when leading a popular band). We also went on to identify a number of social experiences when Gerry had been very much admired (almost revered) for having special gifts. He fondly recalls feeling validated when people said things like, 'Gerry, you've got a special gift'. It became understandable that Gerry might have experienced a conflict: both a fear of having talents, and a fear of them being taken away, and the potential social consequences of that. Perhaps one of Gerry's greatest fears, we wondered, was a realisation that maybe he just had an 'ordinary' brain like everyone else.

Throughout the therapy process we were always ready and looking out for opportunities to bring the 'compassionate self' back in, (e.g., bringing compassion to the fear of being a nobody). The therapist would say, 'So coming back to compassionate self, engaging with grounding, posture, breathing, qualities, etc., can we now begin to compassionately hold that fear in mind? (long pause . . .) And which compassionate qualities in particular do you need to draw upon to be able to hold/tolerate/process that fear?'

Over time, this process of engaging compassionately with the fear allowed us to begin to unlock another important emotion – sadness. A grieving process could begin, and we could then use 'compassionate self' to help facilitate access to feelings of loneliness, emptiness and sadness. In Gerry's therapy, we used two main techniques for this: chair work and imagery. In the chair work, we set up a dialogue between 'compassionate self' and 'sad self', taking plenty of time to settle into the body experiences of each when shifting between the two chairs.

(ii) Voices as protective against a fear

This line of exploration was initiated by asking Gerry about some of the fears that may be linked to his mind-reading and mind-expanding activities. This is illustrated by a transcript of the audio-recorded dialogue between Gerry and Therapist from CFT session 14:

Therapist: On the one hand, it's something that you've sought out in your life, to develop that skill, but then you've also been slightly reluctant to develop this skill because of the negative consequences it brings.

Gerry: That's right. Or failings on my part to control my investigations, or whatever they were.

Therapist: What do you mean by that?

Gerry: Like mind-reading or projecting my thoughts, which I meditated on a lot.

Therapist: So what do you mean by failing to control that?

Gerry: Well I shouldn't have let these people, this voodoo guy, come in in the first place. I should have built up a defence, but I didn't. I went straight in to whatever I was doing, projecting my mind and trying to get out of my body, maybe too much. I suppose it's not a thing you should do alone, you should do it in a group of people, people who have done the same thing, like monks, Buddhist monks or something.

Therapist: So what are the dangers of mind-reading, projecting your thoughts?

Gerry: Well you are opening your mind too much I think, without any curtailments, without any boundaries. So you have to be careful when you do these things I think. In hindsight I think that.

Therapist: So what are the risks? What's the worst that could happen?

Gerry: Well what's happened to me.

Therapist: So you develop a psychosis?

Gerry: Yeah and have a Kundalini experience as well, it's another example of being opened out. It's opened my mind to influences, rather than being mine, inner influences or outer influences, I don't know.

Therapist: OK, so if we take this voodoo character and we think about this. So you've kind of reached the point where you think this might be a part of you that you've created.

Gerry: Well it is.

Therapist: So if we try and understand the psychological and emotional purpose of what your mind's created and why it's created something like this.

Gerry: Uh-hum.

Therapist: And we look at it in terms of what you're worried about, having this skill, this ability, is it too big a stretch of the imagination to think that actually, even though this is a horrendous evil brain-guzzling evil piece of work, that there's some kind of protective function against the dangers of expanding your mind?

Gerry: Could be. Could very well be. Myself. To give myself a shock.

Through uncovering Gerry's fears of mind-expanding, we were able to consider the voices in a protective role. He used the phrase of 'giving himself a shock', which led us to contemplate whether the hostile, gruesome language and tone of the voices might actually be a way of attracting his attention, of pulling him back. Was this Gerry's threat system kicking in to stop him expanding his mind too far? The more horrible the words, the more they succeed in grabbing Gerry's attention; the more effective they were in pulling him back. We could therefore start thinking of the voices as reflecting/communicating a fear of 'going too far'. We could start thinking of their function as protective in that they might be keeping his feet on the ground, protecting him from becoming too immersed in the spiritual world, or perhaps from becoming 'too special'?

Compassionate relating to the voices

Having established hypotheses for the emotional function of voices, we could then focus on the development of a new relationship with the voices, including finding a new way of listening to them, a new way of talking to them, a new role for them in Gerry's life. Again, this was achieved through guided discovery and, for Gerry, these insights into different ways of relating to voices started emerging in session 14:

Therapist: So in terms of compassion and Compassion-Focused Therapy, if we could decode this evil voodoo chap in terms of some protective function, is there room for compassion?

Gerry: Well putting it that way, and knowing that it's me protecting myself, there must be a way. I'd have to say "thank you" to him for helping me, and deal with him at that sort of level. He's only a figment of my imagination anyway, so if he's doing me good, or thinking of me.

Therapist: We're just guessing, but if we followed this hypothesis through, that is something that you could try. And just that slight shift of your relationship to it in terms of thanking – thank you for the warning, thank you for trying to protect me, I don't really need the graphic details of what you're talking about but in principle, I'm grateful for you helping me.

This shift towards more compassionate relating to voices was a significant moment in the therapy. This shift occurred in session 14, but of course relied heavily on all the groundwork, training and compassion practices from previous sessions. This process was marked by Gerry's insight and ability to look behind the hostile exterior of the voices, and into the vulnerability and fear driving the voices. His courage to engage with his threat system, to connect with the pain and vulnerability sitting behind the voices, really opened the door for Gerry's compassion to start flowing. The process of directing compassion was conducted mainly using chair work techniques in the sessions, but was also complemented by compassionate letter-writing and imagery (e.g., imagining Gerry's compassionate self meeting his critical voice in the street).

The remaining 10 sessions of therapy were then a process of Gerry directing compassion to himself and others, in both the present (day-to-day) and in the context of his past experiences and relationships (continuing Stage 5 of the five key stages previously mentioned). He was bringing compassion to all the experiences, memories and people where he felt compassion was needed. Gerry's compassionate self provided the strength, wisdom and commitment to move into these difficult experiences.

My reflections on the experience of CFT

Thank God I (GR) went for this therapy. It lasted six months, and in that time I learnt so much about 'voices'. I learnt that I wasn't alone, that there are thousands of people with this affliction and lots of them having had the same experiences as myself. With the new knowledge I gained, I realised that being at war with the voices was the completely wrong thing for me to be doing. I was actually making war with myself. I was fighting my own consciousness; a self-defeating arrangement. This Compassionate Therapy taught me to soothe these voices if they came back, and also that it was important for me to try to find the source and the cause of these voices. I could not find any reason for them, so I went through my life experiences and forgave every person in every scenario I could find in my memories. I also forgave myself of any blame for any actions I may have taken in the past that might have harmed anyone. I was defragmenting my brain, trying to reset it, and it has worked!

Measures of therapy process and outcome for Gerry

Gerry's CFT took place within the context of a case series research study (led by author CHM, funded by MRC ref. MR/L01677X/1). As such, a number of research measures were used to quantify Gerry's progress through therapy. Gerry provided measures for a six-week (pre-therapy) baseline period, for the 25-week duration of therapy itself, and at eight-week (post-therapy) follow-up. A combination of process and outcome measures were used. This chapter focuses on the two sessional measures that were used every week, and the measure of emotional outcomes (depression, anxiety and stress). Gerry's own remarks, in the following section, will provide a more meaningful illustration of changes with so called 'psychosis symptoms', such as paranoia and voice-hearing.

In terms of process, we were expecting that CFT would help to increase Gerry's experience of social safeness over time, and that as social safeness improved, there would be increasing psychological (internal) integration and reduced dissociation. The 11-item Social Safeness and Pleasure Scale (SSPS) (Gilbert et al., 2009) and a short three-item dissociation measure were administered at the start of every session, as well in the baseline and follow-up periods. Figure 6.1 shows

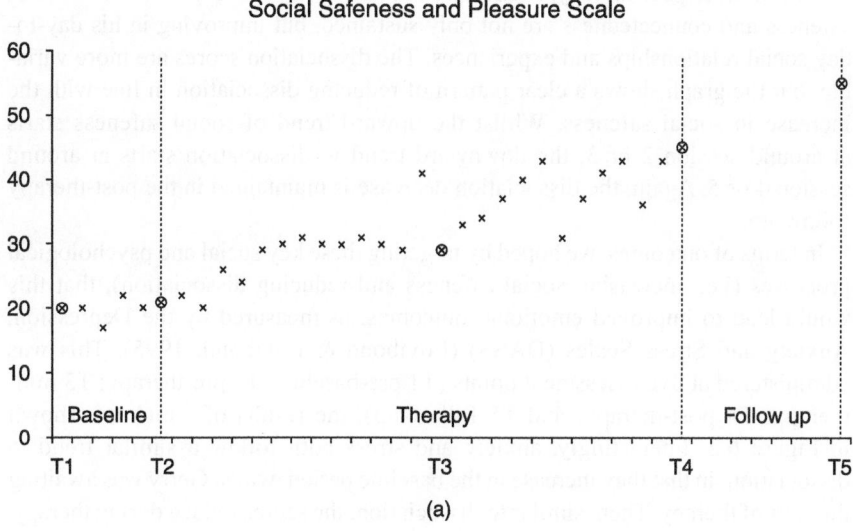

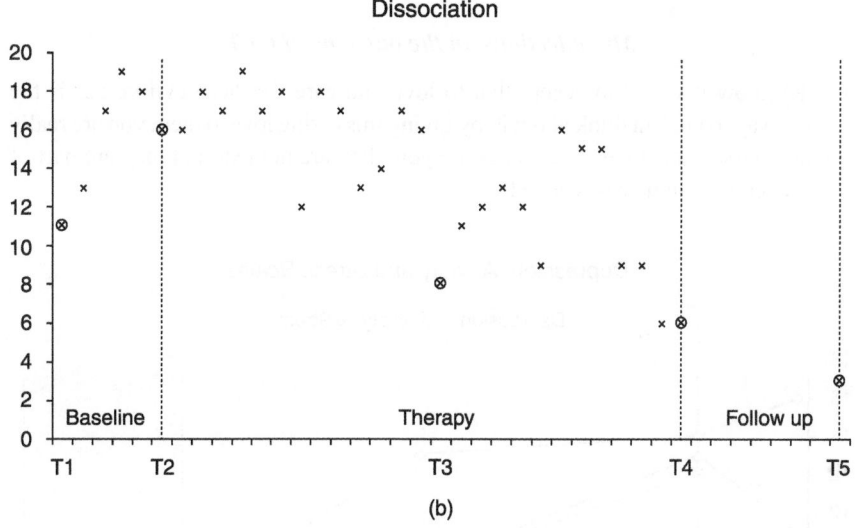

Figure 6.1 Sessional measures: (a) social safeness and (b) dissociation

how the weekly SSPS and dissociation scores changed over time. In the baseline period, there is some variation for SSPS, but a trend of stability around the 20 mark. This trend continues for the first two sessions of therapy, but then starts to increase. By mid-therapy, Gerry's self-rating of social safeness is up to around the 30 mark, and by the end of therapy has risen to over 40. Reassuringly, this upward

111

trend continues post-therapy, suggesting that, for Gerry, his experiences of social safeness and connectedness are not only sustained, but improving in his day-to-day social relationships and experiences. The dissociation scores are more variable, but the graph shows a clear pattern of reducing dissociation in line with the increase in social safeness. Whilst the upward trend of social safeness starts at around session 2 or 3, the downward trend in dissociation starts at around session 4 or 5. Again, the dissociation decrease is maintained in the post-therapy follow-up.

In terms of outcomes, we hoped by targeting these key social and psychological processes (i.e., increasing social safeness and reducing dissociation), that this would lead to improved emotional outcomes, as measured by the Depression, Anxiety and Stress Scales (DASS) (Lovibond & Lovibond, 1995). This was administered at five assessment points (T1 pre-baseline; T2 pre-therapy; T3 mid-therapy; T4 post-therapy; and T5 follow-up), the results of which are shown in Figure 6.2. Interestingly, anxiety and stress both follow a similar trend to dissociation, in that they increase in the baseline period, whilst Gerry was awaiting the start of therapy. Then, similar to dissociation, the scores reduce during therapy, as well as after therapy.

My reflections on the outcome of CFT

I (GR) know it's hard to accept that to love and care for these evil voices is the correct way to go. But think about it, by giving this caring love to them you are really giving yourself this love. The voices are you, they are not external they are part of you. Be compassionate to yourself.

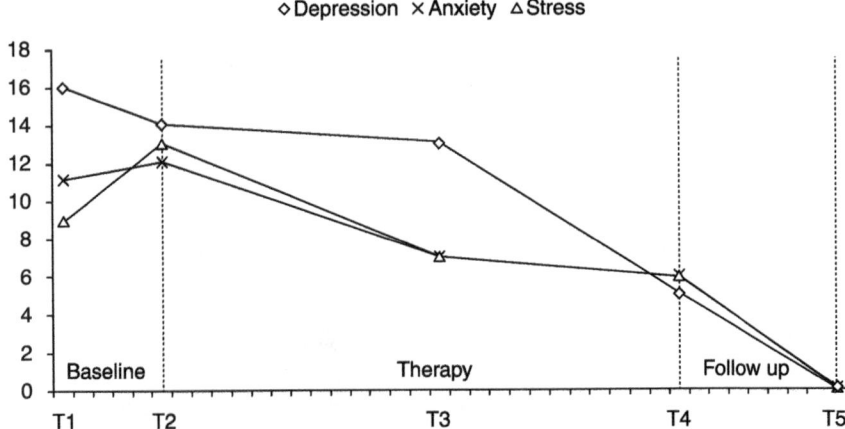

Figure 6.2 Emotional outcome measures: depression, anxiety and stress

I'm back to normal, whatever that means, but after 10 years on the drugs, I learnt some things about myself and this has been added to my new self. I feel I am enhanced and I'm full of the energy I used to have, but I am a bit more tolerant with myself and other people. I love life again!

Gerry came off all anti-psychotic medication two months before the end of therapy, so at the time of his post-therapy follow-up, he had been medication-free for a total of four months. He had not heard any voices, nor experienced any paranoid beliefs. He was enjoying life, feeling more chirpy and socialising more. He felt like his old self; socially confident and having fun.

Conclusions

Individual CFT for psychosis has not yet been subject to a formal evaluation study. However, one of the great strengths of the CFT model is a firm basis in scientific understandings of the human brain, coupled with a clear scientifically-informed roadmap of the bio-psycho-social processes targeted in therapy. It holds much promise in the ongoing quest for clinicians and researchers to improve our therapies of the future. Current research is investigating the question of whether CFT is a feasible intervention for people experiencing distress in relation to psychosis, and this chapter hopefully provides some indication of its acceptability and potentially usefulness for people with these difficulties. This chapter adds to an existing small case series study (n=3) of compassionate mind training with voice-hearers (Mayhew & Gilbert, 2008), as well as another first-person case study of this approach (Ellerby, 2013a, 2013b, 2014a, 2014b; Kennedy & Ellerby, 2016).

It is hoped that this chapter, by using in-depth illustrations and quotations from Gerry's therapy, will help the reader to get a sense of what CFT actually *feels* like, and particularly how it differs from, or enhances, traditional CBT for psychosis. One of the key differences is that CFT works more directly at the emotional and physiological level; slowing down, giving people space to tune into underlying affect and tone (via various sensory modalities) in order to engage their evolved social mentalities and motivational systems.

The CFT approach of exploring the threat-based function and emotional meaning in voices, and also talking directly with the voices, is different to traditional CBT for psychosis, which focuses more on working with the appraisals/ interpretations of voices. This aspect of CFT is more aligned to, and informed by, the Maastricht Approach of Marius Romme and Sandra Escher, who outline a range of interventions – from profiling voices, to making sense of and dialoguing with them (Romme & Escher, 1994, 2010; Romme et al., 2009). What CFT adds to this is to cultivate the part from which the making sense and the dialoguing can take place, (i.e., the compassionate self). The CFT claim is that any explorations into the threat system will be very challenging for people with psychosis, and therefore that training and preparing the mental conditions first (the compassionate mind training) will make this feel more tolerable and safer. The inner 'safe haven'

113

and 'secure base' of the compassionate self helps people to develop the courage and confidence to engage with their own distressing experiences.

References

All URLs accessed March 2018.

Depue, R. A. & Morrone-Strupinsky, J. V. (2005). A neurobehavioral model of affiliative bonding: Implications for conceptualizing a human trait of affiliation. *Behav Brain Sci, 28*(3), 313–350; discussion 350–395. doi:10.1017/S0140525X05000063

Ellerby, M. (2013a). How compassion may help me. *Psychosis, 6*(3), 266–270. doi:10.108 0/17522439.2013.816338

Ellerby, M. (2013b). Schizophrenia, Maslow's Hierarchy and Compassion-Focused Therapy. *Schizophrenia Bulletin, 42*(3). doi:10.1093/schbul/sbt119

Ellerby, M. (2014a). Resisting voices through finding our own compassionate voice. *Schizophrenia Bulletin, 43*(2). doi:10.1093/schbul/sbu035

Ellerby, M. (2014b). Schizophrenia, losers and Compassion-Focused Therapy. *Psychosis, 6*(4), 359–362. doi:10.1080/17522439.2013.876091

Gilbert, P. (2014). The origins and nature of Compassion Focused Therapy. *British Journal of Clinical Psychology, 53*(1), 6–41. doi:10.1111/bjc.12043

Gilbert, P. (2015). An evolutionary approach to emotion in mental health with a focus on affiliative emotions. *Emotion Review, 7*(3), 230–237. doi:10.1177/1754073915576552

Gilbert, P., McEwan, K., Mitra, R., Richter, A., Franks, L., Mills, A., . . . Gale, C. (2009). An exploration of different types of positive affect in students and in patients with bipolar disorder. *Clinical Neuropsychiatry, 6*(4), 135–143.

Gilbert, P., McEwan, K., Matos, M. & Rivis, A. (2011). Fears of compassion: Development of three self-report measures. *Psychology and Psychotherapy, 84*(3), 239–255. doi: 10.1348/147608310X526511

Kennedy, A. & Ellerby, M. (2016). A compassion-focused approach to working with someone diagnosed with schizophrenia. *Journal of Clinical Psychology, 72*(2), 123–131. doi:10.1002/jclp.22251

Kirby, J. & Gilbert, P. (2017). The emergence of the compassion focused therapies. *Compassion: concepts, research and applications.* London: Routledge. 258–285.

Lovibond, S. H. & Lovibond, P. F. (1995). *Manual for the depression anxiety stress scales* (2nd edn). Sydney: Psychology Foundation of Australia.

Mayhew, S. L. & Gilbert, P. (2008). Compassionate mind training with people who hear malevolent voices: A case series report. *Clinical Psychology & Psychotherapy, 15*(2), 113–138. doi:10.1002/cpp.566

Panksepp, J. (1998). *Affective neuroscience: The foundations of human and animal emotions.* New York: Oxford University Press.

Romme, M. & Escher, S. (1994). Hearing voices. *British Medical Journal, 309*(6955), 670.

Romme, M. & Escher, S. (2010). Personal history and hearing voices. In: F. Larøi and A. Aleman, (Eds.), *Hallucinations: A guide to treatment and management,* New York: Oxford University Press. 233–256.

Romme, M., Escher, S., Dillon, J., Corstens, D. & Morris, M. (2009). *Living with voices: 50 stories of recovery.* Ross-on-Wye: PCCS Books, England.

7

A PRINCIPLES-BASED APPROACH
USING THE METHOD OF LEVELS

Sara J. Tai

The Method of Levels (MOL) is an application of Perceptual Control Theory (PCT), which uses three principles (control, conflict and reorganisation) to understand human behaviour (Powers et al., 1960; Powers, 1973, 1990, 1998, 2005, 2008). These principles will be described specifically in relation to understanding psychosis and their application to therapeutic work. This chapter aims to describe exactly what an MOL therapist is required to do when delivering therapy and how MOL might be implemented in everyday clinical practice. The case examples provided are fictionalised, although inspired by real clinical experience.

Control

The foundational premise of PCT is that control is paramount for living our day-to-day lives. In order to survive, all living organisms must be able to exert control (Powers, 2008). What we control might be best described as 'preferred states' – for example, how warm we want to feel, how close to other people we want to be, or how busy we want to be. The term 'preferred state' can be used synonymously with terms such as 'goal', 'value', 'reference' or 'standard'. The salient point is that all living beings strive to maintain these preferred states. One example of control that people might be familiar with is the biological process of homeostasis, through which states such as body temperature are maintained at their optimum levels (Carey et al., 2014). From a PCT perspective, mental health problems develop when we lose control over the things that are important to us.

The link between control and health is well recognised within the literature. Research has demonstrated that when people have less control over their destiny, this negatively affects their physical health; for example, cardiovascular disease (e.g., Marmot et al., 1978, 1991; Tsey et al., 2003; Tsey, 2008). Control is just as important for mental health (e.g., Fiske & Taylor, 1991; Thompson & Spacapan, 1991) – when people seek help from therapists, it is often an attempt to establish some control over behaviours, emotions, thoughts, relationships, or some other aspect of their life (Carey, 2008a). For psychoses, loss of interpersonal control is recognised as a developmental factor (Ballon et al., 2007; Pinkham et al., 2007; Berry et al., 2008); lack of control over life events is both a common precursor (Bentall & Fernyhough, 2008) and consequence of psychosis (e.g., Birchwood et al., 1993), and control of one's life and destiny as a goal or outcome is regarded as the essence of what is required to recover from psychosis (Gumley & Schwannauer, 2006).

Emphasis is usually given to people's need to establish control over their behaviour. For example, therapy manuals frequently advocate behavioural change such as managing actions associated with anger, developing specific social skills, increasing activity levels, or developing specific behavioural attributes like assertiveness. Contrary to this, PCT specifies that people do not directly control their behaviour (nor output), but instead they control their perceptual experiences (or input). Evidence for this comes from research based on simulation and modelling (e.g., Marken, 2001; Powers, 2008). An everyday example, such as riding a bike to work, provides a simple illustration. If you controlled your *behaviours*, such as turning the handlebars in exactly the same way, or stopping peddling at the same precise moment and applying the brakes in the very same way you did the morning before, you would never reach your workplace; certainly not without injury. What you control is not your behaviour, but your sensory experience, or *perception* of how the bike is moving; being the right distance from other vehicles and objects around you, your position on the road, and the speed at which you are travelling. Although the route and journey you make each day remains exactly the same, your behaviour needs to be different each time you make the journey, depending on what is happening around you.

We use our behaviour to minimise any disturbance the environment creates on the preferred states we are trying to maintain. In other words, we are specifically controlling the effects our behaviour has on the way we experience our environment. Control happens through a process of negative feedback. We compare a current experience (perception) to our preferred state and then act to reduce any discrepancy between the two. When discrepancy between a current experience and a preferred state occurs, we experience psychological distress, which in PCT terms is called 'error'. Control is best understood as an on-going process of 'perceiving, comparing, and acting', which is why it is described as a closed negative feedback loop. Because we have many 'preferred states' we are controlling at any one time, there are countless negative feedback loops, which are interconnected and organised hierarchically. Feedback loops lower down in the hierarchy involve control processes specific to concrete actions – *how* we do things. Higher-level feedback loops relate more to personal values and principles – *why* we do things. Actions that might appear to an observer as random behaviours, are actually lower-level processes at work, instrumental for achieving a preferred state. Therefore, we cannot know what is driving another person's actions, nor what their goal is, simply by watching their behaviour.

In the context of psychosis, where to an observer someone's behaviour might appear extreme, erratic, and unintelligible, the principle of control is particularly

116

relevant. From a PCT perspective, psychoses, like other mental health problems, are understood to result from the very same processes involved in the normal realms of behaviour. Symptoms of psychosis are considered to be functional, resulting from an individual's efforts to control an important goal in their life.

To use a case example, Jack was diagnosed with persecutory and grandiose delusional beliefs involving being followed by government agents, whom he thought were intent on killing him. He believed they wanted him dead because they had stolen important, novel, and valuable business ideas that Jack had developed and that were worth a significant amount of money. Jack engaged in behaviours including monitoring particular models of cars that he believed belonged to government agents, leading to car chases and writing letters to prominent politicians, which had brought him into contact with the police. To an observer, these behaviours appeared bizarre, irrational, and unexplainable. For context, Jack came from a family of highly successful business entrepreneurs, who did not consider his talent and interest in music and the arts as a respectable or meritable career. Despite numerous courses to obtain qualifications in business, Jack had made limited progress in establishing himself in this type of career. Two important preferred states (goals) that Jack held were, firstly, to feel he had achieved something that others (particularly his family) valued and regarded as important. Simultaneously, Jack wanted to pursue his own interests and talents, rather than follow in his family's footsteps by being a businessman. Within the context of his unusual beliefs, Jack was engaging in what, from a PCT perspective, is considered to be lower-level actions (in hierarchical terms), such as monitoring the presence of cars he perceived to be following him, getting into car chases, and making contact with prominent politicians and officials. This served the function of enabling him to meet his preferred state of achievement and importance; having achieved something so substantial and valuable that the government was conspiring to steal it from him! Furthermore, the situation provided a justification for Jack to no longer pursue his business ideas without threatening his credibility. From Jack's perspective, to maintain his safety, he would need to retreat from his business plans and do something different with his life. Obviously, psychotic experiences like Jack's and the behaviours associated with such beliefs are problematic because they also incur many unintended negative consequences.

Understanding psychosis as functional for controlling a preferred state does not minimise the problems associated with it as a means of control. However, from a PCT perspective, psychotic experiences are always understood as part of a normal control process whereby individuals are trying to make their experiences fit with how they want their world to be. We all have multiple preferred states we seek to maintain and 'normal healthy functioning' is dependent on the degree to which we can successfully balance numerous preferred states simultaneously (Carey, 2008b; Mansell & Carey, 2009). This is consistent with other normalising approaches in psychosis, such as the 'Maastricht Approach' where symptoms are understood as a consequence of other problems in the person's life (Romme & Escher, 1994; Romme, 1998).

117

In MOL, emphasis is placed on identifying and targeting patients' underlying distress rather than their symptoms. MOL does this through increasing patients' awareness of their preferred states and facilitating them in reaching these. In reality, this might require a degree of problem-solving in order to find novel solutions to control a range of preferred states simultaneously. Understanding how problems with control arise is therefore important in conceptualising and thus directing what the MOL therapist must do.

Conflict

The mechanisms through which people experiencing psychosis lose control are no different to how control is lost for anyone else. For example, damage of a physical or organic nature can compromise a control system, making it difficult to compare a current perception to a preferred state and then produce an action that reduces discrepancy between the two. Similarly, environmental disturbances can be so extreme that an individual's efforts to minimise these disturbances are simply overwhelmed. People with psychosis are much more likely to have encountered disrupting life events such as trauma, and been exposed to life circumstances that are chronically difficult (Varese et al., 2012). However, the most common cause of loss of control is conflict (Carey & Mullan, 2008; Carey, 2008a; Powers, 2005). Because day-to-day life for anyone involves balancing various preferred states simultaneously, it is inevitable that conflict between preferred states will occur. PCT considers distress and discomfort resulting from experiencing a dilemma or having to make a difficult decision as very normal and something that we all experience. Resolving conflicts in order to re-establish control is usually a spontaneous process called 'reorganisation', which is described in the next section of this chapter. However, when conflict remains unresolved, chronic loss of control can occur, which can result in different mental health problems, including psychosis. Earlier, control was described as a closed negative feedback loop with each feedback loop, or 'control system' organised within a hierarchy. Conflict arises when two or more control systems are pursuing incompatible preferred states. When one control system acts to reduce discrepancy between current perception and a preferred state, it can increase discrepancy for another control system. For example, the earlier case of Jack described how he aimed to experience an achievement that would be regarded as important and valuable by other people (particularly his family). His belief that his business plan had been stolen provided the desired sense of achievement whilst also offering him a reason for withdrawing from a potential career in business without losing face. However, his psychotic experiences also served to take him further away from co-existing preferred states of pursuing his own life goals and having a relationship with his family in which he felt believed, approved of, and respected. Jack experienced ongoing conflict between wanting to feel successful whilst pursuing his own life plans but, on the other hand, wanting to please his family and have their respect. Subsequently, his behaviour fluctuated and appeared to observers as chaotic and extreme as he oscillated between preferred states, trying to reconcile incompatible goals. Therefore, he was unable to attain both preferred states and experienced loss of control, causing considerable psychological distress. It is common for an individual to have little awareness of both sides of a conflict. For example, Jack was far more in tune with his desire to gain the approval of his family, but less aware of how he needed to feel important and successful whilst pursuing his own life plans. He also had little awareness of how his behaviour (e.g., monitoring cars, getting into car chases, and contacting politicians), had unintended consequences (such as getting arrested and being hospitalised) that impeded pursuit of his own life goals (e.g., getting a job and establishing meaningful relationships with others).

An alternative way of describing conflict is in terms of 'relativity'. Problematic thoughts, experiences and feelings are only problematic relative to co-existing thoughts, experiences or feelings. Carey (2009) commented that 'the value we attribute to a particular thought is *always* determined by the way in which it measures up to other thoughts, ideas, goals, and beliefs that we have.' (p. 168). For example, if Jack's sense of failure over thwarted attempts at pursuing a career in business were held in isolation, it is unlikely these feelings would have been distressing. However, the problem arose because he simultaneously wanted his family's approval, which he pursued through attempts to demonstrate achievement in business.

Another example is that of Isabelle who sought help for distressing critical voices she heard daily, which repeatedly told her that she was to blame for her brother's suicide. From a PCT perspective, if Isabelle held the belief that she was to blame in isolation, this would be un-troubling. The notion 'I am to blame' becomes problematic in the context of co-existing beliefs and standards held, such as Isabelle's desire to have been able to look after and protect her brother and prevent bad things from happening; standards she equated with being a strong person. This is consistent with research demonstrating that for people who experience hearing distressing voices, it is frequently the incongruence between the voice content and the personal values and goals they hold, which causes cognitive dissonance (Varese et al., 2016). Voices have been explained as internally generated phenomena, which are misattributed to an external source (Morrison et al., 1995; Baker & Morrison, 1998). From a PCT perspective, the degree to which psychotic experiences are problematic or distressing is relative to the preferred states held by an individual. The external attribution of an internally generated phenomenon is a functional means of reducing discrepancy between a preferred internal state one would want to experience (e.g., to feel self-worth), and those actually encountered (e.g., negative thoughts about self).

In PCT, a psychotic experience is functional for at least one preferred state but usually problematic in relation to others. Therefore, a paranoid belief, or an unwanted perceptual experience such as hearing a voice, or a distressing belief such as 'I am worthless', are not considered abnormal, but are attempts to bring the individual closer to a preferred state held at a higher level. For example, Greg

119

heard voices that provided a running commentary on his actions. These voices had started at a time in his life when he felt very isolated and unsure of what to do. On the one hand the voices provided some relief from anxiety in the way they instructed him in what to do next; however, they were equally distressing because Greg perceived the voices to be abnormal and experienced them as intrusive and uncontrollable. MOL therapy aims to help develop awareness of different preferred states and the conflicts between them. In doing so, new potential solutions for balancing preferred states and achieving different goals become possible, through a process known as reorganisation.

Reorganisation: The mechanism of therapeutic change

PCT states that to reduce discrepancy between a preferred state and a current perception of the way things are, we make random changes to our behaviour. This mechanism is a very basic, innate learning process through which change occurs called reorganisation (Marken & Carey, 2015). The process does not involve any decision-making, planning, or analysis of the advantages and disadvantages of either the potential changes that reorganisation causes, or the behaviours involved. Reorganisation is far less complicated and simply involves generating a change and then monitoring the outcome produced by that change. Reorganisation as an activity is never-ending. Random changes are incessantly generated unless discrepancy reduces, in which case no further changes are made. Because goals and intentions are organised within a hierarchical system, change to one preferred state will always have consequences on other inter-related preferred states within that system; and because this system interacts with ever-changing environments, in reality reorganisation never stops. The very purpose of reorganisation is to generate an immediate change; the more creative or divergent an idea, potentially the more chance it has of successfully reducing discrepancy. For this reason, when distressed, people might be more likely to experience ideas and sensory experiences that seem extreme, bizarre, or out of the ordinary. When changes generated during reorganisation are produced very quickly, sufficient monitoring of the effect of actions might not always occur, causing control to be lost. Similarly, changes that are generated too slowly could be ineffective at restoring control adequately. Problems with the timing of reorganisation could result in action that is incongruent with an individual's environment and this is likely to play an important role in the development of psychosis (Carey et al., 2015).

Reorganisation is essentially an innate and automatic problem-solving process. Our attention is naturally drawn to areas of discrepancy and reorganisation occurs wherever mental awareness or 'attention' is focused. From a PCT perspective, what makes any psychotherapy effective in creating therapeutic change is facilitation of mobility of awareness within the hierarchy of interrelated control systems so that reorganisation can occur at the right level (Carey et al., 2012). Reorganisation does not occur in a planned, systematic manner and so one cannot just make it happen as required. Where therapy keeps a patient focused on their problem enough for them to develop awareness of their conflict and generate new solutions, this can increase the chances of that person making changes where necessary (Carey, 2011a). For each individual, distress represents a unique conflict, which will require novel and usually unpredictable solutions developed through a trial and error process.

For example, Jack's conflict between wanting to follow his own interests in music but also wanting to gain the approval of his family through pursuing a business career, would be unlikely to be resolved by merely choosing one option over the other. In reality, once he became aware of both of these preferred states, Jack began to make his own life decisions that were less dependent upon the approval of his family, particularly when he felt less vulnerable. On other occasions, when feeling more vulnerable, he was more proactive in seeking their advice and guidance, as well as that of other people outside of his family whose opinions he also valued. Jack was able to reflect on how to balance both goals, and solutions to doing this were often situation-specific. Jack was eventually able to reflect on some of his psychotic experiences in relation to this conflict. In therapy he discussed how his experiences of having his business plans stolen and then being targeted by the thieves caused him a problem. Jack described how this had made it difficult for him to pursue anything else in his life, including his own musical interests and also served to make him feel further disconnected from his family. However, he also became aware of how his experiences served to protect his own vulnerability and self-esteem and his need to develop his ability to trust his own choices rather than be reliant on the approval of others. As Jack discovered different ways of managing his conflicting preferred states, particularly developing his own musical interests, his unusual beliefs began to dissipate. From a PCT perspective, this change reflects reorganisation.

Reorganisation, specified by PCT as a process of therapeutic change, can and does occur within therapies other than MOL. In fact, PCT would state that wherever a therapy is effective, it is because reorganisation has occurred. MOL focuses exclusively on creating the conditions most likely to facilitate this process. Techniques and methods considered to be important in other therapeutic approaches, such as structured assessments and history taking, specific methods for alliance building, or giving homework, for example, are not considered as requisite within MOL. Also, in MOL there is recognition that distress can only be understood from the perspective of the patient, who has the capacity to generate their own solution.

The Method of Levels in practice

To promote the chances of reorganisation, MOL specifically sets out to help patients express and sustain their attention on a problem they are experiencing. Focusing on the problem needs to occur for long enough to allow the patient to attend to a range of emotions and thoughts about that problem, so they can shift their awareness to higher-level goals and values.

There are two main goals for an MOL therapist in order to help a patient do this. Firstly, the therapist must work to create the required conditions for a patient to be able to talk openly about a problem, or any area of their life that is currently not the way they would wish it to be. The willingness of a patient to talk in an open and honest way is paramount in MOL. It cannot be a coercive intervention. Therapy is a process of exposing a patient to the problem at hand and, from a PCT perspective, exposure is more likely to be therapeutic and beneficial when the process is controlled by the patient as opposed to the therapist (Healey et al., 2017). MOL sessions are therefore client led, even if the discussion focuses on their ambivalence about attending therapy. For example, a patient who attends a therapy appointment because they felt under pressure to do so by a key worker's mention of the Mental Health Act, might not consider themselves to have a problem requiring help. Yet, the same patient might value an opportunity to discuss their experience of feeling under pressure from their key worker, whether the situation troubles them, or exploring why they felt under pressure at all.

The second goal for the MOL therapist is to draw the patient's attention to background thoughts that occur as they are discussing a problem. This involves the therapist noticing signs that might indicate that a patient has experienced a background thought, such as emphasis on certain words, laughing, or pauses as they are speaking, or non-verbal cues such as reduced eye contact, gestures or smiles. The aim is to use these indicators to redirect attention and expose the patient to parts of the problem that would otherwise have only been attended to fleetingly. The emphasis is on helping the patient to express their problem whilst concurrently processing any emotions as they occur. The focus is particularly on the way in which the patient is thinking about a problem, as opposed to drawing out details related to the content of what the person is saying. This experiential process is thought to develop awareness of higher-level goals and conflicts. Although potential solutions to problems might be explicitly discussed in therapy, in reality solutions are often generated spontaneously. Change won't necessarily materialise during a therapy session, but it may do later when the patient has had time to process the discussion further. Time taken to generate workable solutions and resolve conflicts varies considerably between patients. Logical problem-solving and advice is viewed as having limited value and being potentially counterproductive, as it can draw attention to only one side of a conflict rather than helping a patient develop multiple perspectives.

The two goals of MOL therapy – helping the patient talk about a problem and directing attention to background thoughts – remain constant, regardless of what problem is being targeted. The specific actions of an MOL therapist, in order to implement these two goals, will need to vary in accordance with the way in which a patient presents. The three principles of control, conflict, and reorganisation provide a framework in which to understand the patient's experiences. Behaviours that might be attributed directly to psychosis, or the patient being resistant, noncompliant, or avoidant are all understood to be functional in relation to the patient's preferred state. For example, Isabelle often gave very tangential answers, mumbled, and had noticeably reduced eye contact when asked an emotionally salient question by her therapist. Her behaviour could easily have been interpreted as evidence of her responding to a psychotic phenomenon, or being thought disordered (particularly as her responses to questions were so random they were difficult to understand). Her behaviour could also have been attributed to Isabelle being avoidant or disengaged in therapy. Yet Isabelle's preferred states were to stop bad things from happening and be a strong person. Her tangential replies were her attempts to remember and relay information to the therapist about times when she perceived she had succeeded in preventing something bad from happening. Furthermore, by not having eye contact with the therapist, she thought she was able to control how visible her emotions were, and prevent people being able to see how upset she was, giving her a sense of being a strong person. An MOL therapist views all human beings as unique controlling systems and their behaviour is simply the means by which they are maintaining a preferred state. Therefore, one cannot know what another person is *doing* by observing their actions. For an MOL therapist, there is an appreciation that it simply is not possible to know how it is to wear another person's shoes and so the only option is to ask that person detailed questions about their shoes and how they feel.

To maximise the possibility of a patient being able to gain benefit from therapy, it is of great importance that patients feel able to talk openly and honestly about a problem, verbalising the thoughts they experience in real time (Carey et al., 2012). When beginning a session of MOL, the therapist starts by asking if the patient has a problem or something they would like to be different that they feel able to discuss. For example, the session might begin with the therapist asking, 'What would you like to discuss today?' or, 'Is there something on your mind you would feel able to speak about today?'. In MOL, therapists do as much as they can to facilitate the patient being in control so it is important that the patient generates the focus of the session. The therapist's job is to work at retaining the patient's attention on this focus by asking detailed and curious questions. People experiencing psychosis commonly do not want to focus specifically on their psychotic symptoms and choose to discuss other issues, such as financial concerns, relationship problems, difficulties with medication, or the fact that they only attended the therapy session because their family pressured them. Sometimes patients respond by saying, 'I don't know what I want to talk about'. The therapist can still enquire about this experience curiously; for example by asking, 'Does it bother you that you don't know what to talk about?' or, 'Is it difficult to find the words to talk about it?' or even, 'What is it like not to know?'. An example therapy session with Isabelle provides a further illustration of how an MOL therapy might proceed:

Therapist: What would you like to talk about today?
Isabelle: Well, I'm not quite sure because I find it quite hard to think about things that have happened.
Therapist: I'm not asking you to talk about anything you don't want to. Could you tell me what makes it hard to think about things that have happened?

Isabelle:	Thinking about things makes it all start up in my head and then I can't stop. I can't control it and then it's like . . . I'm weak.
Therapist:	What do you mean – weak?
Isabelle:	I mean a weak person . . . like I'm just pathetic and can't handle things. I need to be strong.
Therapist:	Is being strong the same as handling things?
Isabelle:	Yes – if I'm strong and can handle things then I can stop bad things from happening.
Therapist:	What kind of bad things can you stop happening?
Isabelle:	Err . . . ha ha. (laughs)
Therapist:	What occurred to you just then?
Isabelle:	Because of course I can't stop bad things happening. It sounds funny when you say it back to me.
Therapist:	What's funny about it?
Isabelle:	Well it's funny because I can't stop bad things from happening and I need to be strong in order to be able to handle it when they do happen.
Therapist:	And so do you want to be able to handle the things you said you didn't want to think about?
Isabelle:	Yes, and that's why it's funny. Because I said I didn't want to think about them and yet I do . . . because I just want to be able to handle them.
Therapist:	Hmm . . . what do you make of that?
Isabelle:	Well, that maybe I do need to talk about things. It's just that thoughts, images and memories are trying to get into my head. It's just so hard to think about that. Really scary. I want to take what happened and sweep it under the carpet.
Therapist:	Are you trying to sweep them under the carpet as you speak?
Isabelle:	Yes.
Therapist:	How far under the carpet do you need to sweep them?
Isabelle:	Right under as far as I can . . . but . . . (eyes start to tear up)
Therapist:	What just popped into your head?
Isabelle:	That I try and sweep it under the carpet and yet I can still see it. So, it's not really helping me to feel strong. In fact it's making me weaker.

This excerpt illustrates how the therapist does not lead Isabelle to speak about things she does not wish to, but rather maintains the focus on the problem and curiously questions the process of her thinking. It is not necessary for the therapist to ask Isabelle to recall details of her past experiences. Instead, the therapist merely maintains Isabelle's attention on her present moment experience of thinking about those past events – how she currently processes and evaluates these thoughts in the moment, as they occur. For example, the therapist could ask, 'As you are speaking now are you thinking about the things?' or, 'If you sweep those thoughts under the carpet what kind of things are left in your head?' or, 'When you sweep things under the carpet, do they stay there?' The questions asked by the therapist can often appear very direct and literal, as in these examples. The aim is to help patients sustain their attention on the problem, so they are able to consider it in a new way. The patient is also likely to experience new thoughts and feelings as the problem is examined from new perspectives. The therapist will ask about these experiences as they are happening to facilitate exploration, awareness, and discovery.

If required, the patient might choose to use a word or phrase to refer to particular memories, thoughts, or experiences they choose not to discuss. In the example, Isabelle mentioned experiences she did not want to think about and referred to this as 'things'. Sometimes patients choose specific and symbolic labels, such as 'spiky weeds' or 'green apples' so that they can make reference to the very thing they do not want to talk about, without it hindering their ability to express themselves whilst paying attention to the problem they do wish to discuss. This is another example of facilitating the patient's sense of control during therapy. Often when patients perceive they do have control and there is no attempt by the therapist to coerce them into talking about certain experiences, they feel more able to disclose the information anyway.

In the example therapy excerpt, the therapist asks Isabelle about the meaning she intended when using certain words. An MOL therapist aims to avoid making assumptions about what the patient is saying and does not offer reflections or interpretations. Therefore, the therapist also refrains from making comments that might traditionally be regarded as 'empathic'; for example, 'That must be really upsetting for you'. Statements like these are inherently assumptive; without asking Isabelle, there is no way of knowing whether her internal experience of an event was upsetting, frustrating, sad, surprising, or embarrassing. Such attempts at empathy run the risk of misjudging the person and could then inhibit them in expressing their problem. Instead, an MOL therapist adopts a curious style of questioning. The therapist is encouraged to speak at a pace that matches the patient, using short, simple sentences consisting of only one question at a time. This helps to maintain the patient's attention on their immediate experience with as few distractions as possible. Similarly, using terminology only generated by patients helps to sustain attention on their own thinking. Asking what the patient means by their use of certain words helps anchor attention and enables the patient to work out what they mean. For example, the therapist might ask, 'What made you choose the word "scary" to describe the thoughts?'

During therapy the focus is always on the present moment, encouraging patients to express their immediate 'online' experiences in whichever modality they occur, including metaphors or images. Even when the problem at hand relates to past events, it is the individual's present evaluation or experience of the event that is of relevance. Questioning the 'here and now' is not reliant on memory and recall or post hoc analysis of metacognitive processes. Therefore, this is a particularly useful approach when working with individuals who have difficulties with memory, struggle to express themselves, or appear thought disordered. It is also especially suited to processing experiences consisting of unusual and unwanted perceptual phenomena (Tai, 2009).

When patients talk about a problem, they might encounter a range of background thoughts that run in parallel. As described earlier in the chapter, there are usually non-verbal signs – some subtle and others more obvious – which indicate such background thoughts are momentarily popping into consciousness. These might include frowns, smiles, pauses mid-sentence, a stutter, or changes in volume, pace or intonation of speech. In MOL, these are known as 'disruptions' because they can disrupt the flow of expression. When asking about disruptions, if the patient reveals it is unrelated to the problem at hand, the therapist encourages them to continue talking and maintain their focus on the original problem. It is normal for people to have numerous thoughts in quick succession and a background thought about what to have for dinner, for example, might not be fruitful to the problem under examination. Sometimes a patient may wander off-topic, in which case the therapist's job is to keep them on track, asking for example, 'How does that connect to what you were just saying?'. The therapist's goal is to track how the patient's thinking evolves and awareness develops, yet anchor the patient's attention on the problem rather than passively follow the discussion off in tangents. MOL therapists, when pursuing the two goals of MOL, need to be flexible in response to the way in which a patient presents. A patient who talks a lot and loses focus on the problem at hand, for example, might require more frequent interruption to enquire about distractions, which are a form of disruption. Yet, someone who speaks slowly and pauses regularly to think reflectively might find that too many questions about disruptions interfere with their reflective process. The skill of an MOL therapist is in facilitating a patient's awareness of the different aspects of an experience, without 'getting in the way' of the natural fluidity of their thinking process (Carey, 2006).

Evidence for PCT and MOL

The evidence for PCT is multidisciplinary and derived predominantly from simulations and modelling of human behaviour (e.g., Marken, 2001; Powers, 1989, 1999). More detailed descriptions, reviews of the theory and evidence can be found elsewhere (e.g., Marken & Mansell, 2013; Carey et al., 2015). MOL has previously been used to treat a broad range of mental health problems and the evidence for MOL is described elsewhere (e.g., Carey et al., 2009; Carey & Mullan, 2007, 2008; Carey et al., 2013; Tai, 2009). The application of MOL across a wide range of mental health problems means it can be considered a 'transdiagnostic' therapy. Within the context of psychosis, this is particularly beneficial given the extremely common occurrence of co-morbid problems; for example, personality disorders, anxiety disorders, and mood disorders (Buckley et al., 2009). Given that mental health difficulties from a PCT perspective are understood in a non-pathologising way, MOL might be better described as 'adiagnostic'. Evidence for the application of MOL specifically to psychosis is still very much in development. A study by Carey, Tai and Stiles (2013) recruited patients from in-patient and out-patient secondary care mental health services in Australia with a range of diagnoses, including psychosis. The study demonstrated that MOL was equivalent in effect size to other interventions such as cognitive behaviour therapy and more efficient in terms of effect size achieved per session attended. The author of the current chapter has conducted informal and unpublished acceptability and feasibility evaluations with people experiencing psychosis in community mental health teams, early intervention services and acute in-patient services (Tai, 2017). We are also in the process of running a randomised control trial of MOL with people who have experienced a first episode of psychosis. So, research to date has provided preliminary evidence that the approach is acceptable and feasible, with patients reporting they find MOL beneficial and satisfactory.

The MOL Session Evaluation Form (Carey & Tai, 2012) provides an eight-item scale in which the therapist's adherence to MOL can be assessed. Items relate to key therapist goals, such as: asking about disruptions; using questions rather than advising, suggesting, or teaching; asking about the patient's immediate experience; and sustaining the patient's focus in one or more areas. Each item is rated on a 0–10 scale, where higher ratings indicate that a goal was adhered to throughout, where appropriate to do so.

Implementing MOL for psychosis

The structure of MOL therapy is intended to maximise the degree of control a patient has within the therapeutic process. From a PCT perspective, reorganisation is an idiosyncratic process and the timescale in which different people might progress and make changes varies enormously; so appointment scheduling in MOL therapy therefore needs to be flexible. Patients are encouraged to make their own decisions about how many sessions they require, the duration of each appointment, as well as the frequency of their appointments. Patients are asked to lead on arranging their own appointments as and when they choose. Whereas some patients might schedule appointments weekly, others will have much more varied patterns of attendance. Many practitioners have concerns that patient-led appointment scheduling is not feasible due to service restraints and lack of resources, anticipating that demand will outweigh supply. Others fear that some patients will fail to engage with services and high-risk patients could then 'slip through the net'. In the numerous services in which patient-led-scheduling has been implemented, including those for people experiencing psychosis, this has not been the case (Carey et al., 2009; Carey & Mullan, 2007, 2008; Carey et al., 2013). When patients have had more choice about their appointments, this appears to have increased their ability to make appointments when they perceive they need them, which has reduced demand rather than increased it (e.g., Carey et al., 2013; Tai, 2009). Patient-led appointment scheduling could be particularly suitable and empowering for people with psychosis.

Flexibility can still be offered even when service constraints are necessary. For example, placing an upper limit on the number of sessions patients can book, having specified time windows in which people can attend therapy, placing limits on the maximum length of time a session can last, and how often they can be scheduled, can all be set in accord with service restrictions but still enable more patient control. Research suggests that patient-led appointment scheduling has the potential to be more efficient than fixed schedules of treatments; for example, 16 weekly sessions (e.g., Carey & Kemp, 2007; Carey, 2011b). There is evidence that patient-led scheduling has yielded positive benefits to services including reduced waiting times, increased access to psychological therapy for more patients, and is highly acceptable (Carey et al., 2009; Carey & Mullan, 2007, 2008; Carey, Tai & Stiles, 2013).

Assessing and monitoring risk during MOL therapy occurs as it would in any usual clinical practice. If patient-led appointment scheduling is offered to a patient who presents with significant risk, it would be possible to agree a maximum period of time of no-contact before the therapist contacts the patient. Alternatively, for therapists working in teams, it might be possible for other team members to monitor risk so that the specific therapy component of the patient's overall care plan can remain completely in the control of the patient. This is particularly beneficial where integrating psychological therapy with routine aspects of case management can negatively affect the likelihood of a patient engaging in treatment.

Training as an MOL therapist can be achieved through the use of treatment manuals (e.g., Carey, 2006, 2008c; Mansell et al., 2012; Carey et al., 2015), work-shop attendance, and regular supervision. It is also recommended that supervision includes regular role-play practice of MOL, provision of feedback on trainees' video-taped sessions, and trainee observation of therapy delivered by experienced practitioners. Further information and training resources are available at www. methodoflevels.com.au and www.pctweb.org

Conclusions

MOL is a personalised form of cognitive therapy based on PCT principles of control, conflict and reorganisation. PCT provides a framework for understanding the nature of psychotic experiences and the associated distress. MOL is emerging as an effective psychological intervention for a range of psychological problems. MOL appears to be feasible and acceptable for people experiencing psychosis and further research developing the evidence specifically for psychosis is in progress.

References

Baker, C. A. & Morrison, A. P. (1998). Cognitive processes in auditory hallucinations: Attributional biases and metacognition. *Psychological Medicine, 28*, 1199–1208.

Ballon, J. S., Kaur, T., Marks, I. I. & Cadenhead, K. S. (2007). Social functioning in young people at risk for schizophrenia. *Psychiatry Research, 151*(1), 29–35.

Bentall, R. P. & Fernyhough, C. (2008). Social predictors of psychotic experiences: Specificity and psychological mechanisms. *Schizophrenia Bulletin, 34*(6), 1012–1020.

Berry, K., Barrowclough, C. & Wearden, A. (2008). Attachment theory: A framework for understanding symptoms and interpersonal relationships in psychosis. *Behaviour Research and Therapy, 46*(12), 1275–1282.

Birchwood, M., Mason, R., MacMillan, F. & Healy, J. (1993). Depression, demoralization and control over psychotic illness: A comparison of depressed and non-depressed patients with a chronic psychosis. *Psychological Medicine, 23*(2), 387–395.

Buckley, P. F., Miller, B. J., Lehrer, D. S. & Castle, D. J. (2009). Psychiatric comorbidities and schizophrenia. *Schizophrenia Bulletin, 35,* 383–402.

Carey, T. A. (2006). *The Method of Levels: How to do psychotherapy without getting in the way.* Hayward, CA: Living Control Systems Publishing.

Carey, T. A. (2008a). Conflict, as the Achilles heel of perceptual control, offers a unifying approach to the formulation of psychological problems. *Counselling Psychology Review, 23,* 5–16.

Carey, T. A. (2008b). Perceptual Control Theory and the Method of Levels: Further contributions to a transdiagnostic Perspective. *International Journal of Cognitive Therapy, 1*(3), 237–255.

Carey, T. A. (2008c). *Hold that thought! A short introduction to the Method of Levels.* Chapel Hill, NC: Newview Publications.

Carey, T. A. (2009). Dancing with distress: Helping people transform psychological troubles with the Method of Levels two step. *The Cognitive Behaviour Therapist, 2,* 167–177.

Carey, T. A. (2011a). Exposure and reorganization: The what and how of effective psychotherapy. *Clinical Psychology Review, 31,* 236–248.

Carey, T. A. (2011b). As you like it: Adopting a patient-led approach to the issue of treatment length. *Journal of Public Mental Health, 10*(1), 6–16.

Carey, T. A., Carey, M., Mullan, R. J., Spratt, C. G. & Spratt, M. B. (2009). Assessing the statistical and personal significance of the Method of Levels. *Behavioural and Cognitive Psychotherapy, 37*(3), 311–324.

Carey, T. A., Kelly, R. E., Mansell, W. & Tai, S. J. (2012). What's therapeutic about the therapeutic relationship? A hypothesis for practice informed by Perceptual Control Theory. *The Cognitive Behaviour Therapist, 5*(2–3), 47–59.

Carey, T. A. & Kemp, K. (2007). Self selecting first appointments: A replication and consideration of the implications for patient-centred care. *Clinical Psychology Forum, 178,* 33–36.

Carey, T. A., Mansell, W. & Tai, S. (2014). A biopsychosocial model based on negative feedback and control. *Frontiers in Human Neuroscience, 8,* 94.

Carey, T. A., Mansell, W. & Tai, S. (2015). *Principles-based counselling and psychotherapy: A Method of Levels approach.* London: Routledge.

Carey, T. A. & Mullan, R. J. (2007). Patients taking the lead: A naturalistic investigation of a patient led approach to treatment in primary care. *Counselling Psychology Quarterly, 20,* 1–14.

Carey, T. A. & Mullan, R. J. (2008). Evaluating the Method of Levels. *Counselling Psychology Quarterly, 21,* 1–10.

Carey, T. A. & Tai, S. J. (2012). MOL Session Evaluation Form – Revised. In W. Mansell, T. A. Carey & S. J. Tai, *A transdiagnostic approach to CBT using Method of Levels therapy* (pp. 137–141). London: Routledge.

129

Carey, T. A., Tai, S. J. & Stiles, W. B. (2013). Effective and efficient: Using patient-led appointment scheduling in routine mental health practice in remote Australia. *Professional Psychology: Research & Practice, 44*(6), 405–414.

Fiske, S. T. & Taylor, S. E. (1991). *McGraw-Hill series in social psychology. Social cognition.* New York, NY: Mcgraw-Hill Book Company.

Gumley, A. & Schwannauer, M. (2006). *A cognitive interpersonal approach to recovery and relapse prevention.* Chichester: John Wiley and Son.

Healey, A., Mansell, W. & Tai, S. (2017). An experimental test of the role of control in spider fear. *Journal of Anxiety Disorders, 49*, 12–20.

Mansell, W. & Carey, T. A. (2009). A century of psychology and psychotherapy: Is an understanding of control the missing link between theory, research, and practice? *Psychology and Psychotherapy: Theory, Research and Practice, 82*(3), 337–353.

Mansell, W., Carey, T. A. & Tai, S. J. (2012). *A transdiagnostic approach to CBT using Method of Levels therapy: Distinctive features.* London: Routledge.

Marken, R. S. (2001). Controlled variables: Psychology as the center fielder views it. *The American Journal of Psychology, 114*(2), 259.

Marken, R. S. & Carey, T. A. (2015). Understanding the change process involved in solving psychological problems: A mode-lbased approach to understanding how psychotherapy works. *Clinical Psychology & Psychotherapy, 22*(6), 580–590.

Marken, R. S. & Mansell, W. (2013). Perceptual control as a unifying concept in psychology. *Review of General Psychology, 17*(2), 170.

Marmot, M. G., Rose, G., Shipley, M. & Hamilton, P. J. (1978). Employment grade and coronary heart disease in British civil servants. *Journal of Epidemiology and Community Health, 32*(4), 244–249.

Marmot, M. G., Stansfeld, S., Patel, C., North, F., Head, J., White, I., . . . & Smith, G. D. (1991). Health inequalities among British civil servants: The Whitehall II study. *The Lancet, 337*(8754), 1387–1393.

Morrison, A. P., Haddock, G. & Tarrier, N. (1995). Intrusive thoughts and auditory hallucinations: A cognitive approach. *Behavioural and Cognitive Psychotherapy, 23*(3), 265–280.

Pinkham, A. E., Penn, D. L., Perkins, D. O., Graham, K. A. & Siegel, M. (2007). Emotion perception and social skill over the course of psychosis: A comparison of individuals "at-risk" for psychosis and individuals with early and chronic schizophrenia spectrum illness. *Cognitive Neuropsychiatry, 12*(3), 198–212.

Powers, W. T. (1973). Feedback: Beyond behaviorism. *Science, 179*(4071), 351–356.

Powers, W. T. (1989). Random-walk chemotaxis: Trial and error as a control process. *Behavioral Neuroscience, 103*(6), 1348–1355.

Powers, W. T. (1990). Control theory: A model of organisms. *System Dynamics Review, 6*(1), 1–20.

Powers, W. T. (1998). *Making sense of behavior.* New Canaan, CT: Benchmark.

Powers, W. T. (1999). A model of kinesthetically and visually controlled arm movement. *International Journal of Human-Computer Studies, 50*(6), 463–479.

Powers, W. T. (2005). *Behavior: The control of perception.* (2nd edn.) New Canaan, CT: Benchmark.

Powers, W. T. (2008). *Living control systems III: The fact of control.* Escondido, CA: Benchmark.

Powers, W. T., Clark, R. K. & McFarland, R. L. (1960). A general feedback theory of human behavior. Part II. *Perceptual and Motor Skills, 11*, 309–323.

Romme, M. & Escher, S. (1994). Hearing voices. *BMJ: British Medical Journal, 309*(6955), 670.

Romme, M. (1998). Listening to the voice hearers. *Journal of Psychosocial Nursing and Mental Health Services, 36*(9), 40–44.

Tai, S. J. (2009). Using Perceptual Control Theory and the Method of Levels to work with people who experience psychosis. *The Cognitive Behavioural Therapist, 2*, 227–242.

Tai, S. J. (2017, July). A principles based approach to adapting engagement and therapy within in-patient settings. Paper presented at the 45th Annual Conference of the British Association for Behavioural and Cognitive Psychotherapies, Manchester, UK.

Thompson, S. C. & Spacapan, S. (1991). Perceptions of control in vulnerable populations. *Journal of Social Issues, 47*(4), 1–21.

Tsey, K. (2008). The 'control factor': Important but neglected social determinant of health. *The Lancet, 372*(9650), 1629.

Tsey, K., Whiteside, M., Deemal, A. & Gibson, T. (2003). Social determinants of health, the 'control factor', and the Family Wellbeing Empowerment Program. *Australasian Psychiatry, 11*, 34–39.

Varese, F., Smeets, F., Drukker, M., Lieverse, R., Lataster, T., Viechtbauer, W., . . . Bentall, R. P. (2012). Childhood adversities increase the risk of psychosis: A meta-analysis of patient-control, prospective-and cross-sectional cohort studies. *Schizophrenia Bulletin, 38*, 661–671.

Varese, F., Tai, S. J., Pearson, L. & Mansell, W. (2016). Thematic associations between personal goals and clinical and non-clinical voices (auditory verbal hallucinations). *Psychosis, 8*(1), 12–22.

Part 3

CRITICAL PERSPECTIVES

8

A STEP IN THE RIGHT DIRECTION OR A MISSED OPPORTUNITY?

Rachel Waddingham

I was first introduced to Cognitive Behavioural Therapy (CBT) whilst seeing a psychologist for help with the intense anxiety and emotional struggles I was facing at university. My memories of our two or three sessions together are largely positive – she was warm, easy to talk with and I got the sense that she really cared. I remember her giving me a sheet – *10 common thinking traps* – that left me feeling like she had an uncanny ability to read my mind. I could, almost effortlessly, give examples of each of them within my life. Naming these struggles felt helpful – it was as if we could target each one in turn, challenge it and return my mind to a place of sanity. Of course, she had no idea that I was struggling with voices and believed that I had an alien inside me that had the power to control me. It never came up in conversation.

There was something about the rationality of CBT that really appealed to me. Its solid structure felt like it had the potential to take something that was very messy (my life), untangle it and neatly file it away as thoughts, feelings and behaviours – so some years later, when my community psychiatric nurse (CPN) invited me to work through a CBT for Psychosis (CBTp) workbook with her I was happy to oblige. Still, working alongside someone who was as clueless as me didn't inspire confidence and I was soon inventing answers to questions that seemed irrelevant and unhelpful. I tried to show progress to keep the nurse happy, yet in truth I couldn't connect the dots between the worksheets and my experience. They seemed as if they were on different planets, and the nurse simply wasn't equipped to help me navigate the space between.

Thankfully, I had the privilege to meet a skilled CBTp practitioner whilst working in a service to support children and young people who hear voices. Coupled with a good working knowledge of dissociation and trauma, I recognised their deep respect for the client's own wisdom. I valued their willingness to work outside of the box rather than blindly follow the worksheets that constrained my own therapy. Still, I wondered how much of the healing I witnessed came via the quality of the therapeutic relationship, rather than the tools of the trade. I came to view CBTp as a potentially useful vehicle to enable practitioners to have useful conversations around difficult experiences. I saw it as a way of encouraging practitioners to pay attention to someone's relationship with the voices they hear and the beliefs that surround them. Some seemed able to use this structure to creatively engage with another human being; others found themselves wedded to an approach that was a poor fit for the person they were trying to help.

I have deeper concerns about the model of CBT. Its language, filled with terms such as 'misattribution', 'cognitive distortions', 'maladaptive', 'errors', 'biases' and 'faulty' hurt the part of me that has had to fight to recognise my experiences as meaningful and adaptive. This professionalised psychobabble, backed up with peer reviewed articles and Randomised Controlled Trials (RCTs), has the power to steal and reframe my own way of making sense of my story in a kindly formulation. It's an effort to sit with these feelings and gather the generosity of spirit needed to allow myself to look beyond this and acknowledge what CBTp can offer. It has, I believe, helped to place psychological approaches to psychosis within mainstream mental health practice. It has helped to make it okay for practitioners to talk about voices and engage with people's beliefs, pushing back against those long-held fears of collusion that have influenced so much of mental health practice. It helped provide a useful framework for many people I consider allies. Yet it is not perfect.

A limitation that many recognise in CBTp is its focus on rationality and cognitive processes, when so much of what we believe and do as humans goes beyond this. Like many, I have the amazing ability to ignore the evidence and listen to my gut. This ability can be useful – it has led me to fight against the odds and take steps forward when others felt I would surely fail. However, it also means that all the rationality in the world won't provide me with lasting reassurance if my gut is consumed by terror. At those times, so-called rational thoughts feel like ill-fitting clothes whereas the feeling itself resonates with my core. Sure, sometimes the way I think can modify how I feel about something. But, with the deep stuff – shame, terror and rage – this approach barely scrapes the surface. Instead, attempts to modify my thinking merely promote a state of dissonance where I begin to disown or disavow my feelings-core. Given a choice between rational-me and feelings-me, I might understandably choose the rational one as it brings with it the promise of control. Yet such a separation is impossible to sustain in the long-term. Those feelings don't simply disappear, they fester underneath the surface and are handed back to me in a metaphorical and exaggerated form by the voices and the content of my overwhelming beliefs. Such emotional suppression gives my voices and beliefs more fuel.

Ushering in the third wave

I first heard about third wave CBT approaches at the 2012 World Hearing Voices Congress in Wales. During a hot debate around CBTp, I heard Rufus May speak about the new third wave developments and their focus on emotions and compassion. Instantly, I perked up. Compassion and curiosity have been essential companions in my own journey and the idea of CBTp embracing these principles sounded promising. Since then, I've noted an increasing number of those practitioners I respect begin to speak of mindfulness, compassion-based approaches and Acceptance and Commitment Therapy. Their enthusiasm left me with the impression of a fresh approach that is a dramatic departure from the rationalisation valued in CBT. Yet despite being around these approaches for a while, when I came to write this chapter my biggest challenge was articulating what these approaches were. After months of staring at a page filled with half-written sentences and a brain left muddled by an array of YouTube lectures and papers on a plethora of 'third wave' approaches, I had to face a worrying truth – I knew nothing. Or, in a less dramatic sense, I knew very little about this third wave and was confused by the little I did know.

There's something about these approaches that can feel intangible and slightly hippy-ish when described in person, yet reads as almost cold and formulaic in academic journals. The combination of scientific sounding theories, clinical terminology and evidence-based practice contrasts sharply against talk of compassion, values and mindfulness. This felt conflict begs the question: Can such approaches really be integrated within a psychology that is concerned with scientific validity, or are they at risk of being subsumed into larger theoretical frameworks that dilute and warp their nature?

As diverse as third wave approaches are, they represent a move away from attending to the specific content of voices, visions and beliefs. When someone is feeling troubled by the content of the voices they hear, a CBT practitioner may feel moved to zoom in and examine the experience in detail – supporting the person to explore, understand and evaluate it in the context of their life experiences. Third wave approaches, rather counter-intuitively, encourage us to zoom out – focusing our attention on the way in which someone relates to, or responds to, their experience rather than getting caught up in the experience itself.

The following threads seem to weave, in different ways, through each third wave approach:

- Acceptance: Being willing to experience the things that we find difficult, rather than seeking to avoid them.
- Mindfulness: Noticing experiences in the present moment, without judging them. Letting experiences drift in and out of one's awareness without trying to hold on to them or push them away.
- Compassion: Based on a Buddhist perspective where one cultivates 'a sensitivity to suffering in self and others with a commitment to try to alleviate and prevent it'.

My experiences through the 'third wave' lens

To help me get inside the third wave and make sense of its strengths and limitations, I'm going to explore what one approach – Acceptance and Commitment Therapy

(ACT) – could offer in terms of understanding, and navigating, some of my own experiences.

The experiment

Walking down the corridors of the ward I felt certain that every move I made was being watched. I knew the staff were keeping notes about me – but it was more than that. The ward was full of cameras and privacy simply didn't exist. I was admitted there as part of 'the experiment'. I had lived with an alien inside of me since the age of 14. Initially, back home, it was okay. I could feel it growing inside me and influencing my body, yet I could cope. I pulled out my hair and cut myself to wrestle back control. I kept it secret, unsure of how to even begin talking about it.

It was only when I went to university that I began to understand the extent of the problem. As I had moved away from my home, those monitoring the experiment were forced to set up a network of cameras across the campus. They watched every aspect of my life. I could feel their gaze – a prickly sensation on the back of my neck that left me feeling exposed. Then, one day, I heard them talking about me – keeping track of my movements and, at times, ridiculing me amongst themselves. I knew that I could hear them because of an implant in my neck – it felt like a mistake, as if I was listening in on a conversation that I should not be aware of.

The reach of those conducting the experiment was mind-blowing. At home, at university, in town – they could see me no matter where I went. Not only did I feel crushed by their judgements, I felt terrified of where all this was heading. The only respite I got were the times when I went out clubbing with friends – the intoxicating mix of alcohol, rock music and dancing helped to temporarily take my mind off the enormity of what was happening.

Prior to my admission, things began to spiral further out of control. I began to pay more and more attention to the subtle changes in the voices of three men responsible for monitoring me. Their tone sometimes changed in response to what I was doing. I remember walking through the supermarket and, when I reached out for items, noticing that their tone became more foreboding. Walking up and down the aisles, surrounded by people, I tried to determine whether this was their attempt to warn me about something or if they were, more worryingly, trying to push me into buying something specific by scaring me away from items that were safe. It was exhausting, and often I left that shop with only a few items – cheese, milk and orange juice – unable to make eye contact with the checkout staff in case they were in on it too.

My fear of being poisoned increased, so much so that the food-parcels left by my worried parents became a tower of untouched boxes in the corner of my bedsit. I'd long since stopped showering for fear of being seen naked on the cameras. My thoughts raced around my head, fragmented, and I felt completely and utterly powerless. It was at this point my parents came and, with the support of my sisters and friends, moved me back home. It was at this point I went to see a psychiatrist and, with my dad sitting beside me, the events of the last few years began to tumble out of my mouth. The psychiatrist was kind and reassuring, encouraging me to come in to hospital so that they could treat my illness. Of course, I didn't believe I was ill and felt sure it was all part of the experiment I was trapped in. However, for a moment at least, I really wanted it to be true.

Acceptance and Commitment Therapy (ACT)

In stories like mine, it could easily be assumed that the voices and unusual beliefs I struggled with (aka my 'symptoms') were a sign of a deeper problem – an underlying illness. As such, a successful intervention would involve treating the illness, resulting in the reduction or elimination of the symptoms in order to enable me to move forward with my life. An ACT practitioner, however, might be more interested in the way in which I related to my experiences. They might locate the source of my difficulties as a state of 'psychological inflexibility', thinking that I had become entangled with the content of my anomalous experiences and that I was unable to reach my valued goals. They would have had a point; back then I was so occupied with my survival that the idea of any goals beyond this was off the agenda.

An ACT practitioner might also note multiple examples of 'experiential avoidance' in my story – times when I tried to escape from uncomfortable or painful inner experiences. They may have viewed my self-harm as futile attempts to avoid the horrible feeling of having an alien inside me. These actions came with the promise of some semblance of control over an intensely disempowering situation. Similarly, my place of sanctuary (nightclubs) could be seen as a way of avoiding the experience of the voices – literally drowning them out with loud music and dancing. So many of my actions during this time could fit inside the experiential avoidance box. From an ACT perspective, our ability as humans to create webs of words and meaning in absence of physical stimuli meant that every time I avoided something I simultaneously re-created it in my head and reinforced it as something truly frightening and powerful. I was stuck in a loop.

When I look back through hindsight's lens this all makes sense. However, I can't shake the feeling that it somehow sidesteps a crucial point – at the time I was not avoiding inner experiences, I was trying to survive real-world harms. When I refused to eat, I was not avoiding the uncomfortable inner experience of feeling that I was being poisoned – I was avoiding being poisoned. My reality was constituted of those experiences outsiders might categorise as 'inner' or 'private'. Within an ACT framework, this might be viewed as evidence of 'cognitive fusion' – that I was responding to my experiences (thoughts, perceptions and beliefs) as if they were unquestioningly true. It could be argued that I became trapped in a web of personal meanings that I then, unknowingly, superimposed on to the world around me; that these meanings prevented me from seeing the world as it really was. My fears became my reality.

Had I seen an ACT practitioner, these are some of the processes we might have worked on together to help increase this psychological flexibility that would hopefully help me identify, and reach, my goals:

- Contacting the present moment: The goal of this process would have been to help me connect with the sensations I experience (mental and physical) in the present moment, noticing them rather than judging or creating stories about them. In an ACT group or session, I might have been taught some mindfulness exercises – beginning with physical sensations and then moving on to noticing my inner states. This is a fundamental skill that I would be encouraged to develop throughout the therapy, hopefully extending it to more worrying or frightening experiences as I learn more about the approach.
- Defusion: The aim of this phase would be for me to have moved away from seeing my voices and beliefs as true, towards being able to notice them as experiences without attaching myself to their content. Within ACT, it's this attachment – a state of cognitive fusion – that can cause problems. The hope would be that by learning the skill of defusion, I would gain enough space to make more flexible choices as to how I respond. Building on the mindfulness skills I would have been introduced to, an ACT practitioner might have encouraged me to play with the idea of there being some separation between myself and the content of my experiences through the use of metaphors and practical activities. I might have tried imagining the contents of my mind appearing on a computer screen, or being relayed to me by a chatty co-pilot. I'd have been encouraged to see the extent of information that is given to me during my day and, gently, begin to recognise the possibility of questioning how useful or accurate it is.
- Self-as-context: Rather than defining myself in terms of the content of my thoughts, preferences and beliefs, this process would encourage me to recognise that there is always a part of myself that is noticing that I'm having an experience. Similar to defusion, the aim of developing an awareness of one's self-as-context would be to reduce the tendency for me to get caught up in the immediacy and reality of my experiences. Instead I'd be encouraged to see these things as mental events that are, by their nature, transient.
- Acceptance: In order to help me become free to pursue my goals, ACT would have encouraged me to develop a state of willing acceptance of unwanted or unpleasant experiences. This acceptance would hinge on me beginning to utilise and value those processes that develop space between myself and my experiences. If I was to still believe them to be fully and concretely true, I could imagine that discussions around the futility of my survival strategies

would leave me feeling defeated and powerless to escape my fate. Acceptance without defusion feels like a very lonely and sad place to be.

- Values: In this framework, values can be understood as the things which are important to us and add value to our lives. Given the difficulty I had with imagining values outside of survival, a skilled practitioner might help me connect with these through exploration of my fears. The fear of powerlessness and loss of autonomy flow through so many of my experiences, meaning that autonomy and independence were some of the values most important to me at that time. By helping me consider how my attempts to control or avoid my experiences were leading me into situations where control was taken away from me, I would be encouraged to think how acceptance might be a valid alternative.

- Committed Action: This part would involve me choosing specific actions and committing to them, knowing that this involved a willingness to experience difficult things in order to live a life in accordance with my values. It would be about me making choices when I act – living intentionally. In line with my value of autonomy, I might choose a goal like 'cook a meal for a friend'. Such goals are not end points, they are simply tangible enactments of the values that guide our lives.

So, assuming I had successfully completed a course of ACT – where might I be?

If I lived these experiences according to an ACT approach I would notice that I was hearing voices. I would notice that I had the thought that people were watching me. I would notice that I had a sensation in my neck that felt uncomfortable. I would notice that I was having the thought that someone had placed something in my neck. I would notice a lot of things, and I would notice my uncomfortableness with these noticings. However, I would have a little more distance from the intensity of these experiences and, hopefully, enough space to make choices about my responses. Aware of the drawbacks of using experiential avoidance strategies, I would be making a conscious effort to choose to do the things that I'd decided add value to my life. Perhaps, in time, the unwanted experiences might fade – but there would be no guarantee of that, and the acceptance thread might leave me suspicious of the virtues of having that as an aim.

There are parts of this that chime with a path I instinctively carved out to escape the cycle of hospital admissions I got lost in. I chose not to chase my beliefs down the rabbit hole, recognizing that my search for the truth only led me back to the ward. I chose to accept my feelings and resist the urge to untangle or explain them further. Whilst I was more able to keep on track, this path came at a cost. It was exhausting, requiring me to turn my back on my survival instincts and cut myself off from experiences that were literally shouting to be heard. It was ultimately unsustainable. However, noticing my experiences without fully attending to them left me unable to learn from them. I was able to function, more or less, but I felt incomplete. I had erected an artificial barrier to protect me from hospitalisation, yet I had no conception of how to engage with my experiences in a more flexible way. Had I met an ACT therapist at such a vulnerable point in my life I wonder if I would have ever realised that delving into the content of my voices was a valid and useful option.

Things have changed, dramatically, since I looked behind the barrier and began to explore my experiences. I have affection for those three voices that narrate me, and sometimes speak so harshly about myself and those around me. I see them as a reflection of the difficulties I have with groups, having learnt early on that groups of people can be dangerous. I see them as part of my heightened sense of risk-awareness – that they're trying to silence me sometimes in order to keep me safe. I see them, sometimes, as reflections of that insidious type of bullying where your friends speak about you as if you're not there. Most of all, I see them as meaningful and I choose to attend to the content, sometimes, so I can learn from it. I talk with the voices, even though they don't talk back. I see the alien experiment experiences as a canny metaphor for the sense of powerlessness and violation I experienced via childhood abuse (outside of my family). I see it as a reflection of holding a secret that I felt none of the people who loved me could ever know – of living in an alternative universe where those adults most trusted by society were the ones causing me harm. Focusing on the content of my experiences, using creativity and peer support, has enabled me to find ways of viewing them that enrich my life.

The 'Not Yets'

I am curious to consider how ACT might relate to the 'Not Yets' – a group of violent voices that I still struggle with. How might this compare with my own way of living with such difficult experiences?

> A few years ago, I remember lying in bed one morning whilst my husband made coffee. My body felt overwhelmed with unwanted sensations. I could feel people touching me; sharp stabbing pains in sensitive areas. My lips started to tingle and I knew I needed to get out. As I tried to move I realised that my body was frozen to the spot. I could move my head, but nothing else. I heard a woman's voice describing what was going to happen to me – in detail. She called me vile names and I felt like I wanted to vomit. Although it only lasted for minutes, it felt like hours. Afterwards, when my husband returned, I was unable to tell him. I kept it secret for years.
>
> From that day, I began to hear different voices talk about things that left me feeling such intense shame. Some threatened me directly, talking about violent and sexual things that would happen to me. Some spoke as if I wasn't in the room, reciting monotone descriptions of the ways in which people can be hurt; fragmented and repetitive – almost hypnotic in their tone. Some, the ones I find most abhorrent, describe how people around me want to be hurt in very graphic and upsetting ways.

Sometimes these voices are accompanied by body sensations – pain, tingling, burning.

Unsurprisingly, these voices are hard to hear and even harder to talk about with others. In therapy, I grouped them together and named them the 'Not Yets', giving my therapist the clear message that this was a 'no go' area. At times, when I heard them, I would feel consumed with panic. I felt like I was slipping in to another world, a world where I was a bad person who did bad things. At times I felt physically nauseous after hearing them. Even now, they are the most challenging of all the voices I hear – and the ones that I have the most challenging relationship with. Even writing about them in this chapter feels like a huge risk.

ACT and the 'Not Yets'

One of the hardest challenges I might face in ACT would be developing a willingness to experience unwanted and torturous painful physical sensations, and those voices that tell me to hurt the ones I love. The other would be the sad fact that I would be unlikely to ever bring these experiences to therapy. Saturated with shame, it is hard to imagine building the degree of trust needed to offer these experiences as examples to work with in a time-limited therapy.

Yet, in my own way, I have come to accept their existence. The distance I have found comes from framing my experiences as an echo of something I don't yet understand. Whenever I have a painful physical experience, I tend to my body when needed (often using massage) and remind myself that this is an echo of something that hurt. I (sometimes) talk to my younger voices inside and remind them that I'm there and that – in the now – they are safe. I might surround myself in a blanket, or cuddle a fluffy owl. Ultimately, I wait for it to pass.

The 'Not Yets' speak to me with such certainty and power that I can find myself flinching. The idea of listening to them is difficult and I have found all kinds of ways to avoid this. Whereas ACT may encourage me to distance myself from their difficult content – casting them as a thought and simply noticing their presence – the most progress I have ever made with these voices came from getting uncomfortably close. Counterintuitively, the 'Talking with Voices' approach facilitated the creation of a completely different kind of space. By allowing one of the voices to speak with a practitioner, a trusted colleague, I had the opportunity to hear the voice in a new way. More than that, I heard another person respond to it with firm compassion and curiosity. I felt its hesitation, its lack of connection. The transformation this engendered in me is hard to verbalise, but I left that session with a deep sense of sadness for this voice that cannot yet connect. I began to see it as stuck in a role it does not know how to get out of.

This depth of engagement with this difficult voice held more transformative potential than simply letting it pass me by, as if it was a passenger on my bus. By letting the voice take the wheel for a while I was able to take part in a kind of experiential learning that is slowly changing how open I feel I can be to that particular experience. This experience leaves me wondering if ACT's emphasis on defusion may be missing a trick. After all, do I really need to see my experiences as verbal events/thoughts in order to become more flexible in my responses? My voices are real. They are part of my reality. Defusion is only one way of relating to experiences in a vast array of possibilities. Compassion is another. Neither, in and of itself, is a goal nor a symbol of success. In my journey these ways of being have emerged as consequences of a larger and more meaningful changing relationship to myself, the world and my experiences. It feels almost nonsensical to package these as a desirable skillset, as if we are focusing on a specific detail but missing the bigger picture.

Critique of ACT and other third wave approaches

So, whilst there is much about ACT and its brethren that I appreciate – and some of its techniques echo things I have found helpful in my own journey – I am left with a number of concerns.

CBT's ever-growing umbrella

When first preparing this chapter I was rendered almost motionless by the array of approaches that can be termed 'third wave CBT'. Whilst they are linked by some obvious themes and values, their theoretical underpinnings and practice are diverse. Both ACT and Compassion-Focused Therapy (CFT), for example, encourage people to connect with difficult experiences rather than attempt to avoid them – teaching mindfulness and utilizing experiential exercise to facilitate this. However, when one looks underneath the hood it is clear that they are based on radically different theories. Whereas ACT was derived from Relational Frame Theory and is thus concerned with promoting psychological flexibility, proponents of CFT cite neuroscientific insights into affect-systems as underpinning their practice. It is this understanding that drives CFT's focus on developing people's ability to access or activate their soothing systems, enabling them to be kind and compassionate with themselves.

If the roots of these two approaches are so different, why gather them together under the same umbrella? It's at this point a cynical part of me raises its hand and wonders if the link is the identity of the CBT practitioners who champion them, not attributes of the therapies themselves. I could imagine that trained CBT practitioners each developed their practice using ideas from other fields and cultures, weaving them into their work to address growing concerns about the neglect of emotional life and prioritisation of the rational in second wave CBT. An even more cynical part of me is curious about whether ACT, CFT and the other approaches sheltering under the third wave umbrella would have their current place in mental health services if they were not considered a development of an already accepted treatment approach (CBTp). Whilst there is a growing evidence base for these approaches, does their conceptualisation as a 'third wave' provide a veil of acceptability that lessens the likelihood of them being relegated to the fringes? Is there a strength in numbers that would be lost if we spoke about them in isolation?

If this is the case, I am mostly glad that these approaches are becoming more accepted or credible through their association with CBTp. However, it does bring with it the concern that CBTp is crowding out the wider range of psychotherapies and social support options available in our so-called evidence-based and under-funded mental health services. In growing like a town that absorbs its surrounding villages, CBTp leaves little room for innovation and approaches that are messier or less easily evidenced. I've found it increasingly hard to argue for the development of Hearing Voices Groups within services that view time-limited ACT for Psychosis groups as a good value evidence-based option. How many Early Intervention in Psychosis services encourage longer-term psychotherapy when they have limited resources and guidelines that necessitate the provision of CBTp? In an ideal world this competition would not exist, with services being sufficiently resourced to offer a menu of need-adapted options. Yet we live in a world where one therapy can squeeze out others and, albeit unintentionally, the growing third wave umbrella could hasten this. In stretching to include elements of other approaches, third wave CBTp risks becoming the psychotherapeutic equivalent of an all-you-can-eat buffet; a cheap but not particularly tasty alternative to choosing a specific cuisine.

Misappropriation or a melting pot?

Many of the principles now core to these approaches are ones that I have learnt through discussions with voice hearers and other survivors in the Hearing Voices Movement – long before they became psychological therapies. My own journey of healing, described above, is peppered with practices that can be found in both ACT and CFT. I came to these outside of formal therapy, in conversations with other people with lived experience and through our collective knowledge base. Are these similarities a coincidence, developing independently, or has there been some cross-fertilisation? The answer to this question is, in many ways, unimportant – they are useful approaches and their spread within mental health services can help many in distress. The current context of mental health provision is challenging enough without engaging in turf wars with allies, fighting to own the provenance of a particular idea of technique. However, the potential for survivor expertise to be colonised by the psychological disciplines cuts me deeply.

This is not an idle worry. I regularly hear psychologists (and other mental health professionals) remark that my way of working with voices – developed through the Hearing Voices Movement – is similar to ACT, CFT, psychological formulation, psychodynamic, or whatever approach floats their particular boat. I get the feeling that these words are intended as gifts, appreciative and validating. I imagine that, sometimes, they can be peppered with a wish to gain a similar gift from me – the recognition that they are already working in a way that values lived experience.

However, my experience of these moments is that they steal survivor expertise by recasting it as a diluted form of professional expertise. It feels a little like an adult patting a child on the head when they play dress-up and mimic adult chores. In our society, professional expertise has the power to drown out those survivors. History, as they say, is written by the victors. This is not inevitable, yet its navigation requires a great deal of reflection coupled with an awareness of power and privilege.

A missed opportunity for learning

In its focus on the way we relate to our thoughts and experiences, rather than the experience themselves, third wave approaches may leave little space for exploration and understanding. Yet it is this sense of curiosity and a willingness to engage with the content of my experiences in some creative and unconventional ways that has been so fruitful in my own life. I've found the use of art to communicate with voices rather than simply express them, for example, to provide fertile soil for beginning to dialogue in a more traditional sense. Exploring the different potentials for relating to the voices I live with, and the ways in which they can relate to each other, using characters from graphic novels, has opened up new possibilities for collaboration.

The ability to be able to distance myself from my experiences has been crucial, but it was only one step amongst many. In a culture of short-term therapy, I wonder what can realistically be achieved in six, twelve or twenty-four sessions. I wonder whether practitioners have the chance to encourage curiosity about the content of experiences, or whether they feel the need to keep things simple and limit their aim to one of mindful acceptance. There is a danger that in promoting a sense of detachment from one's voices and thoughts, practitioners could communicate an implicit message that engagement with the voices is therefore 'bad'. Such a message could, combined with distressing voice-content, leave someone hearing voices for years but never really listening to them. Whilst this is a step up from a sole focus on suppressing voices (which can carry the implicit message that voices and beliefs are so powerful and dangerous that they can only be caged by equally powerful drugs), it is a long way from the careful engagement that has helped me reclaim my past, present and future.

Maintaining the expert position and propping up the status quo

Whilst looking at YouTube videos on third wave approaches, I was shocked at some of the overtly medical language and assumptions used to describe those of us who struggle with voices, unusual beliefs and other experiences labelled as psychosis. In side-stepping engagement with the content of people's experiences, there is a risk that the third wave is also side-stepping debates on the meaningfulness of our experiences and the deep insult that is labelling people as 'severely and enduringly mentally ill'. With a pragmatic focus on people's quality of life, third wave approaches may be part of maintaining the status quo and leaving people forever cast as patients who simply need to have a different relationship to their so-called symptoms. Where is the potential for revolution?

The therapist role can be cast as the one of expert, there to teach the patient a healthier way of thinking to effect change. Whilst this can be enacted in a compassionate and supportive manner, the kindness of the therapist does not erase the potential for such therapies to replicate the power imbalances found in mainstream mental health services. With successful therapy contingent, in part, on the patient adopting the therapist's way of thinking about difficult experiences, the client's voice may be silenced if they intuit that their existing framework is not welcome nor valued in the space.

Are people encouraged to consider the social causes of their distress, and to gather together to change it? Are issues of class, gender, race, prejudice, poverty, sexuality, disability and other social inequalities attended to? Whilst these are blind spots of many therapies, the third wave emphasis on acceptance can make these issues particularly problematic. Changing the way I feel about my experience of injustice may help me feel better in the short-term, but without the fire in my belly it provokes I may lose the drive I need to fight against it. Moreover, this way of thinking about experiences may promote the individualisation of societal problems. If we have a therapy that eases experiences of injustice and helps people accept their lot, why bother spending money on addressing structural inequalities and preventing childhood abuse? Just as mindfulness in Buddhism is connected with a strong ethical framework, third wave practitioners need a firm commitment to human rights and social justice to help guide their work. What happens inside the therapy room is deeply connected to our wider social and political worlds.

The imposition of ways of thinking and being in the world

Third wave approaches are particularly intriguing to me as they seem to teach particular ways of thinking about our experiences, our selves, and what constitutes wellbeing. They go beyond tools used by therapists to aid exploration to become a set of skills and principles to implement, on which one's health is supposedly contingent. In ACT a combination of acceptance of distressing experiences, detachment from these experiences and a commitment to acting in accordance with one's values is prioritised. In Compassion-Focused Therapy, the emphasis is on developing the ability to sit with one's distress and feel compassion for oneself. These are all valid paths through distress, yet they represent a mere fragment of the many ways people can 'be' in this world.

> ACT clients are encouraged to abandon any interest in the literal truth of their own thoughts or evaluations; instead, they are encouraged to embrace a passionate and ongoing interest in how to live according to their values.
>
> Hayes (2004)

147

If someone feels overwhelmed with experiences that they cannot avoid, the idea of teaching people different ways of relating to these feels helpful. However, if we teach one path in isolation and disregard other possibilities we risk preventing people finding a way forward that is uniquely suited to them. We might impose frameworks that are culturally or spiritually loaded, chock full of assumptions that might not chime for those we try to squeeze into them. There is a potential for these approaches to convey a moral stance towards ways in which we 'should' relate to our experiences, with some clients learning that engagement with experiences is unenlightened or 'bad'. Are these approaches really as benign as they sound?

Given that these approaches each teach different ways of thinking about experiences that go beyond exploration, I would argue that it is crucially important for potential clients to make an informed choice about which approach they wish to try. However, in modern mental health services such a choice is rare indeed. People are lucky if they get offered CBTp, and the particular third wave approach they encounter will often depend on the preference of the practitioner they are allocated to. This is an issue for counselling or psychotherapy in general – clients rarely get a choice over the specific modality of the therapist. However, in more exploratory approaches the modality shapes the way in which the therapist interacts with, and understands, the client – not a particular way of being that the client is encouraged to adopt.

In an ideal world, I could imagine a potential client having multiple taster sessions to try out different therapies. I imagine the role of a therapy broker whose role is to aid informed choice, demystifying different approaches and transparently setting out their particular assumptions, values and goals. I imagine a potential client receiving the message that these are simply different paths we can take on our journey, rather than the holy grail of healing. Of course, this would involve the widespread availability of a multitude of approaches – short and long-term. Whilst I think this is something we should fight for, in the meantime the responsibility sits with individual practitioners and teams to conduct themselves in as reflective and ethical a way as possible. By keeping up-to-date with some of the many alternative ways of working with distressing experiences, practitioners may be better able to resist the temptation to mentally stick to a single approach as the 'answer'. By supporting alternatives such as Hearing Voices Groups, Talking with Voices or the creative therapies, practitioners can help to widen out the space in psychological services. Rather than be content with psychological, social and psychotherapeutic approaches fighting for scraps from the biomedical table, let's work together to embed them at the heart of mental health care.

Where can we go from here?

The drive for therapeutic interventions to be grounded in scientifically tested models feels like an artefact of the push for clinical psychologists to be defined as scientific practitioners – of the boundary-keeping of a profession that is hard to differentiate from its brethren. It feels as if psychological therapies are being boxed into a corner, competing against biological treatments that are backed up by multiple RCTs that appear to support their places as the cornerstone of treatment, despite significant concerns around their efficacy and long-term safety. Psychological and psychotherapeutic work is not, to me, a prescription we can take. Attempts to compare it like for like risk missing the creativity and fluidity of therapy that I value so deeply. I do not want to adhere to a particular model of thought. I want the flexibility to integrate some of the ideas, practices and skills found in third wave approaches as if they're on a buffet table in front of me and have the freedom to customise a meal that suits my needs. As a client and practitioner, I want choice not dogma.

I want to try some ACT, but I don't want a focus on living in line with my personal goals and values – that feels like a lot of pressure. I want to use mindfulness, but I don't want to lose my intensity and depth of connection with my experiences. I want to be compassionate, but I also want to draw a line in the sand and feel okay to be angry. This anger can be a fire that drives me. I can use it. I do not want to be detached and accepting. I want to learn from my voices as teachers – even the ones that tell me to hurt people (I just want to listen to them in a way that means I can make choices about how I interpret them).

Most of all, I long for approaches that can balance the teaching of skills and techniques with an exploratory attitude that does not define what is – or isn't – important to attend to. I imagine psychologists and other practitioners becoming trusted guides whose focus is on helping the person in distress find their own path through the messiness of being human. I long for the use of tools without a grounding wider theory, adapting around the person. I want to rip up the protocols that can provide practitioners with a sense of stability, and exchange them for a focus on connecting with people where they are at . . . and increasing the trainee's ability to tolerate 'not knowing' and, perhaps, even to embrace it. Ultimately, I want psychological, social and spiritual approaches to take up a bigger space in our mental health systems. I want this space to be as pluralistic as possible, so we don't simply swap narrow biological responses for narrow psychological ones. This is a time for choice.

References

Hayes, S. C. (2004). Acceptance and Commitment Therapy, Relational Frame Theory, and the Third Wave of Behavioral and Cognitive Therapies. *Behavior Therapy, 35,* pp. 639–665.

9

WHERE NEXT FOR CBT
AND PSYCHOSIS?

Caroline Cupitt and Anne Cooke

The arrival of the third wave of CBT has been a gradual process and its status remains contested. Arguably it has given greater attention to a person's relationship to their experience and the processes which contribute to distress. However, some (e.g., Hofmann et al., 2010) have questioned whether this is truly a new wave, and have suggested that the key elements can in fact already be found in the broader family of CBT approaches. Do the approaches described in this book collectively merit the term 'third wave'?

What's new (and what's not)?

This book has included meta-cognition as the starting point for third wave approaches. However, whether or not it should be seen as part of the third wave is a matter of some debate. Hayes et al. (2006) consider it such, specifically mentioning Wells' (2000) Meta-Cognitive Therapy (MCT). However, Wells himself does not, considering MCT to be an extension of, but part of, traditional CBT (Hofmann & Asmundson, 2008). He has a point, since CBT has for a long time encouraged people to notice the effect of their thinking and in particular the counterproductive effects of thought suppression. Traditional CBT has also acknowledged the importance of higher-order meanings, sometimes called modes or schemas, which organise our relationship to individual thoughts or events. For example, as early as 1993 John Teasdale suggested that alongside any direct gains from challenging negative thoughts in traditional CBT, 'it may be that the very action of attempting to deal with negative thoughts, in common with other active coping procedures, leads to the synthesis of schematic models related to taking control' (Teasdale, 1993). Arguably CBT has never simply been a mechanistic approach to changing the content of thoughts, as Hayes (e.g., 2004) appears to imply.

Acceptance and Commitment Therapy (ACT) has its roots in radical behaviourism, albeit with a welcome added emphasis on internal events and their context. Hayes (2004) states that, 'ACT is neither from the first wave of behavior therapy nor the second, although it builds upon both' (p. 645). However, despite its distinctive theoretical justification being based on Relational Frame Theory, it could be argued that it ends up in a similar place. For example, a central focus is the role of experiential avoidance. Tackling avoidance is hardly a new focus for CBT: indeed exposure is one of the most effective elements of the first wave of Behaviour Therapy. Although Hayes (2004) claims that, 'acceptance and willingness in ACT leads to a different kind of exposure: experiencing actively and fully in the present' (p. 656), no doubt adherents of the first wave would argue that they have always asked that people fully expose themselves to their feared stimulus (e.g., Marks, 1979). What ACT appears to add is a broader conceptualisation of that stimulus to include present moment experience.

Likewise it could be argued that the ACT term 'cognitive fusion' describes the same rapid, automatic thinking characterised in the second wave as 'negative automatic thoughts' and from which the therapy aims to help the individual disengage. In traditional CBT this is done by promoting awareness, writing down thoughts and then reviewing their content and effects. The ACT idea of 'defusion' appears similar: people are invited to approach their thinking in a less literal way and not to act on particular cognitions. Thus whilst the content is not directly challenged, a person's relationship to it is changed. This is clearly helpful, but is it a distinctively new approach? Having received traditional CBT someone may also continue to experience the same negative automatic thoughts, but no longer believe or be swayed by them as before. One could therefore argue that what ACT brings is a refinement of traditional models, rather than an innovation (Greenwood, 2017). However, by expressing the task in new terms it has certainly captured the interest of a new generation of therapists.

Eastern influences

A common feature of ACT, mindfulness approaches, and Compassion-Focused Therapy (CFT) is that they all look to Eastern psychologies for inspiration. Eastern traditions such as Buddhism are founded on individual exploration of mental phenomena, rather than scientific empiricism, and as such bring an understanding of subjective cognitive process to CBT. However, the integration of these ideas is at an early stage and it is not always clear what is meant when cross-over terms are used. For example, within ACT there is an emphasis on self as context, described as a transcendent self which is 'a no-thing' (Hayes, 2004, p. 656). This appears to draw on the Buddhist idea of non-self (Sanskrit: *anatman*), which refers to the experience of the absence of a permanent and stable self, but at the same time is described as a safe place from which to experience difficult content. From a Buddhist perspective this 'safe place' is perhaps more likely to be a refinement of the ordinary constructed self; perhaps a version of 'the watcher' or observer of thoughts rather than non-self (Trungpa, 1992). It is therefore hard to be sure what is meant by the ACT notion of 'a transcendent self'. Is it more than the idea that it is possible to observe one's thinking?

151

Mindfulness approaches can also find themselves in some confusion about the difference between Eastern and Western conceptions of the practice. For example, in many Buddhist traditions, such as Zen, meditation to merely improve one's health is viewed as the shallowest form of the practice. Such a mundane goal is very much secondary to the main purpose of Buddhist meditation, which would always be spiritual realisation. In transposing mindfulness into CBT, this philosophy underpinning the technique has been lost, including the teaching on non-self. As Grossman (2011) points out, the goal of the practice then becomes unclear: is it just about increasing wellbeing by means of attentiveness in everyday life, or something more profound? Without clarity about the nature of self in relation to experience, it is difficult to know.

Perhaps CFT has given the most emphasis to its Eastern links, and in this case they primarily come from Mahayana Buddhism. Paul Gilbert has co-authored books with Tibetan Tulkus (Buddhist teachers) and quotes the Dalai Lama in his writing (e.g., Gilbert, 2005). However, despite the references, the extent to which Buddhist teachings have actually influenced the approach is unclear. Buddhism after all does not own exclusive rights to the promotion of compassion, which has been an important part of all world religions and indeed an important part of psychotherapy for a long time. It is also a word which can be used very differently in different contexts. When CFT uses the term, it appears to be referring to an active engagement with difficult experience at an emotional level. This focus on emotion stems from the influence of evolutionary psychology and attachment theory, and is an important contribution to the practice of CBT, especially in the context of psychosis. Traditional CBT tended to emphasise appraisal of voices and re-evaluating unusual beliefs, without much attention to emotion except in relation to triggering events. More recently both CFT and ACT have stimulated interest in how our emotional responses can become part of the problem, particularly if we seek to suppress or avoid them. Skills in accepting and soothing emotional distress are therefore now developing an important place in the repertoire of a CBT therapist working with an experience of psychosis (see Chapter 2).

Universal processes

The therapeutic developments included in this book all pay more attention to process than traditional CBT, which was arguably more focused on the content of cognition. In making this shift away from content, CBT is beginning to address universal processes which underlie distress. For example, the Method of Levels (MOL), although clearly a meta-cognitive form of therapy, is different in making its focus the control of perceptual experience rather than behaviour. However, in practice a session may look rather similar to CBT: for example, the therapist redirects awareness using techniques not dissimilar to Socratic questioning. Implicit within it is the normalising assumption that everyone experiences conflict and emotional distress from time to time and that everyone has the capacity to reorganise psychologically to resolve this. This conception of a universal process may be more significant than it first appears.

Part of the underlying philosophy of ACT is an acceptance that suffering is inherent to life. This has allowed the therapy to avoid getting too involved with illness labels, which has both contributed to a normalising stance and encouraged a trans-diagnostic approach. Both CFT and MOL also claim to address universal psychological processes and have quickly found application across many different forms of distress. These new forms of therapy have reawakened interest in universal psychological processes of suffering, which more symptom-focused CBT by its nature had neglected.

Does all this constitute a 'third wave' of CBT? The answer all depends on how one defines a wave. It does not appear to be a wave quite like the previous two. If this is indeed a third wave, its contribution is perhaps not to add a whole new sphere to CBT, but rather to bring out and to emphasise certain elements and present them again, this time better understood. As such it is clearly an important stage in, and vehicle for, the evolution of CBT.

Better outcomes?

As yet we do not know whether this renewed focus on underlying psychological processes actually improves outcomes. As many commentators on second wave research have found, identifying the effective elements of a CBT approach is a challenging task. Those who have tried have often suggested that the most effective elements within the second wave may be those derived from the first; for example, behavioural activation and exposure therapy (Longmore & Worrell, 2007). However, as Hofmann et al. (2010) point out, failure to demonstrate that change occurs by explicitly changing cognitions does not necessarily mean that cognitions are not the mediators of change. It may well be that cognitive processes are central to effectiveness.

There have been some meta-analyses of the effectiveness of third wave behavioural therapies (Öst, 2008), ACT (Powers et al., 2009) and mindfulness (Khoury et al., 2013). Öst criticises the rigour of Randomised Controlled Trials (RCTs) of third wave approaches and therefore finds it impossible to describe them as evidence-based. Powers et al. conclude that receiving ACT is more effective than being on a waiting list or receiving a placebo, but not more effective than established interventions such as traditional CBT. As more research has been undertaken, the American Psychological Association (2012) has designated ACT as an empirically supported therapy for psychosis with modest research support (in contrast to CBT, which they assess as having strong research support). Khoury et al. (2013) describe a meta-analysis of mindfulness interventions for psychosis and find some moderate effect sizes, but their conclusions are weakened by the heterogeneity of the trials. More recently, a systematic review of mindfulness interventions for psychosis (Aust & Bradshaw, 2017) includes a number of new clinical trials but draws similar conclusions, asking for more rigorous, larger trials to be conducted. Chadwick et al. (2016) reported results from the first RCT of Group Person-Based Cognitive Therapy (a form of mindfulness-based CBT for psychosis), which found that the most significant sustained effect was on mood. As yet, the National Institute for Health and Care Excellence (NICE) guidelines in the UK do not recommend ACT nor any other third wave approach for psychosis (NICE, 2014).

It may yet be too early to say whether evidence will emerge showing that the third wave enhances the effectiveness of more traditional CBT for psychosis. However, we are already more than ten years into many of these ideas. Thus far we can perhaps conclude that third wave approaches can achieve outcomes equal to those of more traditional CBT but that there is as yet little evidence that they produce better ones (Kahl, 2012). The question therefore remains whether the third wave really has more to offer? Indeed, for some third wave approaches (e.g., ACT) it is possible that their effectiveness rests on operant conditioning, and thus may derive from the basic behavioural components of all CBT. For example, mindfulness-based approaches are said in part to be effective because they counter the experiential avoidance which can often powerfully maintain psychological difficulties (see Chapter 4). The practice effectively requires someone to expose themselves to provoking stimuli rather as Behaviour Therapy used loop tapes, resulting in habituation of fearful responses.

Some have argued that focus on cognitive change in CBT is unnecessary because simple behavioural techniques can produce the same degree of success (Longmore & Worrell, 2007). However, of course that does not mean that for the individuals receiving behavioural interventions, cognitive change is not occurring. In the same way, it may be that the similarity of outcomes often reported between second and third wave CBT reflects the fact that the same changes are occurring, whether they are explicitly targeted or not. Seen from this perspective, what the third wave may contribute is not necessarily better outcomes, but a better understanding of how those outcomes come about.

The importance of meaning in psychosis

Third wave approaches are characterised by a focus on people's relationship to their experiences rather than the experiences themselves. In the case of psychosis, this perhaps risks losing something, namely an exploration of the meaning and possible value of the experiences. There have always been examples of people who have found meaning in the content of their psychotic experience (e.g., Campbell, 2010; Jackson et al., 2011). They may not wish to mindfully let go of that content, but (or in addition) wish to explore its relationship to their life history in order to learn from it.

With some notable exceptions (e.g., McGowan et al., 2005) there has been little research into service users' experience of CBT for psychosis or what people find most helpful about it. A study by Kilbride et al. (2013) however, is particularly helpful in being service-user led. The authors conducted in-depth interviews with nine people and identified five major themes, one of which was 'CBT as an active process of structured learning'. Participants described the value of re-evaluating psychotic experiences within the wider context of their life experiences as part of the process of formulation. Another theme related to 'improved personal under-standing of both psychosis and self'. People spoke of the value of the therapy's normalisation of their experiences: '[the therapist] helped me to see that the thoughts weren't crazy, after looking at what happened' (p. 95). The authors conclude that such normalisation is of central importance in CBT for psychosis.

There are different ways to normalise psychotic experience, but here participants are clearly valuing a detailed exploration of the content in relation to life events. There appears to be some danger of losing this aspect as the focus is taken away from content and towards process. This study suggests that opportunities to explore the meaning of such experiences need to be preserved within CBT for those who want them.

Trans-diagnostic approaches

One of the welcome features of third wave CBT is an increasing tendency to look beyond diagnosis. In the early Beckian model (Beck et al., 1979) each 'emotional disorder' had its own maladaptive cognitions, be it a fear of dying in panic attack or a fear of social embarrassment in social anxiety. Whilst this symptom-focused approach has led to important developments, it has also tended to mean that the diagnostic system itself has avoided criticism from within the CBT community. Elsewhere it has come under increasingly intense scrutiny and attracted widespread critique, particularly since the launch of DSM 5 (Kinderman et al., 2017). It is therefore refreshing that many of the third wave CBT approaches, such as ACT, are not reserved for specific diagnostic groups.

Even within the current diagnostic framework, there has been recent research on the benefits of using CBT to address common problems such as sleep or worry within the context of psychosis, with promising results. Waite et al. (2016) describe using a standard CBT intervention for insomnia (Espie, 2006) to improve sleep for people who have received a diagnosis of schizophrenia. Despite the use of the diagnostic term, this approach cuts across the Beckian idea that treatment needs to target cognitions specific to the diagnosis in order to work. Instead they find that helping people with their sleep can, 'reduce the frequency and intensity of distressing psychotic experiences and improve coping capacity' (p. 282). Such approaches do not fall into the category of the third wave, but appear to be part of a wider movement towards more trans-diagnostic CBT interventions. By their nature they also contribute to normalising the experiences of people experiencing psychosis, by suggesting that they can benefit from the same interventions as the general population.

Likewise, Freeman et al. (2015) have demonstrated that a brief worry inter-vention significantly reduced both worry and persecutory delusions, even though the strategies did not involve challenging the persecutory beliefs themselves but were based on a standard CBT worry-reduction intervention (Freeman & Freeman, 2013). Recipients of the intervention found the focus on worry helpful and agreed that they had this problem, giving it high face validity. Interestingly, only eight people assessed as having persecutory delusions did not have sufficient worry to be included in the study. The authors speculate that although they found significant effect sizes for persecutory delusions, potentially there could be many more benefits to be gained from reducing worry. The approach also has the advantage of being more acceptable to the many people who do not see themselves as psychotic nor wish to enter into a dialogue about their 'delusional beliefs', per se.

One striking aspect of both of these developments is the brevity of the interventions. At six to eight sessions, they are much shorter than the usual length of CBT for psychosis (which UK NICE guidelines suggest should be at least 16 sessions), and yet they appear to produce lasting change for people. This suggests that one means to empower CBT interventions for psychosis might be to make them less condition-specific and instead target common psychological processes. This fits with what service users themselves have said about the importance of the normalisation of their experiences in therapy (Kilbride et al., 2013) and opens it up to those who do not view their problems as psychosis nor wish to accept a diagnostic label. This is a very common (Jansen et al., 2015) and understandable reaction given the current social construction of psychosis (Schomerus et al., 2014). Perhaps in the future CBT may no longer view people through the lens of diagnostic categories, and dividing CBT into branches such as CBT for psychosis will become unnecessary.

A fourth wave?

Given that we are now already many years into the development of third wave CBT, it is interesting to speculate about the future direction for CBT and of a possible fourth wave.

If the first wave took behaviour as its focus and the second cognition, the multiple strands of the third certainly suggest that as CBT matures it is becoming more able to address the complexities of mental distress. For example, it has begun to break down old divisions between psychosis and 'normality' and the binaries of diagnosis. Thus far, however, the focus of both theory and intervention remains largely at an individual level. The obvious next step is to look outside the individual to consider the effect of the social context and our relationship to it in shaping experience.

Over the last twenty years, psychological theories of psychosis in the cognitive tradition have increasingly acknowledged the importance of the social environment – the events and circumstances of people's lives, and especially of their early lives – in the aetiology and maintenance of psychosis (e.g., Bentall et al., 2012; Dillon et al., 2014; Hardy et al., 2016). Empirical studies have provided ample support. Varese et al., (2012) for example, found that experiencing multiple childhood traumas appears to give approximately the same risk of developing psychosis as smoking does for lung cancer.

This emphasis on the role of the environment has been slow to develop and is still not ubiquitous, perhaps because of fears of a return to the 'mother-blaming' theories of the 1950s and 1960s. One of the authors (AC) remembers a prominent theorist, Richard Bentall, attracting fierce criticism from clinicians and researchers in the audience at a British Association for Behavioural and Cognitive Psychotherapies (BABCP) conference in the late 1990s for suggesting that adverse early experiences within the family could play a role in the genesis as well as the maintenance of psychosis (Bentall, 1999). In the intervening years, however, their role has been increasingly acknowledged and UK NICE guidelines now suggest that services should assess for 'reactions to trauma because people with psychosis or schizophrenia are likely to have experienced previous adverse events or trauma associated with the development of the psychosis' (NICE, 2014).

Some current authors go further and now stress the need to avoid psychocentrism; that is, the excessive focus on internal, psychological factors as opposed to the social and material environment (LeBlanc & Kinsella, 2016; Rimke, 2016). In a way it could be argued that this focus on the events and circumstances of people's lives is a return to the behavioural roots of CBT in that the role of the environment (albeit often somewhat more narrowly understood) is of central importance in behavioural theory.

A related development has been an increasing acknowledgement of complexity and heterogeneity of psychotic experiences, and of the 'complex interactive dance of nature and nurture' (Kinderman, 2015) that calls for humility and for aetiological agnosticism in any particular case. In the words of the recent British Psychological Society report, to which many CBT researchers and practitioners contributed:

> The causes of a particular individual's difficulties are always complex. Our knowledge of what might have contributed, and what might help, is always tentative. Professionals need to respect and work with people's own ideas about what has contributed to their problems.
>
> (Cooke, 2017, p. 103)

Taking the emphasis on the environment even further, a third development that has been suggested (and this has been a step too far for some) is the abandonment of the idea of psychosis itself. If 'psychotic' experiences are often no more and no less than a natural reaction to traumatic events, the argument goes, then invoking the idea of mental illness or psychosis may be unhelpful and tantamount to victim blaming. For example, Johnstone (2011) suggests:

> there is growing evidence that the experiences service users report . . . are, in many cases, a natural reaction to the abuses they have been subjected to. There is abuse, and there are responses to the abuse. There is no additional 'psychosis' that needs explaining.
>
> (p. 106)

This renewed focus on understanding the role of trauma has recently become central to the development of a conceptual alternative to psychiatric diagnosis, *The Power Threat Meaning Framework* (Johnstone & Boyle, 2018).

Therapeutic possibilities for a fourth wave

There are a number of implications for individual and group therapy connected to the idea of a fourth wave of CBT.

A not-knowing approach

Facilitating cognitive change where needed will remain important. However, acknowledgment of aetiological complexity, heterogeneity and indeterminacy implies the need for a 'not knowing' approach to therapy (Anderson & Goolishian, 1992) where the client is seen as the expert on their own problems, and formulation and treatment are co-constructed. In the language of ACT, therapists may need to help people to defuse from the clinical meaning of psychosis and find their own language. This may involve engaging with their values, which might, for example, include an interest in altered states of mind. At the same time, people often need support with the emotional impact of what is happening to them, especially if they have come from a background of adversity and have not come to expect a compassionate response from others.

This is a very different approach to that adopted by some of the standardised, diagnosis-driven 'treatment packages' traditionally on offer. It is likely to mean that therapists will more commonly work within belief systems that would conventionally have been labelled delusional, bringing CBT closer to approaches such as the Hearing Voices Movement.

Focus on current life circumstances

Secondly, it is likely that therapy will increasingly focus on the events and circumstances of people's lives in addition to internal, psychological factors such as attributions or people's relationship to their thoughts. There has been some criticism of third wave approaches, such as mindfulness, when used with people in difficult life circumstances; for example, poverty or homelessness. Critics argue, is it right to ask people to just notice and let go of their depressed thoughts when they have no job, little money and few prospects? Might it not be more helpful to support people to better their situation so that they can begin to look forward to the future?

Whippman for example, suggests that:

> Mindfulness . . . which on the face of it advocates paying attention to the outside world, urges it in only its most apolitical form – a 'non-judgmental awareness' of whatever is directly in front of us right this second,

deliberately renouncing analysis, critical thinking or wider imaginative empathy. . . . But this level of self-focus has come at the expense of outward engagement. Our narrative of wellbeing has become divorced from community, social justice or wider political responsibility. . . . What we urgently need now is not inner exploration, but outward engagement. Not 'non-judgmental awareness' but critical thinking.

(2017)

This criticism has become more acute as the politics of 'austerity' have increased levels of poverty and social inequality. Clinical Psychologist Masuma Rahim, for example, has written movingly about her experience of 'trying to do therapy when your patient has no food or money', suggesting, 'If basic needs haven't been met, what the hell is a bit of therapy going to do?' (Rahim, 2014).

Within ACT, for example, there is an important emphasis on activating someone's pursuit of their values. However, what ACT does not explicitly address is the very real difficulties someone might have in attempting to do so. People who have experienced psychosis are often held back by a lack of opportunity, by poverty, and by the view society takes of them and their distress. Therapy needs to be informed by this, which may mean widening the focus from thoughts and feelings to helping people with practical issues. It also suggests that therapists could usefully devote some energy to changing societal views and narratives about psychosis: this is addressed below.

The emphasis on the family and social environment also implies that family or even community-level interventions may at times be more helpful than individual approaches. In the past, family interventions have often been used alongside individual CBT. Recent developments include Open Dialogue (Lakeman, 2014), an approach to family therapy which incorporates the 'not-knowing' stance referred to above and is consistent with the recent theoretical developments in CBT described here. A large-scale trial is currently underway in the UK (Razzaque & Stockmann, 2016).

Focus on trauma

Therapy may also increasingly focus not only on the general circumstances of people's lives, but also on specific traumatic experiences. Partly this will be about being 'trauma-informed', making sensitive questions about trauma a part of every first contact with mental health services – but also providing CBT that explicitly helps people to process traumatic events from their past that may have been a large part of the reason they developed psychosis. The means to do this are already being developed within CBT (e.g., Keen et al., 2017) and the chapters of this book also contain ways to meet this challenge, in particular CFT with its focus on addressing the neuro-developmental consequences of early trauma (see Chapter 6). Many therapists still have concerns about the potential harm they may cause by directly targeting trauma in the context of psychosis. There is evidence that these barriers can be overcome with specialised training and supervision (e.g., van den Berg et al., 2016), and there is an urgent need for these to be more widely available.

Support for supporters

As mental health services move away from interventions that seek to suppress psychotic symptoms and towards a better understanding of the wider context of someone's distress, supporters trying to connect with someone in a confused and frightened state of mind need to be well-equipped themselves. 'Third wave' approaches such as mindfulness and a focus on compassion have the potential to be hugely beneficial for therapists and others trying to support people in states of extreme distress. Indeed, within the Buddhist tradition from which the movement has so often borrowed, they are more likely to be seen as useful for those in supporting roles (e.g., Podvall, 2003). There is now widespread adoption of the idea that reflective capacity is an essential aspect of professional practice and yet many of the tools used to promote it are as yet unevaluated (Mann et al., 2009). In future, CBT is likely to need to expand this repertoire and develop and evaluate new ways to sustain supporters.

Beyond therapy: A public health approach to psychosis

Prevention

Increasing appreciation of the role of the social and material environment in the genesis of psychosis leads naturally to a focus on prevention. As Read (2014) pithily summarised it, 'Why do we neglect prevention? The best way to reduce rates of psychosis would be to reduce childhood adversity'. Harper (2016) has made a cogent and well-evidenced argument for therapists also to become involved in prevention; for example, by specialising in public health. There may always be a need for therapy, but without concomitant efforts at prevention, just offering treatment to those already affected equates to 'mopping the floor faster while ignoring the source of a leak' (Marsh & Cooke, 2017). Cooke (2014) argues that psychology needs to adopt a public health approach. Drawing an analogy with the public health physicians who eliminated cholera from Western Europe in the 19th century by improving housing and drainage, she suggests that the psychological equivalents of these basic necessities might be basic safety and equality (Wilkinson & Pickett, 2009).

Of course, such criticism of the focus on individual psychological interventions, rather than addressing the events and circumstances of people's lives, is not new. Psychologists have tried before to develop approaches which recognise the social realities of people's lives (e.g., Holland, 1992; Holmes, 2010; Midlands Psychology Group, 2014; Rhodes, 2015). However, they have often been seen as the domain of community psychology rather than as part of the cognitive behavioural tradition.

The theoretical and empirical developments described here suggest that this may change over the next decade. Harper (2016) asks:

> What might a preventative intervention informed by a socially con-textualised Cognitive Behaviour Therapy look like? (We) could start by going out more to where people conduct their everyday lives. . . . We could encourage more 'bottom-up' rather than expert-driven 'top-down' approaches, like supporting the development of self-help and peer support groups. And we could seek to reduce income inequality. This requires action in the political realm, not only as individual citizens but also using our knowledge and status as professionals who are familiar with this research and the pernicious effects social injustice has on the lives of those who use our services.
>
> (p. 444)

With respect to psychosis, it is good to see links being established between CBT researchers and community-/peer-led initiatives such as the Hearing Voices Network (part of the Hearing Voices Movement: www.hearing-voices.org), the Mad Studies Network (https://madstudies2014.wordpress.com) and the Paranoia Network (e.g., Psychosis Research Unit, 2016).

Changing society's whole approach to understanding psychosis

A recent survey of just over 1,000 members of London's population asked about people's understanding of psychosis (Early Intervention in Psychosis London, 2015). There was 38% agreement with the statement, 'I don't know what psychosis is, and would not recognise someone experiencing psychosis'. Despite this, most people said that they would encourage a friend or relative to seek help (78%) and nearly half were optimistic about recovery (46%). About a third (31%) thought that people could recover from psychosis without taking medication. There were differences of view between groups, with women and older people sharing a higher awareness and more empathy. People in the age range 16–24 were the most pessimistic. This is of course the age when many people experience psychosis for the first time. Many will have witnessed peers develop difficulties, which as yet have an uncertain outcome.

Perhaps the most interesting thing about this survey is the confusion surrounding the term 'psychosis', in the context of otherwise fairly positive attitudes. Like other terms such as 'schizophrenia', it has a social as well as a clinical or 'official' meaning, and is widely used in the popular media to denote evil.

The poor quality of available public information impacts not only on public attitudes but also directly on how people who experience psychosis come to see themselves and their problems. It can reduce or remove the basic safety described above which is necessary for recovery. For example, the book, *Think you're crazy? Think again* (Morrison et al., 2008), described as 'a resource book for cognitive therapy for psychosis', very helpfully explains the evidence for viewing psychosis as on a continuum with normal, healthy functioning. However, outside the world of therapy it is difficult to find anything as good. It is more likely that people's first experience is like that of Jonny Benjamin – 'I felt like I'd been given a life sentence. All I knew was what I read in the papers that people with schizophrenia are violent and incapable of recovery' (O'Hara, 2013).

Discourses which denigrate 'insanity' can function similarly to the metacognitions that we know serve to maintain other forms of psychological distress, such as anxiety. The therapeutic task is therefore both to question these beliefs and metacognitions with the individual, and also within wider society.

The effects of societal discourses regarding psychosis can be particularly toxic for those whose identities are also already devalued in other ways, for example women or people from Black and Minority Ethnic (BME) backgrounds. In a study of voices' use of gender, race and other social categories to undermine female voice-hearers, Haarmans et al. (2016) argue that current CBT models have woefully neglected the socio-political context of the phenomena. They found that almost all of the women who participated in their study experienced voice content that undermined their self-worth in specifically gendered ways. In addition, more than half of the BME women also experienced voice content that denigrated their racial identity. As women who also experienced psychosis, they were doubly or triply marginalised within society and their voices told them so repeatedly.

Across cultures, we find that unusual experiences are either valued or labelled mad in differing ways. The fear of 'going crazy' underlies a great deal of distress, not just in psychosis but also other more common mental health problems. It is perhaps surprising therefore, that the idea of changing societal appraisals of unusual experience has not received more attention within CBT as a means to reduce individual distress. It is a natural extension of meta-cognition, as we move from considering an individual's beliefs about their thoughts to society's beliefs about the individual.

There is an urgent need for CBT therapists and researchers to provide good public information and to become involved in the public debate by writing for the public and by broadcasting and podcasting. A good example is the recent British Psychological Society report *Understanding Psychosis* (Cooke, 2017) to which many well-known CBT researchers contributed.

The normalising approach inherent to CBT is very helpful with respect to such initiatives and contrasts with the 'othering' approach, premised on the idea of an 'illness like any other', for which anti-stigma campaigns have been criticised (e.g., Cooke & Harper, 2013). It is possible that the word 'psychosis' can be reclaimed in the way that words like 'queer' have been reclaimed by the communities they were previously used to deride. An alternative point of view is that the social meaning of the word (like that of schizophrenia) is so entrenched that reclamation is unlikely and that alternative terms are needed, perhaps drawing on the Hearing Voices Movement's idea of using ordinary, rather than clinical, language and people's own preferred terms.

162

There is evidence that social attitudes are starting to change and become more open. This appears to result from greater knowledge and increased social contact, particularly if this is between adults, face-to-face (Corrigan et al., 2012). The engagement of people who have experienced psychosis in the task of changing societal beliefs is therefore vital. Although CBT has always identified itself as a collaborative form of therapy, the actual involvement of people with an experience of psychosis has thus far been limited. Greater involvement is the natural extension of the normalisation element already established within CBT. For the fourth wave to be successful it is now an essential component.

Conclusions

CBT has promoted the idea that psychosis is understandable in psychological terms in a similar way to anxiety or depression. More recent developments have increasingly acknowledged that psychosis is often a reaction to adverse events and circumstances. In the further evolution of CBT there is a need to validate people's reactions to adversity and be careful about language which locates problems within people, since this could undermine their efforts to cope. In addition, there is an urgent need to increase prevention – in particular addressing those events and circumstances such as child abuse which we know contribute to forms of distress such as psychosis. Finally, CBT offers a variety of techniques which could be adapted to the task of changing societal discourse about psychosis and ultimately about the origins of distress, promoting more acknowledgment of aetiological complexity.

References

American Psychological Association (2012). *Acceptance and Commitment Therapy for Psychosis* [online]. Available at: www.div12.org/psychological-treatments/treatments/acceptance-and-commitment-therapy-for-psychosis [Accessed 12th July 2017].

Anderson, H. and Goolishian, H. (1992). The client is the expert: A not-knowing approach to therapy. In S. McNamee and K. Gergen, K. (Eds.), *Social construction and the therapeutic process*. Newbury Park, CA: Sage. pp. 25–39.

Aust, J. and Bradshaw, T. (2017). Mindfulness interventions for psychosis: A systematic review of the literature. *Journal of Psychiatric and Mental Health Nursing, 24,* pp. 69–83.

Beck, A. T., Rush, A. J., Shaw, B. F. and Emery, G. (1979). *Cognitive therapy of depression.* New York, NY: Guildford Press.

Bentall, R. P. (1999). Self-discrepancies, attributional stability and family relations in paranoia: Expanding the model. Paper presented at British Association for Behavioural and Cognitive Psychotherapies Annual Conference, Bristol, 15th July.

Bentall, R. P., Wickham, S., Shevlin, M. and Varese, F. (2012, April). Do specific early-life adversities lead to specific symptoms of psychosis? A study. *Schizophrenia Bulletin, 38*(4) pp. 734–740 [online]. Available at: http://schizophreniabulletin.oxfordjournals.org/content/early/2012/04/09/schbul.sbs049.full.pdf+htm [Accessed 5th July 2017].

Campbell, P. (2010). Surviving the system. In T. Basset and T. Stickley, (Eds.), *Voices of experience: Narratives of mental health survivors*. Chichester: Wiley-Blackwell. p. 29.

Chadwick, P., Strauss, C., Jones, A-M., Kingdon, D., Ellett, L., Dannahy, L. and Hayward, M. (2016). Group mindfulness-based intervention for distressing voices: A pragmatic randomised controlled trial. *Schizophrenia Research, 175,* pp. 168–173.

Cooke, A. and Harper, D. (2013). When the ads don't work. [Blog] Discursive of Tunbridge Wells. Available at: https://blogs.canterbury.ac.uk/discursive/when-the-ads-dont-work/ [Accessed 29th July 2017].

Cooke, A. (2014). A response: So what do we need to do? *Clinical Psychology Forum, No. 256,* pp. 22–25.

Cooke, A. (ed.) (2017). *Understanding psychosis and schizophrenia: Why people sometimes hear voices, believe things that others find strange or appear out of touch with reality, and what can help* (Revised edition). A report by the British Psychological Society Division of Clinical Psychology. Available at: www.understandingpsychosis.net [Accessed 13th July 2017].

Corrigan, P. W., Morris, S. B., Michaels, P. J., Rafacz, J. D. and Rüsch, N. (2012). Challenging the public stigma of mental illness: A meta-analysis of outcome studies. *Psychiatric Services, 63,* pp. 963–973.

Dillon, J., Johnstone, L. and Longden, E. (2014). Trauma, dissociation, attachment and neuroscience: A new paradigm for understanding severe mental distress. In E. Speed, J. Moncrieff and M. Rapley, (Eds.), *De-medicalizing misery II: Society, politics and the mental health industry*. London: Palgrave Macmillan UK.

Early Intervention in Psychosis London (2015). *Attitudes to psychosis: Mental Health London Bus Survey.* London: Verve Communications and the Early Intervention in Psychosis London programme. Available at: www.myhealth.london.nhs.uk/sites/default/files/Attitiudes-to-Psychosis-London-Survey-Report-2.pdf [Accessed 13th July 2017].

Espie, C. A. (2006). *Overcoming insomnia and sleep problems: A self-help guide using cognitive behaviour techniques*. London: Constable and Robinson.

Freeman, D. and Freeman, J. (2013). *How to keep calm and carry on*. Harlow: Pearson.

Freeman, D., Dunn, G., Startup, H., Pugh, K., Cordwell, J., Mander, H., Cernis, E., Wingham, G., Shirvell, K. and Kingdon, D. (2015). Effects of cognitive behaviour therapy for worry on persecutory delusions in patients with psychosis (WIT): A parallel, single-blind, randomised controlled trial with a mediation analysis. *Lancet Psychiatry, 2,* pp. 305–313.

Gilbert, P. (Ed.) (2005). *Compassion: Conceptualisations, research and use in psychotherapy*. Hove: Routledge.

Greenwood, K. (2017). Psychological treatments for psychosis: Invited commentary on . . . psychological treatments for schizophrenia spectrum disorder, *British Journal of Psychiatry Advances, 23*(1), pp. 24–26.

Grossman, P. (2011). Defining mindfulness by "how poorly I think I pay attention during everyday awareness" and other intractable problems for psychology's (re)invention of mindfulness. *Psychological Assessment, 23*(4), pp. 1034–1040.

Haarmans, M., Vass, V. and Bentall, R.P. (2016). Voices' use of gender, race and other social categories to undermine female voice-hearers: Implications for incorporating intersectionality within CBT for psychosis. *Psychosis, 8*(3), pp. 203–213.

Hardy, A., Emsley, R., Freeman, D., Bebbington, P., Garety, P., Kuipers, E., Dunn, G. and Fowler, D. (2016). Psychological mechanisms mediating effects between trauma and psychotic symptoms: The role of affect regulation, intrusive trauma memory, beliefs, and depression. *Schizophrenia Bulletin, 42*(suppl.1), S34–S43.

Harper, D. (2016). Beyond individual therapy. *The Psychologist, 29,* pp. 440–444 [online]. Available at: https://thepsychologist.bps.org.uk/volume-29/june/beyond-individual-therapy [Accessed 13th July 2017].

Hayes, S. C. (2004). Acceptance and Commitment Therapy, Relational Frame Theory, and the third wave of Behavioral and Cognitive Therapies. *Behavior Therapy, 35,* pp. 639–665.

Hayes, S. C., Lucoma, J. B., Bond, F. W., Masuda, A. and Lillis, J. (2006). Acceptance and commitment therapy: Model, processes and outcomes. *Behaviour Research and Therapy, 44,* pp. 1–26.

Hearing Voices Network (2017). *Hearing Voices Network: For people who hear voices, see visions or have other unusual perceptions.* Available at: www.hearing-voices.org [Accessed 12th July 2017].

Hofmann, S. G. and Asmundson, G. J. G. (2008). Acceptance and mindfulness-based therapy: New wave or old hat? *Clinical Psychology Review, 28,* pp. 1–16.

Hofmann, S. G., Sawyer, A. T. and Fang, A. (2010). The empirical status of the 'new wave' of cognitive behavioural therapy. *Psychiatry Clinics of North America, 33,* pp. 701–710.

Holland, S. (1992). From social abuse to social action: A neighbourhood psychotherapy and social action project for women. In J. Ussher and P. Nicholson, (Eds.), *Gender issues in clinical psychology.* London: Routledge.

Holmes, G. (2010). *Psychology in the real world: Community-based groupwork.* Ross-on-Wye: PCCS Books.

Jackson, L., Hayward, M. and Cooke, A. (2011). Developing positive relationships with voices: A preliminary grounded theory. *International Journal of Social Psychiatry, 57*(5), pp. 487–495.

Jansen, J. E., Pederson, M. B., Hastrup, L. H., Haahr, U. H. and Simonsen, E. (2015). Important first encounter: Service user experience of pathways to care and early detection in first-episode psychosis. *Early Intervention in Psychiatry.* doi:10.1111/eip.12294

Johnstone, L. (2011). Can traumatic events traumatize people? Trauma, madness and 'psychosis'. In M. Rapley, J. Moncrieff and J. Dillon (Eds.), *De-medicalizing mental illness, psychology, psychiatry and the human condition.* Basingstoke: Palgrave Macmillan.

Johnstone, L. and Boyle, M. with Cromby, J., Dillon, J., Harper, D., Kinderman, P., Longden, E., Pilgrim, D. and Read, J. (2018). *The Power Threat Meaning Framework: Overview.* Leicester: British Psychological Society.

Keen, N., Hunter, E. C. M. and Peters, E. (2017). Integrated trauma-focused cognitive-behavioural therapy for post-traumatic stress and psychotic symptoms: A case-series study using imaginal reprocessing strategies. *Frontiers in Psychiatry, 8*(92). doi:10.3389/fpsyt.2017.00092 [Accessed 6th March 2018].

Khoury, B., Lecomte, T., Gaudiano, B. A. and Paquin, K. (2013) Mindfulness interventions for psychosis: A meta-analysis. *Schizophrenia Research, 150,* pp. 176–184.

Kilbride, M., Byrne, R., Price, J., Wood, L., Barratt, S., Welford, M. and Morrison, A. P. (2013). Exploring service users' perceptions of cognitive behavioural therapy for psychosis: A user led study. *Behavioural and Cognitive Psychotherapy, 41,* pp. 89–102.

Kinderman, P. (2015). Mental health is a complex, interactive dance of nature and nurture. *The Conversation* [online]. Available at: https://theconversation.com/mental-health-is-a-complex-interactive-dance-of-nature-and-nurture-38003 [Accessed 6th June 2017].

Kinderman, P., Alsopp, K. and Cooke, A. (2017). Responses to the publication of the American Psychiatric Association's DSM-5. *Journal of Humanistic Psychology.* Published online 15th March.

Lakeman, R. (2014). The Finnish open dialogue approach to crisis intervention in psychosis: A review. *Psychotherapy in Australia, 20*(3), pp. 28–35, [online]. Available at: http://search.informit.com.au/documentSummary;dn=267467486046068;res=IELHEA. ISSN: 1323–0921. [Accessed 14th March 2017].

LeBlanc, S. and Kinsella, E. (2016). Toward epistemic justice: A critically reflexive examination of 'Sanism' and implications for knowledge generation. *Studies in Social Justice, 10*(1), pp. 59–78.

Longmore, R. J. and Worrell, M. (2007). Do we need to challenge thoughts in cognitive behaviour therapy? *Clinical Psychology Review, 27*, pp. 173–187.

Mad Studies Network (2017). *Mad Studies Network: A collection of resources and posts bringing together an international network of mad studies endeavours.* Available at: https://madstudies2014.wordpress.com [Accessed 12th July 2017].

Mann, K., Gordon, J. and MacLeod, A. (2009). Reflection and reflective practice in health professions education: A systematic review. *Advances in Health Sciences Education, 14*(4), pp. 595–621.

Marks, I. (1979). Exposure therapy for phobias and obsessive-compulsive disorders. *Hosp Pract, 14*(2), pp. 101–108.

Marsh, I. and Cooke, A. (2017). The politics of suicide. [Blog]. Discursive of Tunbridge Wells. Available at: https://blogs.canterbury.ac.uk/discursive/the-politics-of-suicide/ [Accessed 5 June 2017].

McGowan, J. R., Lavender, T., Garety, P. A. (2005). Factors in outcome of cognitive-behavioural therapy for psychosis: Users' and clinicians' views, *Psychology and Psychotherapy, 78*, pp. 513–529.

Midlands Psychology Group (2014). The draft manifesto. *Clinical Psychology Forum, No. 256*, pp. 3–7.

Morrison, A. P., Renton, J. C., French, P. & Bentall R. P. (2008). *Think you're crazy? Think again: A resource book for cognitive therapy for psychosis.* London: Routledge.

NICE (2014). *Psychosis and schizophrenia in adults: Treatment and management.* NICE clinical guideline 178. London: NICE.

O'Hara, M. (2013). Schizophrenia: 'I felt like I'd been given a life sentence'. *The Guardian*, 18th September.

Öst, L. G. (2008). Efficacy of the third wave of behavioural therapies: A systematic review and meta-analysis. *Behaviour Research and Therapy, 46*(3), pp. 296–321.

Podvall, E. (2003). *Recovering sanity: A compassionate approach to understanding and treating psychosis.* Boston, MA: Shambhala.

Powers, M. B., Zum Vorde Sive Vording, M. B. and Emmelkamp, P. M. (2009). Acceptance and commitment therapy: A meta-analytic review. *Psychotherapy and Psychosomatics, 78*, pp. 73–80.

Psychosis Research Unit (15th November 2016). *Dr Eleanor Longden joins the Psychosis Research Unit.* Available at: www.psychosisresearch.com/news/dr-eleanor-longden-joins-psychosis-research-unit/ [Accessed 12th July 2017].

Rahim, M. (2014). On trying to do therapy when your patient has no food or money. [Blog] Masuma Rahim. Available at: https://masumarahim.wordpress.com/2014/03/01/on-trying-to-do-therapy-when-your-patient-has-no-food-or-money/ [Accessed 5th June 2017].

Razzaque, R. and Stockmann, T. (2016). An introduction to peer-supported open dialogue in mental healthcare. *British Journal of Psychiatry Advances, 22*(5), pp. 348–356.

Read, J. (2014). Creating evidence-based, humane mental health services: Overcoming barriers to a paradigm shift. Paper presented at From Diagnosis to Dialogue, ISPS-UK biennial residential conference. Leicester: ISPS.

Rhodes, E. (2015). Walking the talk and looking to be heard. *The Psychologist,* Vol. 28 [online]. Available at: https://thepsychologist.bps.org.uk/volume-28/august-2015/walking-talk-and-looking-be-heard [Accessed 5th June 2017].

Rimke, H. (2016). Introduction – mental and emotional distress as a social justice issue: Beyond psychocentrism. *Studies in Social Justice, 10,* pp. 4–17.

Schomerus, G., Matschinger, H. and Angermeyer, M. C. (2014). Causal beliefs of the public and social acceptance of persons with mental illness: A comparative analysis of schizophrenia, depression and alcohol dependence. *Psychological Medicine, 44,* pp. 303–314.

Teasdale, J. (1993). Emotion and two kinds of meaning: Cognitive therapy and applied cognitive science. *Behaviour Research and Therapy, 31*(4), pp. 339–354.

Trungpa, C. (1992). *Transcending madness: The experience of the six bardos.* Boston, MA: Shambhala.

van den Berg, D. P., van der Vleugel, B. M., de Bont, P.A., Thijssen, G., de Roos, C., de Kleine, R., Kraan, T., Ising, H., de Jongh, A., van Minnen, A., van der Gaag, M. (2016). Exposing therapists to trauma-focused treatment in psychosis: Effects on credibility, expected burden, and harm expectancies. *European Journal Psychotraumatology,* doi:10.3402/ejpt.v7.31712

Varese, F., Smeets, F., Drukker, M., Lieverse, R., Lataster, T., Viechtbauer, W., Read, J., van Os, J. and Bentall, R. P. (2012). Childhood adversities increase the risk of psychosis: A meta-analysis of patient-control, prospective- and cross-sectional cohort studies. *Schizophrenia Bulletin, 38*(4), pp. 661–671.

Waite, F., Myers, E., Harvey, A. G., Espie, C. A., Startup, H., Sheaves, B. and Freeman, D. (2016). Treating sleep problems in patients with schizophrenia. *Behavioural and Cognitive Psychotherapy, 44*(3), pp. 273–287.

Wells, A. (2000). A cognitive model of generalised anxiety disorder. *Behaviour Modification, 38,* pp. 318–345.

Whippman, R. (2017). Be happy, not mindful. *The Guardian* [online]. Available at: www.theguardian.com/lifeandstyle/2017/jan/01/be-happy-not-mindful [Accessed 5th June 2017].

Wilkinson, R. and Pickett, K. (2009). *The spirit level: Why more equal societies almost always do better.* London: Allen Lane.

INDEX

Indexer: Dr Laurence Errington.

acceptance 2–3; in mindfulness 65, 66, 67, 70, 74–5; patient's perspective 137, 140–1
Acceptance and Commitment Therapy (ACT) 3, 4, 79–97, 139–48, 150–1, 153; adaptations 88–91; development 80–1; empirical studies 85–6; patient's perspectives 139–48; values and 82, 84, 88, 89, 91–2, 93, 141, 159
actions (and responses): committed 91, 141, 147; values-based 82, 88, 92; workability of (to experience) 84, 86, 88, 89, 91
addition (in Acceptance and Commitment Therapy) 89
adult attachment 32, 33
Adult Attachment Interview (AAI) 32, 34, 35
affect see mood and affect
affiliation 98, 99, 100
anxieties and worries 155–6; Compassion-Focused Therapy 112; see also fear
anxious/fearful attachment 31, 32, 33, 34
appreciation (in Acceptance and Commitment Therapy) 89
attachment 25–44; adult 32, 33; anxious/fearful 31, 32, 33, 34; avoidant 31, 32, 33, 34; disorganised 31–2, 33, 34, 35, 36, 37, 38; dissociation and 25–44; insecure 26, 31, 32, 33; secure 31, 32, 33, 34, 35, 36, 37
attention (and awareness): on/of body see body; on/of breath see breath; training 105
attribution (styles) 48, 54; external 48, 119

austerity, politics of 159
automatic thoughts, negative 151
avoidance, experiential, patient's account 2, 84, 139, 141, 151, 154
avoidant attachment 31, 32, 33, 34
awareness of other peoples' minds see theory of mind

background thoughts 122, 126
behaviour: Acceptance and Commitment Therapy and 80–1, 82; change in see change; Methods of Levels and control over 116–17; see also contextual behavioural science
Behaviour Therapy 1, 3, 151; Acceptance and Commitment Therapy as 80, 93
behavioural activation 3, 56, 80
behavioural component of Compassion-Focused Therapy 99
being: imposition of ways of being in the world 147–8; mode of mind 65, 66, 74
beliefs, changing, in Metacognitive Training 51–2
betrayal trauma 28–9
biases 47–63; cognitive, targeting 47–63; social 48, 49, 57
bio-psycho-social approach 98–9
Black and Minority Ethnic (BME) persons 162
body (and its posture, attention on/awareness of): in Compassion-Focused Therapy 105; in mindfulness 69, 72
body language 55
brain, emotional systems 99, 101, 104

breath/breathing (attention on): Compassion-Focused Therapy 98, 100, 103, 105; in mindfulness 68, 69, 70, 72, 73
Buddhism 137, 147, 151, 152, 160

caring for carers (support for supporters) 160
centring 66
chair work in Compassion-Focused Therapy 107, 109–10
change (therapeutic/behavioural/cognitive) 82, 116, 120–1, 154; antipsychotic drugs and mechanisms of 54; in Metacognitive Training, in beliefs 51–2; Method of Levels and mechanisms of 120–1; mindfulness and mechanisms of 64, 65, 75; not-knowing approach and 158
childhood see attachment; interpersonal adversity; trauma
CHIME framework 92–3
client see patient
cognition, social 11, 12, 55
Cognitive Attachment Model of Voices (CAV) 33, 34, 35
cognitive behaviour therapy/CBT (general aspects) 1–4, 47–8; current cognitive theory 65; first wave 1, 151, 156; fourth wave 156–60; future perspectives see future perspectives; patient's perspectives 135–49; second wave 1, 144, 153; third wave 3, 4, 19, 37, 67, 79, 93, 136–7, 137–9, 144–8, 150, 153
cognitive biases, targeting 47–63
cognitive change see change
cognitive fusion 83, 84, 140, 151
committed actions 91, 141, 147
compassion: blocks and resistances to 106; patient's perspectives 137
Compassion-Focused Therapy 3, 4, 98–114, 152; patient's perspectives 144
compassionate curiosity in mindfulness 64, 66
Compassionate Mind Training 104, 113
compassionate self 100, 101, 104–5, 106, 107, 110, 113, 114
complexity of experiences 157
confirmation bias 51
conflict (in Perceptual Control Theory) 118–19, 121, 122, 128

connection: in Acceptance and Commitment Therapy 89, 92, 143; in Compassion-Focused Therapy 101, 104
construction (in Acceptance and Commitment Therapy) 89, 91–2
context (of actions and behaviour), Acceptance and Commitment Therapy 82, 83–4; see also self-as-context
contextual behavioural science 80–1, 93
control (attempts to/wanting to be in): Acceptance and Commitment Therapy and 91; mindfulness and 73, 74; patient's account 141; Perceptual Control Theory and Method of Levels and 115–18, 118, 119, 120, 122, 123, 127, 135; see also Perceptual Control Theory
cultural issues 162

decentering/decentration 2, 65; in Metacognition Assessment Scale 11; in Metacognition Assessment Scale-Abbreviated 12; in mindfulness 64, 65, 68, 69, 74
defusion in Acceptance and Commitment Therapy 140, 141, 151
delusions (delusional thinking) 46–7, 47–60; Acceptance and Commitment Therapy and 85; definition 47; Metacognitive Therapy and 57–9; Metacognitive Training and 48–57; persecutory 117, 155–6
depersonalisation and derealisation 27
depression/depressed mood: Compassion-Focused Therapy and 112; Metacognitive Training and 48, 55–6
diagnosis, looking beyond 155–6
Diagnostic and Statistical Manual of Mental Disorders (DSM-5) 47, 155
disconfirmatory evidence, bias against (BADE) 48, 51–2, 55, 57
disorganised attachment 31–2, 33, 34, 35, 36, 37, 38
disruptions: metacognitive 13; in Method of Levels 126
dissociation 35–44; Compassion-Focused Therapy and 100–1, 110–12; conceptualisation 27
Dissociative Experiences Scale 28, 33, 35
doing mode of mind 65, 66, 71, 75
DSM-5 47, 155

Eastern influences 151–2
efficacy *see* outcomes
emotional outcome measures in
  Compassion-Focused Therapy 112
emotional systems of brain 99, 101, 104
empathy and Method of Levels 125
empowerment (in Acceptance and
  Commitment Therapy) 93
environment 116, 118; family *see* family;
  material 157, 160; social 157, 159
errors, overconfidence in, Metacognitive
  Training and 48, 49, 52–4, 55
ethnic minorities 162
evidence *see* outcomes
experiences (self-experiences) 135–59;
  avoidance *see* avoidance; being open to
  71–2, 80, 85; complexity and
  heterogeneity of 157; in Metacognition
  Assessment Scale-Abbreviated
  (MAS-A) 15; in Metacognitive
  Reflection and Insight Therapy 19;
  patient's account 135–59; perceptual,
  control *see* Perceptual Control Theory;
  reflection about *see* reflection;
  workability of responses and action to
  84, 86, 88, 89, 91
expert: patient/client as (and survivor
  expertise) 146, 146–7, 158; therapist as
  (professional expertise) 147, 147–8
exposure therapy 151, 153
external attribution 48, 119
eye contact, reduced 122, 123

facial expressions: Compassionate Mind
  Training and 105; Metacognitive
  Training and 55
family 159; conflict 118, 121
fear and Compassion-Focused Therapy
  106, 107–9; *see also* anxieties
fearful/anxious attachment 31, 32, 33, 34
fourth wave CBT 156–60
future perspectives 150–67; attachment
  and dissociation 34–5; metacognitively-
  oriented therapies 20; patient's view
  148–9

goals: fluidly emerging with time 16; in
  Metacognitive Therapy, establishing
  58; in Method of Levels 115, 116, 117,
  119, 120, 121, 122, 126, 127;
  traumatised people with disorganised
  attachment patterns 37
grounded theory (in mindfulness) 66–7

grounding: Compassion-Focused Therapy
  98, 100, 103, 105, 107; mindfulness
  practice 67, 70, 72
group-based metacognitive training 2, 4,
  48–57

hallucinations and dissociation 30, 32,
  33, 35
health: being in control of 115–16; public
  160–3
hearing voices 3, 29–31, 98–114, 135–49;
  Acceptance and Commitment Therapy
  and 83–4, 85, 88, 90, 93; Compassion-
  Focused Therapy and 98–114;
  compassionate relating to voices
  109–10; dissociation and 29–31, 32, 33,
  34, 35; exploring possible functions of
  voices 106–9; general population 2;
  mindfulness and 66, 68, 69, 70, 71, 73,
  74, 75; patient's perspectives 135–49
Hearing Voices Congress in Wales
  (World) (2012) 136
Hearing Voices Movement 145, 158, 161,
  162
here and now *see* present moment
heterogeneity of experiences 157
historical background 1; Acceptance and
  Commitment Therapy 80–1;
  metacognition disturbances 13
hope (in Acceptance and Commitment
  Therapy) 92

identity (in Acceptance and Commitment
  Therapy) 91, 92
imagery in Compassion-Focused Therapy
  103, 105–6, 106, 107, 110
information, public 161–2, 162
insecure attachment 26, 31, 32, 33
interpersonal adversity (in relationships)
  25–44, 29; early/childhood 25–30, 31;
  see also trauma
intersubjective elements and processes: in
  Metacognitive Reflection and Insight
  Therapy 19–20; promoting reflection
  on 16–17

judgment and non-judgment: Acceptance
  and Commitment Therapy 88, 90;
  mindfulness 74–5, 158–9
jumping to conclusions bias 48, 50–1, 58

language and Acceptance and
  Commitment Therapy 82, 86

learning: fostering, in Acceptance and Commitment Therapy 90; missed opportunities with therapies 146; operant 81

letting come and go: in Acceptance and Commitment Therapy 92; in mindfulness 65, 66, 68, 70, 71, 72–4

liberation in Acceptance and Commitment Therapy 94

life: focus of current life circumstance 158–9; meaning and purpose (in Acceptance and Commitment Therapy) 82, 89, 93

lost (sense of being) in psychosis, mindfulness and 66, 68, 71–2

Maastricht Approach 113, 117

Mad Studies Network 161

Mastery 11, 15; in Metacognition Assessment Scale 11; in Metacognition Assessment Scale-Abbreviated 12, 15

May, Rufus, 136

meaning: in psychosis, importance 154–5; and purpose in life (in Acceptance and Commitment Therapy) 82, 89, 93

medical language and assumptions 146–7

medication (treatment for psychosis) 43, 57; patient's account of experiences with 102; voice-hearing and 84, 101, 113

memory practices in Compassion-Focused Therapy 105–6

mental health, being in control of 115–16

mentalising 11

meta-analyses 29, 153–4; metacognitive capacities and 13; metacognitive training 57; third wave CBT/therapies (in general) 153–4; see also systematic reviews

metacognition 2, 3, 9–24, 47–63, 150; capacity improvement over time as a target 13–14; construct of 10–11; definition 10; enhancing treatment 13–14; operationalisation 11–12; reduced/disturbed capacities 10, 11, 12–13; therapies matching a patient's capacity 14–16; therapies targeting 17–20, 47–63

Metacognition Assessment Scale (MAS) 11–12

Metacognition Assessment Scale-Abbreviated (MAS-A) 11, 12, 14–15

Metacognitive Reflection and Insight Therapy (MERIT) 17–20

Metacognitive Therapy (MCT+) 57–9, 59–60

Metacognitive Training (MCT) 2, 4, 48–57, 59–60, 150

metaphors used in Acceptance and Commitment Therapy 87, 90

Method of Levels (MOL) 4, 115–31, 152–3; evidence for 126–7; implementing 127–8; in practice 121–7

mind: being mode 65, 66, 75; Compassionate Mind Training 104, 113; doing mode 65, 66, 71, 75; habits, familiarity with 73; theory of see theory of mind

mindfulness 2, 4, 64–78, 152, 153–4, 154, 158–9; in Acceptance and Commitment Therapy 89–90; adaptations 67–8; in Compassion-Focused Therapy 105; guiding 69–70; inquiry after practice 70–1; introducing 68; judgment and non-judgment 74–5, 158–9; key psychological processes 65–7; Metacognitive Reflection and Insight Therapy compared with 19; patient's perspectives 137; present moment in 72, 137

MOL Session Evaluation Form 127

monocausal attribution biases 48, 54

mood and affect: depressed see depression; regulation by brain 99

Mountains of Life metaphor, Two 87

multiple selves (concept) 104

negative automatic thoughts 151

negative feedback process in control 116, 118

non-judgment see judgment and non-judgment

non-reaction 73

non-self 151

not-knowing approach 158

now see present moment

operant learning 81

operationalisation of metacognition 11–12

other people's minds, awareness of see theory of mind

outcomes (and evidence of/measurement/ efficacy) 1, 153–4; Acceptance and

Commitment Therapy 85; Compassion-Focused Therapy 112–13; improving 153–4; Metacognitive Therapy 58–9; Metacognitive Training 56–7; Method of Levels 126–7; *see also* meta-analyses; systematic reviews
overconfidence in errors, Metacognitive Training and 48, 49, 52–4, 55

paranoia and dissociation 31, 32–3, 35
Paranoia Network 161
parental loss and dissociation 33
Passenger on the Bus metaphor 90–1
past trauma *see* trauma
patient/client/service user: as expert 146, 146–7, 158; personal experiences *see* personal experiences
Perceptual Control Theory (PCT) 115, 116, 117, 118, 119, 120, 121, 122, 128, 152; evidence for 126–7
persecutory delusions 117, 155–6
personal experiences of service users 135–49, 154–5; Compassion-Focused Therapy 101, 110, 112–13; research into 154–5
perspective-taking by therapist 86
physical health, being in control of 115
politics of austerity 159
Positive and Negative Syndrome Scale (PANSS) 1
posture *see* body
preferred states 115, 116, 117, 118, 118–19, 120, 121, 122, 123
present moment (here and now): in Acceptance and Commitment Therapy 80, 84, 88, 140; in Method of Levels 125–6; in mindfulness 72, 137; patient's perspectives 140
prevention 160–1
processes: in Compassion-Focused Therapy, measures of 110–12; universal 152–3
protection *see* threat and protection
psychocentrism 157
psycho-education: Compassion-Focused Therapy 100, 104; Metacognitive Training 49
psychological component of Compassion-Focused Therapy 98–9
psychological flexibility 79–80, 88, 89, 92, 93; lack (inflexibility) 84, 85, 86, 139; patient's account 139, 140, 144; therapist's skills 86

psychosis: abandonment of term 157; definition/meaning 156, 161, 162–3; self-definition 74
Psychosis Attachment Measure (PAM) 34, 36
psychotherapies: future perspectives 148–9, 150–67; multiple taster sessions of different types 148; recovery-oriented 9–24
public health 160–3
purpose and meaning in life (in Acceptance and Commitment Therapy) 82, 89, 93

randomised controlled trials 1, 136, 153–4; Acceptance and Commitment Therapy 79, 85, 153; Metacognitive Reflection and Insight Therapy 18–19; Metacognitive Therapy 58–9; Metacognitive Training 57; Method of Levels 127–8
rationality of CBT, patient's perspectives 135
reaction, stepping out of (non-reaction) 73
reality testing 30, 48, 58
recovery 9–24; Acceptance and Commitment Therapy and 17, 89, 91, 92–3; developing forms of therapies oriented towards 9–24; obstacles to 9–10
reflection/self-reflectivity 10–11; in Compassion-Focused Therapy 110, 112–13; on intersubjective processes, promoting 16–17; joint 19; in Metacognition Assessment Scale 11; in Metacognition Assessment Scale-Abbreviated 15; *see also* Metacognitive Reflection and Insight Therapy
relapse prevention in Metacognitive Therapy 58
Relational Frame Theory (RFS) 81, 86, 144, 151
relationships *see* interpersonal adversity; therapeutic relationship
relativity and conflict 119
reorganisation (Perceptual Control Theory) 115, 118, 120–1, 122, 127, 128
repetition (in Acceptance and Commitment Therapy) 89

resilience 25, 45
risk (of therapies) *see* safety and risk considerations
role-play in Metacognitive Therapy 58

safeness 98, 99, 100; social 98, 100, 103–4, 110–12
safety and risk considerations: Method of Levels 128; mindfulness 67
schizophrenia, conceptualisation of concept of 13
secure attachment 31, 32, 33, 34, 35, 36, 37
self (selves): compassionate self 100, 101, 104–5, 106, 107, 110, 113, 114; multiple selves 104; transcendent 151
self-as-context 140
self-disclosure (therapist) 92
self-esteem and Metacognitive Training 56
self-experience *see* experience
self-management (in Acceptance and Commitment Therapy) 93
self-protection *see* threat and protection
service user *see* patient
sleep improvement 155
social attitudes 163
social biases 48, 49, 57
social causes of distress 147
social cognition 11, 12, 55
social component of Compassion-Focused Therapy 99
social environment 157, 159
social safeness 98, 100, 103–4, 110–12
Socratic discussion/questioning 48, 58, 152
soothing 99, 100, 103, 104, 144, 152
stigma 20, 100, 162; Metacognitive Training and 50, 56
still, being (in mindfulness) 68, 69, 70, 71–2
stress and Compassion-Focused Therapy 112
struggling: Acceptance and Commitment Therapy and 85, 86, 89, 90, 91, 92; mindfulness and 68, 72–4; patient's account of 135
support for supporters 160
symptom, voice hearing as or not as a 2
systematic reviews 29; mindfulness 153–4; *see also* meta-analyses

theory of mind (awareness and understanding of other peoples' minds) 23, 54–5; deficits 48, 54–5; Metacognition Assessment Scale-Abbreviated (MAS-A) 12, 15
therapeutic change *see* change
therapeutic relationship 86–8; Acceptance and Commitment Therapy and 86–8; attachment and 36, 37; Compassion-Focused Therapy and 100; Metacognitive Reflection and Insight Therapy and 19; mindfulness and 67
thinking: delusional *see* delusions; imposition of ways of thinking in the world 147–8; patient being given *10 common thinking traps* sheet 135; thinking about *see* metacognition; *see also* thoughts
third wave CBT/therapies 3, 4, 19, 37, 67, 79, 93, 150, 153; array of approaches 144–5; criticisms 47–8, 93, 144–8, 158; outcomes *see* outcomes; patient perspectives 93, 136–7, 137–9, 144–8
thoughts: background 122, 126; negative automatic 151; *see also* thinking
threat and protection 71, 99–100, 101; Acceptance and Commitment Therapy and 84; Compassion-Focused Therapy and 99–100, 100–1, 103, 105, 106, 107, 108, 109, 113
three circles model of brain systems 99
three-minute breathing space 70
transcendent self 151
trauma (past/early incl. childhood) 25–38, 157, 158, 159–60; dissociation and 28–9; focus on 159–60
Two Mountains of Life metaphor 87
tyrannical relationship with psychosis, mindfulness and 66, 71–5

universal processes 152–3

value(s) 119, 121, 122; Acceptance and Commitment Therapy 82, 84, 88, 89, 91–2, 93, 141, 159; Method of Levels 115; patient's account 141
voice(s): hearing *see* hearing voices; tone in Compassion-Focused Therapy 105

workability of responses and actions to experience 84, 86, 88, 89, 91
worries *see* anxieties; fear